SETON HALL UNIVERSITY

10001481 8

D1532400

DATE DUE	
DEC 0 9 1994	
DEC 1 1 1994	
4765634	DEC 0 8 1999
DEC 3 1 2001	
GAYLORD	PRINTED IN U.S.A

When
Part of the Self
Is Lost

CONSTANCE HOENK SHAPIRO

When
Part of the Self
Is Lost

HELPING CLIENTS HEAL
AFTER SEXUAL AND REPRODUCTIVE
LOSSES

Jossey-Bass Publishers · San Francisco

SETON HALL UNIVERSITY
McLAUGHLIN LIBRARY
SO. ORANGE. N. J.

RC
455.4
.L67
S37
1993

Copyright © 1993 by Jossey-Bass Inc., Publishers, 350 Sansome Street,
San Francisco, California 94104. Copyright under International, Pan
American, and Universal Copyright Conventions. All rights reserved.
No part of this book may be reproduced in any form—except for brief
quotation (not to exceed 1,000 words) in a review or professional
work—without permission in writing from the publishers.

For sales outside the United States, contact Maxwell Macmillan
International Publishing Group, 866 Third Avenue, New York,
New York 10022.

Manufactured in the United States of America.

The paper used in this book is acid-free and meets the
State of California requirements for recycled paper
(50 percent recycled waste, including 10 percent
postconsumer waste), which are the strictest guidelines
for recycled paper currently in use in the United States.

10% POST
CONSUMER
WASTE

Library of Congress Cataloging-in-Publication Data

Shapiro, Constance Hoenk.
    When part of the self is lost : helping clients heal after sexual
and reproductive losses / Constance Hoenk Shapiro.
        p.   cm. — (The Jossey-Bass social and behavioral science
series) (The Jossey-Bass health series)
    Includes bibliographical references and index.
    ISBN 1-55542-485-6
    1. Grief therapy.   2. Sex (Psychology)   3. Loss (Psychology)
I. Title.   II. Series.   III. Series: The Jossey-Bass health series.
RC455.4.L67S37   1993
155.9'37—dc20   92-17610
                                                                CIP

FIRST EDITION
HB Printing   10 9 8 7 6 5 4 3 2 1   *Code 9285*

A joint publication in
The Jossey-Bass
Social and Behavioral Science Series
and
The Jossey-Bass
Health Series

To the memory of my mother,
Mary White Hoenk

CONTENTS

**Part Three: The Expanding Role
of the Helping Professional**

PREFACE

"I think I'm going crazy." "My family says I should get on with my life, but I just can't." "I feel as if I've lost a part of myself." These are some of the sentiments expressed by my clients in response to the intense grief caused by their sexual and reproductive losses. Are these clients unusual? Are their presenting problems unique? Not at all. The clients I see are people with AIDS, infertility problems, spinal cord injuries, and chronic illnesses; victims of sexual assault; cancer patients; couples who have suffered pregnancy losses; and people whose sexuality has been affected by the course of normal aging. All these conditions have grief and sexual loss as a common denominator.

Many books have been written on these two topics separately, but this is the first book to address their interrelationship. Grief and sexuality were prominent themes in my recent book *Infertility and Pregnancy Loss: A Guide for Helping Professionals* (1988), and in many ways that book served as an impetus to expand my attention to those themes. The reader may note that I have drawn some material from my earlier book, notably on the topics of infertility, pregnancy loss, and stillbirth, and have used this material to enrich the content of *When Part of the Self Is Lost*.

A major purpose of this book is to present sexual and reproductive losses in a bio-psycho-social perspective; such an approach is crucial for professionals who may be working as members of a team in an effort to coordinate services for a client or a patient. Second, by providing case vignettes throughout the book, I have tried to move the professional beyond the *facts* of the client's condition to the *feelings* of loss and grief associated with the conditions discussed. Finally, the book provides detailed information about the counseling and therapeutic skills necessary for work with clients who are grieving a loss.

Despite its emphasis on the intensely private areas of grief and sexuality, this book is not intended to be morose or depressing. The reader is encouraged to think of griefwork as an opportunity to help clients heal and reclaim their lives. The attention to sexual losses is balanced by an emphasis on how to help clients redefine their sexual needs and find joy in new or expanded forms of sexual expression. And, most important, since many clients feel extremely isolated when they are grieving their sexual losses, this book is written to help the professional empathize with the client's emotional pain, develop systems of support, and find creative ways to help clients work through their grief and empower themselves in spite of the losses they have endured.

Who Should Read This Book?

Many different helping professionals can offer emotional support to people experiencing sexual and reproductive losses. Social workers, psychologists, psychiatrists, oncologists, gynecologists, obstetricians, nurses, midwives, family counselors, other medical professionals, and rehabilitation providers such as speech, occupational, and physical therapists are likely to be consulted as men and women from many walks of life experience a sexual loss, mourn for what has been lost, contemplate the implications of the loss, and confront the ongoing life decisions that they must make. Clergy of all faiths are in a special position to offer support and solace when parishioners turn to them in times of despair, loss of faith, and anger that their prayers are not being heard.

The following professionals, paraprofessionals, and volunteers in a variety of facilities and agencies may also find this book helpful: staff in women's clinics and counseling programs, crisis intervention programs, nursing homes, hospice programs, AIDS clinics, convalescent hospitals, retirement communities, and programs that offer support and self-help groups. As an educator of students in social work and the human services, I believe that this book is also appropriate for students preparing for careers as helping professionals.

Professionals reading this book need to be aware of the importance of working in tandem with other professionals involved in the client's recovery from loss. A fragmented delivery of medical and emotional interventions undermines a person's courage as he or she undertakes the difficult griefwork precipitated by a sexual or reproductive loss.

Overview of the Contents

The book is organized into three parts. The first part (Chapters One and Two) provides an overview of theoretical material that the professional can use as a guide when organizing interventions with clients. These chapters provide information on attachment and loss in the context of sexuality, including in-depth attention to the dynamics of grief and coping.

Chapter One offers a framework for conceptualizing certain sexual and reproductive life events as losses, thereby sensitizing both client and professional to the griefwork that will become an important part of the recovery process.

Chapter Two presents several theoretical models of the mourning process and emphasizes a range of coping strategies that clients can be encouraged to use as they resolve their losses and reconstruct their lives.

Part Two (Chapters Three through Ten) provides information on the sexual and reproductive dimensions of specific injuries, medical conditions, and the process of normal aging.

Chapter Three illustrates the various sexual losses experienced by clients who have had hysterectomies and enterostomies and clients with diabetes, endometriosis, and paraplegia.

Chapter Four presents concrete information on cancer and AIDS and discusses the emotional needs of the client who alternates between feelings of despair over the diagnosis and the wish to maximize periods of good health and remission. This chapter concentrates on cancer of sexual and reproductive body parts: the breast, prostate, uterus, ovary, and testis. Special attention is given to feelings and attitudes of professionals who work with terminally ill people.

Chapter Five emphasizes the attachment formed by an infertile couple to a fantasy baby, as yet unconceived, and details the disruptions caused by the diagnostic workup and treatment efforts. This chapter also notes the common themes of loss that occur in the infertility struggle and suggests specific ways in which the professional can help couples to cope.

Chapter Six examines the concept of symbolic attachment and the ways in which it becomes an integral part of the mourning process following an elective abortion, miscarriage, or ectopic pregnancy. Although the woman often bears a unique burden in reproductive losses because of her incapacity to give birth to a healthy child, this chapter also emphasizes her partner's response to their shared loss.

Chapter Seven addresses the emotional anguish felt by couples whose baby is born dead. This chapter pays attention to the immediate needs of the couple while the woman is still in the hospital, as well as the ongoing emotional needs once the woman is discharged to return home with empty arms.

Chapter Eight emphasizes the needs of the sexually abused young person within the context of the family. Using the clinical perspective of posttraumatic stress disorders and referring to the phases of the rape trauma syndrome, the author familiarizes the reader with the expectable reactions of children and adolescents who have been sexually abused. The reader is reminded that other professionals probably will be working with the child and the family (child protective services and legal and medical personnel); consequently, each professional must be clear about the boundaries of his or her role so that the child does not feel confused, betrayed, or further traumatized.

Chapter Nine uses the framework of rape trauma syndrome to conceptualize the adult's response to rape. Whether the assault was by a stranger, an acquaintance, or a spouse, the survivor will have a series of losses to acknowledge and work through. This chapter highlights the therapeutic implications of the losses experienced by adult males and females who have survived a sexual assault.

Chapter Ten explores the concerns of older persons as they come to terms with many losses, some of which tend to eclipse their sexual needs. This chapter encourages the professional to explore with older clients *all* of the losses, including the sexual ones, that cause them regret or distress in their later years.

Part Three (Chapters Eleven through Thirteen) contains chapters that examine the role of the professional beyond therapeutic efforts with clients.

Chapter Eleven uses a developmental perspective to remind the reader of sexual and reproductive issues at each stage of the life cycle. The chapter encourages the professional to consider the client's needs from a broad bio-psycho-social framework rather than adhering too narrowly to any one professional area of expertise.

Chapter Twelve challenges the professional to look beyond individual circumstances to the community in which clients must maintain their coping strategies. The chapter raises questions about organizational barriers that professionals must surmount in their roles as educators, advocates, and change agents.

Chapter Thirteen discusses the need for professionals to maximize their therapeutic helpfulness by continually improving their knowledge base, increasing their intervention skills, and gaining personal replenishment. This chapter emphasizes self-awareness, assessment of one's own areas of resilience and vulnerability, and the importance of developing support networks so that psychological energy can be replenished on an ongoing basis.

Acknowledgments

A number of people have been very helpful and supportive as I have written this book. I am especially indebted to Karen Dashiff Gilovich, Heidi Dana Lipson, Wendy Robertson, M.D., Sue Rochman, and Bonnie Shelley for their willingness to share professional literature with me and, later, to make incisive comments on the first drafts of specific chapters. I also appreciate the precision with which Seana Rolland helped me with the many references contained in this book.

Since all my clients are struggling with sexual or reproductive losses, I have learned an immense amount from them as they courageously mourn their losses and seek new ways of coping with altered life hopes.

And, of course, I owe a special thanks to my family: to my husband, Stuart, who offered constant encouragement; to my children, Adrienne and Daniel, who were accommodating in juggling our use of the family computer; and to Glenna Vangeli, who provided loving care to my children while I was immersed in the research that has culminated in this book.

Ithaca, New York　　　　　　　Constance Hoenk Shapiro
September 1992

THE AUTHOR

Constance Hoenk Shapiro is chair of the Department of Human Service Studies in the New York State College of Human Ecology at Cornell University, where she is also professor. She received her B.A. degree (1969) in sociology from Wellesley College, her M.S. degree with distinction (1971) from the Columbia University School of Social Work, and her Ph.D. degree (1978) in education from Cornell University.

Shapiro's main research activities have been in the area of human sexuality, with particular focus on adolescent pregnancy, infertility, and pregnancy loss. She has received numerous teaching awards and has published extensively in professional journals. She is the author of two books: *Adolescent Pregnancy Prevention: School-Community Cooperation* (1981) and *Infertility and Pregnancy Loss: A Guide for Helping Professionals* (1988). In 1989, she was coeditor of her most recent book, *Adolescent Sexuality: New Challenges for Social Work* (with P. Allen-Meares).

Shapiro has been on the faculty at Cornell University since 1974, serving as the director of its social work program from 1986 to 1992. She is on the board of directors of the Ferre Institute in Utica, New York, and was a founding member of the Central New York Chapter of RESOLVE, Inc. She also serves as a consultant to federal, state, and local organizations on issues relating to human sexuality. In addition to teaching, consulting, and research, Shapiro maintains a private practice for infertile individuals and couples.

When
Part of the Self
Is Lost

PART 1

Loss and Grief

1

Attachment and Loss
in the Context of Sexuality

Coming to grips with losses in American society is a challenging task for several reasons. First, Americans tend to value the stoic image of the person who "bears his loss well." People who have experienced a loss are said to be "making a good recovery" if they resume their normal activities shortly after the loss, make few and unemotional references to the loss, and do not disconcert others by their efforts to adjust to the loss.

Second, our increasingly mobile society disrupts our ties with families and stable neighborhood networks, traditionally sources of solace for persons coming to grips with a loss. The sacrifice of physical closeness with loved ones who have given comfort during periods of childhood loss, adolescent change, and adult transition is significant. Comfort now must be gleaned through long-distance telephone calls or truncated visits in the midst of a crisis; also sacrificed are the day-to-day comfortings that can cushion the pain of loss: child care, a healthy casserole, transportation, a dinner invitation, a lingering cup of coffee. The cycle of reciprocity that encourages families in close contact to comfort one another over life's losses is broken for many families today.

A third challenge that we face in coping with loss is to *define* a variety of life events as representing losses. The early literature on loss tended to focus almost exclusively on the death of a loved one. Later, notably in the work of Elisabeth

Kübler-Ross, that definition was extended to include one's *own* impending death as a loss to be mourned. More recently, loss has been broadened to include symbolic losses, life transitions, and the loss of physical functioning. However, even mental health professionals do not agree about what should be viewed as a loss or how it should be treated. Largely because of the seminal work of Erich Lindemann (1944), who studied people's responses to the deaths of loved ones in a Boston nightclub fire, counselors now recognize that a catastrophic loss can precipitate certain emotional reactions. However, the literature on crisis intervention, which had its roots in Lindemann's research, tends to ignore the individual's need to confront grief and loss and favors instead the goal of returning the person to normal functioning.

In this book, loss is defined as the disruption of an attachment—an attachment to other people, to body parts, to inanimate objects, to fantasies, to habits, and to life-styles. Perhaps Peter Marris (1974) conveys the broadest meaning when he reminds us that we feel immediately threatened if our basic assumptions and emotional attachments are challenged. Parkes and Weiss (1983) observe that persons threatened with loss typically intensify, rather than give up, attachment behaviors.

Peretz (1970) groups the concept of loss into four major categories: the loss of a significant or valued person, the loss of a part of the self, the loss of external objects, and developmental loss. Let us explore these losses in the context of life events concerned with sexuality and reproduction.

Loss of a Significant Person

The early work on responses to loss focuses on loss of significant others, with a concomitant emphasis on grieving the loss. Although death is often cited as the most final kind of loss, other life events disrupt relationships enough to cause a profound feeling of loss. Examples include physical separation from a loved one (caused by hospitalization, a jail term, family members leaving home, a geographical move to a new home);

dissolution of a relationship (a broken engagement, placing a child for adoption or foster care, divorce); loss of a symbolic attachment (pregnancy loss, infertility); and dramatic personality changes that sever the original attachment (changes resulting from psychiatric illness, an accident, or the aging process). The loss of the loved one may be total or partial, permanent or temporary. There may also be a loss of some special aspect of the person, even though the person is still physically present.

Sarah, an eighty- year-old woman, speaks of her life after she placed her ill husband in a skilled nursing facility:

> While he was home, I kept so busy just taking care of him. But my doctor finally told me that I would kill myself if I kept it up, so I arranged to put him in a nursing home. Do you think I did the right thing? I keep thinking of our wedding vows and the words "In sickness and in health till death do you part." So now I putter around doing nothing all day. My daughter takes me to see him once or twice a week, but we have no privacy, and all I can do is give him a kiss hello and a kiss good-bye. I wear his pajamas to bed at night to help me remember what it was like to snuggle up with him in the night.

When we think of ways in which the loss of a significant person bears on one's sexuality, we tend to think of a lover or a spouse. But the emotional response of grieving a loss almost always affects one's capacity for sexual intimacy (Orfirer, 1970; Simos, 1979; Shapiro, 1988). Thus, professionals need to be aware that changes in sexual practices and preferences are common when a client is mourning *any* loss, not only the loss of a sexual partner.

Loss of a Part of the Self

Our sense of identity, which encompasses our beliefs about our physical attributes and our worth as human beings, is shaped over a lifetime of interactions and personal growth. Many events occur that change our perception of ourselves, and we are often prepared for these changes by associations with others who have handed down folk wisdom and educational information on everything from menstruation to parenthood. However, when these changes involve losses that we have not anticipated, the adjustments may be especially difficult.

Loss of health is one area in which both sexual and reproductive functioning may be threatened. If this loss of health is accompanied by the loss of a body part, such as a breast or a colon, the direct impact on sexual functioning cannot be ignored. Yet it is easy for health professionals to focus on physical recovery from an illness or an operation without ever attending to the sexual adjustment that the patient must make in response to the loss.

Jack, who was diagnosed at age sixty-two with colon cancer, now has a colostomy. In a counseling session he says:

> No one ever told me how humiliating it would be to have to deal with this damned bag. Oh sure, the nurses told me how to empty it, and the doctor talked to me about my diet, and in my support group we talk about how to avoid embarrassing situations in public. But no one has talked with me about how to make love with the damned appliance hanging off of me! My wife and I try to have a sense of humor about it, but there's nothing funny about an accident in the middle of an orgasm. Sometimes I figure it would be easier to be celibate than to risk the awkwardness and humiliation of it all.

Injury also may bring with it a sense that a part of the self has been lost. For a young woman forced into an incestuous relationship, the loss of virginity may provoke feelings of anguish, in addition to the sense that she has been robbed of the pleasures that accompany most adolescents' awareness of their emerging sexuality: "While other girls in my class were anticipating their first real kiss, I was worrying about whether my father was going to come into my bed that night." The woman who has been raped also suffers a number of losses. In addition to the physical damage that may have been caused, there is a resulting inability to trust, which is often perceived as a loss of one's way of viewing the world. These losses are often compounded by society's attitude toward rape victims, which suggests that they were somehow negligent by getting into a situation where the rape could occur. As they contemplate whether they will ever be able to experience the pleasure of lovemaking without the toxic specter of their past, survivors of rape and incest anticipate possible future losses that will affect their ability to view themselves as fully responsive human beings.

People suffering from other injuries, most notably spinal cord injuries, also anticipate future losses. These clients will be grieving many current losses related to their physical inabilities to perform tasks that others take for granted. The loss of sexual and reproductive potential is difficult for clients to discuss, yet it is of immense concern. The fear that they will be viewed as asexual causes many individuals to avoid intimate relationships, or, at best, to need support and reassurance about their sexuality and their capacity to express it.

Aging brings with it losses such as diminished feelings of attractiveness, pride, and independence—all of which can have an impact on one's sexuality. Even more debilitating are the implicit societal attitudes suggesting that people who are elderly, ill, or disabled are not entitled to be sexual human beings. Even if these individuals have found a way to cope with their own limitations, such attitudes can have a devastating effect on their creative efforts.

Changes in social roles also may represent a loss of part of the self. People whose family and occupational roles have changed may regret the loss of important statuses associated with these roles. Role losses also are worthy of attention if they represent dashed hopes and dreams, such as the incapacity of an infertile couple to become parents. Likewise, the very concrete role loss that a recent widower faces will include the absence of a sexual partner.

Loss of External Objects

Although the loss of external objects is not usually a prominent loss, the area of finances can be troublesome and stressful for some people. A person's financial status and the availability of medical coverage for important procedures are critical to getting quality care in areas of sexual and reproductive health. Spending personal income for such expenses as in vitro fertilization, chemotherapy, or years of psychotherapy to resolve the issues associated with incest can deplete one's savings and change financial priorities in unanticipated ways.

An infertile couple recount:

> We've used up all our savings, borrowed on our life insurance, and still we haven't conceived. After eight years, six surgeries, five cycles of artificial insemination, and two attempts at in vitro fertilization, we finally realize that we don't even have enough money saved to explore the possibility of adoption. We're not getting any younger, and now we're so emotionally worn out from all the infertility treatments that we don't see any possibility of ever becoming parents. Who's going to give a baby to a couple who are in debt, emotionally exhausted, and depressed?

Loss of external objects also occurs after a change of residence; perhaps a rape survivor moves to a different neighborhood to maximize future physical safety, or illness forces a person to relinquish the comforts of home for the care of a skilled nursing facility. A change in residence also may be accompanied by a loss of familiar possessions and the memories that they evoke.

Developmental Loss

Sexual losses actually begin in childhood, when parents exhort their children to stop certain socially unacceptable behaviors— cavorting around naked, playing "doctor" with a neighbor or sibling, or masturbating. Children then begin to form impressions of themselves as sexual beings and to accept the losses of behaviors that might have been acceptable at an earlier age. The shroud of secrecy that surrounds sexuality lifts at puberty, as the schools (and sometimes the parents) prepare young people for the biological changes their bodies will soon experience. This period, although full of curious anticipation for some, is also replete with losses. Girls complain that their fathers never seem to want to hold them on their laps anymore, and boys are increasingly awkward about kissing their mothers in public. As Simos (1979, p. 16) points out, "The adolescent on his way to maturity . . . must relinquish (lose) the infantile body, the infantile identity and role, and the childhood image of his parents. The failure to work through these losses results in a person who has achieved chronological but not emotional maturity."

The dilemma for young people is that their bodies are sexually ready and responsive far before their sense of responsibility is fully developed. The losses faced by an adolescent girl who has an unplanned pregnancy range from abortion, to placing her child for adoption or in foster care, to raising the child and losing the experiences of peer socialization that would help shape her sexual view of herself. Also in adolescence girls are encouraged to abandon their earlier trusting relationships with male peers and to be watchful lest the young men in their lives take advantage of them sexually. Boys, too, face developmental losses that influence their view of themselves as sexual people. Males in American society are socialized to be stoic about their emotions, to offer strong shoulders for females to lean on, and to seek solace in their work and hobbies. So, while females are permitted, and even encouraged, to demonstrate emotional vulnerability, males are seen as attractive when they are in control of their emotions. This loss is a profound one, since many males lose touch with their emotions altogether and do not even know when they are emotionally bereft. All this in the interest of fulfilling societal stereotypes!

Other losses can be expected as one grows older: sexual partners change as one falls in and out of love; divorce, separation, or the injury or death of a partner may cause one to feel sexually unfulfilled; physiological aging brings about changes in one's sexual and reproductive capacities; and the meaning of one's sexuality also alters as needs change over the life cycle. Certain changes, such as menopause, may be perceived as

losses by some and as mere transitions by others; the response
to other developmental changes, such as the loss of capacity to
perform sexually, may depend on whether one has an available
sexual partner. These examples emphasize that losses are based
on each person's unique perception of the experience.

Secondary Losses

Many losses tend to have other losses associated with them.
These secondary losses may be less apparent to observers but
may be highly significant to the person experiencing the loss.
For example, a woman having a hysterectomy for uterine cancer has lost not only her reproductive organs but a whole host
of other aspects of herself that she may have valued. While in
the hospital, she has lost the familiar comforts of home and
neighborhood. If she is employed outside the home, she will
have losses, both personal and financial, associated with recuperation time away from work. In the hospital setting, she will
be placed in a dependent position, needing to follow the
instructions and schedules determined by others; and this loss
of autonomy and control can be very debilitating for many
women. Once she returns home, she may not feel physically or
emotionally ready to resume her sexual relationship with her
partner. She and her family members may not even regard
these secondary losses as losses; yet they influence her recovery
from the hysterectomy in ways that demand attention by professional caregivers.

    Rando (1988) points out the many secondary losses that
accompany the illness of cancer: loss of autonomy, predictability, bodily functions, body parts, productivity, pleasure, identity,
intimacy, social contacts, and mobility. Again, the professional
must pay attention to these secondary losses, whether the client
initially perceives them or not. Only when these associated
losses are recognized and grieved will the client and loved ones
be able to work through the emotional impact of the total loss
experience.

Symbolic Losses

Symbolic losses are associated with the psychological aspects of a physical loss. They are abstract and therefore easy to miss, especially if a person is more preoccupied with the concrete aspects of the loss.

Following a mastectomy, the symbolic losses for a woman are separate from the loss of a valued body part. She may feel losses of sexuality, security, independence, and control. It is often the symbolic losses that need careful attention, because society offers sympathy and support for concrete losses without necessarily validating the symbolic losses that also need to be mourned.

There are some kinds of losses for which society provides few rituals and only brief comfort. People experiencing pregnancy loss often are encouraged to view it as a medical event rather than as a loss. Because of the "disenfranchised" nature of this loss (Doka, 1989), the prospective parents rarely receive the comfort and permission for mourning that they need. In addition to the very real loss of their child, they face the symbolic loss of the expanded family roles they had anticipated, the loss of confidence in their reproductive capacities, and the loss of control over life choices.

Symbolic losses can also be understood as secondary losses, in that the person experiencing the primary loss must also confront the loss of important future experiences. The client with a spinal cord injury perceives his immediate losses soon after the diagnosis is communicated; however, the secondary symbolic losses relating to sexuality and reproduction can be both more elusive and profoundly depressing: the inability to have a carefree dating relationship; the complications associated with sexual arousal; the questions about fertility and pregnancy; and, perhaps most troubling, the anticipation that no one will want to have a loving and physically intimate relationship with someone who is physically damaged. These symbolic losses need to be acknowledged as valid and deserving careful emotional attention in order for the person to work through his feelings and gain perspective and emotional resilience to face the future that now takes such a different shape.

Reawakened Earlier Losses

A current physical or symbolic loss often reawakens memories of earlier losses. These losses may be similar to the current loss; for instance, menopause may remind an infertile woman that her reproductive hopes are forever lost. Or, as often occurs, the current loss may make one emotionally vulnerable to earlier losses and unable to defend against them as they mingle with the current loss. A woman grieving her stillborn child may find that the grief of her mother's death many years earlier becomes more fresh at this time, when the symbolism of lost motherhood is most poignant. Or a man mourning the loss of his wife and sexual partner may find himself also working on issues of loss that he never successfully resolved years ago when his fiancée broke their engagement. Here the feelings of abandonment and loss of intimacy are so interwoven that the passage of years does not erase the original pain.

Professionals should be highly sensitive to the earlier losses that may need to be grieved concurrently with the immediate physical or symbolic loss. If the old loss is an unresolved loss, the client may need help in resolving it, so that it does not intrude in a disruptive way on the efforts to come to terms with the current loss. If the earlier loss is one that was mourned satisfactorily, the client may be able to apply to the current loss some of the same coping mechanisms that worked well in an earlier situation. Sometimes the professional will need to point out that the current life disruption also represents a loss, so that the client can remember how he has grieved earlier losses. The professional can then enumerate the strengths that the client brings to the present experience, including the knowledge that grief diminishes with time and careful attention to the loss.

Factors That Influence One's Response to Loss

Loss is truly an issue that should be viewed from a bio-psycho-social perspective. The resilience and social support that one is able to draw upon at a time of loss will influence both the ability to grieve and the capacity to cope. Conversely, physical depletion, psychological vulnerability, or lack of social validation can make the mourning experience an exhausting and isolating time. Professionals will want to assess the strengths and limitations of their clients, taking into consideration the factors discussed in the following sections.

Biological Factors

There is a wealth of literature suggesting that mourning a loss makes one more vulnerable to illnesses. This literature, much of it building on Selye's stress theory (1956), suggests that the immune system's responses are inhibited by chemical changes generated by the body's reaction to stress, thus causing persons under stress to contract illnesses that add further to the stress with which they must contend.

If we acknowledge that the stress of loss is physiologically taxing, one area that we will want to explore with clients is their physical well-being. If they have been grappling with the loss for some time before seeking professional help, areas of inquiry would include how well they are sleeping, how much rest they are getting, and how well they feel physically; whether they are eating well-balanced meals and getting regular exercise; and the extent to which they are using alcohol, drugs (including prescription medications), caffeine, and tobacco. As we will see in later chapters, normal grieving causes a number of somatic complaints. It is important for the professional to assess how troublesome these symptoms are and how disruptive the client finds them in her efforts to regain a perspective on life after the loss.

If a client seeks or accepts professional help immediately upon learning of the loss, the professional will need to assess the ways in which the physical loss is causing distress. A diagnosis of cancer, an ectopic pregnancy, a spinal cord injury, a rape, a hysterectomy, and many other physical losses will dramatically alter the client's sense of bodily well-being. The professional will want to work closely with medical staff to ensure that the client is helped to manage physical pain and, at the same time, to become educated about his particular loss. Clients should be encouraged to ask questions, to seek out reading material, and to meet others who have coped with losses like theirs. An organization called Reach to Recovery, which arranges visits to mastectomy patients and their families from women who have had mastectomies, provides an excellent model for ways in which clients may gain strength from others who have grappled with similar worries and fears. This model is especially valuable because it assumes that the woman's sexual partner and other family members will be vitally affected by her cancer diagnosis and subsequent surgery.

In addition to determining the effect of a physical loss on the client, the professional's assessment should include attention to symbolic losses as well. What does it mean for a client to be in a physically dependent situation? How will the client's roles at home and at work change as a result of any symbolic losses? How have the client's future hopes and dreams been altered by the accompanying symbolic losses? Since symbolic losses are often hard to identify as losses, and even harder for society to validate, clients may need special support in recognizing the impact of these losses and in garnering social support for themselves during their period of adjustment.

Joe, recovering from a recent heart attack, reminds us of the role reversals that are occurring in his life:

> Hell, I don't feel like a man anymore! My wife won't let me drive, and I go nuts when she's behind the wheel. She's cooking me all these tasteless, low-fat meals and bustling around the house like a regular nurse. When she doesn't hear me snoring at night, she shakes me to make sure I'm still breathing. And, worst of all, she won't have anything to do with sex even though the doctor has given us the go-ahead. I can complain to my friends about my diet, but who's going to want to hear me complain about the death of my sex life?

Psychological Factors

The professional will want to ask the client to describe his life, including satisfactions and disappointments, before the loss, and then to anticipate how his life will be altered by the loss.

Attachment. It is especially important to inquire about the degree of attachment the client had to what was lost. In general, the stronger the attachment, the more intense the feelings of loss will be. A person with a sedentary life-style and a love of books is likely to feel less investment in robust physical good health than is someone who is athletic and depends on sports participation for his sense of identity and social support. A woman past her reproductive years may feel less a sense of loss after a hysterectomy than a young single woman whose uterus is removed and who fears rejection from men when they learn of her incapacity to bear children.

The impact of a particular loss will also depend on the client's degree of ambivalence toward the individual or the object that is lost. The loss of a clear-cut relationship, whether filled with love or hatred, is easier to mourn than the loss of a relationship characterized by mixed emotions or ambivalent feelings. An infertile couple who build their family through adoption, thereby gaining a rewarding sense of parenthood and loving relationships with their children, have learned to live without attaching reproductive outcomes to their sexual activity. The woman in this couple probably will feel less ambivalent toward menopause than the woman who has no children and who is still undergoing infertility treatments when she enters menopause. This second woman will have more losses to grieve, and she and her husband may have more difficulty finding satisfaction in their sexual relationship, since it is so intertwined with their desire to conceive.

Unfinished Business. When speaking of relationships that are ended through death, professionals often refer to the unfinished business that is left between the survivor and the deceased—those matters that were never addressed or settled. When there is little or no unfinished business, an individual can more easily accept the inevitable closure of a relationship that was ended by death. Unfinished business is a source of anxiety and causes the survivor to search for opportunities to achieve some sense of closure.

Other losses, especially symbolic secondary losses, also are rendered more poignant by one's consciousness of unfinished business. Any person who has a condition that affects his sexual and reproductive functioning will need to come to terms with lost hopes and dreams for the future. A person with a spinal cord injury may be faced with a diagnosis that, in effect, closes the door on any hopes for experiencing sexual pleasure. A woman who has had a mastectomy may believe that she has forever lost her most sensitive source of sexual arousal. A person with AIDS may conclude that safer sex should, in fact, be no sex, and she will feel sharply the unfinished aspect of her sexual self that may have brought great satisfaction before she contracted AIDS. The sense of time urgency is especially frustrating in the case of serious illness such as cancer and AIDS, when the client fears that life itself may end long before she has accomplished all she had set out to do.

Unfinished business is always an issue with pregnancy loss, and may be still further complicated by any feelings of ambivalence that the prospective parents felt. Adults who had not planned a pregnancy and who must grapple with their negative or ambivalent feelings will have complicated emotional work to do if the pregnancy is lost. Most will feel guilty at the sense of relief they feel that the issue has been resolved for them. Others will feel that they needed more time to resolve their ambivalence and that the loss deprived them of the chance to exert their own control over the situation. Still others will be haunted by the fear that their negative feelings actually contributed to causing the pregnancy loss. Such unfinished business can be very troubling in a relationship, especially when partners have differing reactions to the pregnancy, since they will therefore have different struggles in resolving their feelings about the loss.

Most pregnant women who permit themselves to enjoy the beginning bonding with their fetus will speak of the specialness, and even the secrecy, of their relationship with the baby-to-be. Now that medical technology permits prospective parents to see sonograms of their babies in utero, they have more awareness of a "real baby," who can be seen sucking his thumb, gulping amniotic fluid, and turning somersaults! Even for parents who do not request a sonogram, the vivid fantasies attached to this baby may have created a powerful psychological bond during even the earliest months of the pregnancy. If the pregnancy is lost, there will be many feelings of unfinished business, which will be discussed in greater detail in Chapter Six.

Personal Characteristics. A client with good coping strategies, a healthy personality, and sound mental health will have important strengths on which to draw in resolving losses. However, these strengths may diminish as stresses occur in the client's life; so the professional will want to make a broad assessment of family functioning in order to determine the context in which the current loss occurs. If there are financial troubles, other recent or unresolved losses, a dearth of social supports, or any other stressors, the professional will need to help the client attend to these at the same time. Rando (1988) asserts that bereaved people tend to grieve in much the same manner as they conduct the rest of their lives. Asking a client how she has coped with past crises or how she has come to terms with past losses can give the professional some useful insight about strengths and limitations that the client already has in her repertoire.

Joanne, a physical education teacher suffering from breast cancer that has metastasized, relates:

> I'm trying to keep going and to keep physically fit because once I put myself to bed, that'll be the end of me—I'll just waste away. So I've signed up for some classes in low-impact aerobics and some yoga, and I've asked a nutritionist to help me find foods that will fight this cancer. I'm also going to treat myself to a massage whenever I can afford it. My breasts may be gone, but I still have enough life in me to beat this cancer!

It is also useful to ask clients how satisfied they have felt in the past about their efforts to resolve losses. If client and professional can jointly identify vulnerable areas that need careful attention, the client will be able to learn new strategies for coping more effectively with the current loss. On the other hand, if the professional can identify strengths that the client has used in the past, the client—who, like most clients mourning a loss, may feel highly inadequate—will become aware that she is still using excellent coping strategies, painful as they may be.

Sex-Role Conditioning. Rando (1988) and Greil (1991) remind us of the important impact that sex roles have on the way we mourn losses. Although there is much support these days for helping males become more expressive about their emotions, societal conditioning in Western culture values the male who is in control and who avoids the expression of feelings. In addition, since "being in control" implies that they are managing well, males are discouraged from reaching out to others for help. In turn, males often do not know how to offer support, believing instead that they should either discount the loss or try to "fix things." Anger, considered socially acceptable for males to vent and discouraged in females, is a valid emotion associated with expressing loss. However, when males are restricted to anger as one of the few acceptable emotional outlets in grieving a loss, and when females are denied that emotion as integral to their mourning, both are shortchanged. In general, women experience less conflict between their sex-role conditioning and the behaviors that are most functional in resolving a loss. However, this sex-role conditioning can cause frustrating dynamics in a marital relationship.

Julie, recently injured in an automobile accident, is currently confined to a wheelchair and must devote at least two hours a day to physical therapy. Her husband, Alan, has rearranged his life to accommodate to her efforts at recovery. He recounts:

> When I come home from work at lunchtime to take Julie to the
> therapist, I can often tell she's been crying and she seems with-
> drawn and tense. I try to jolly her out of it, telling her we're in

this together, but sometimes I wonder if I'm not pulling more than my share of the load. I find myself getting pretty short-tempered with her doctor and her physical therapist because they can't give us any different answers about how long her recovery will take and how fully she will recover. So I lash out at them, she tries to calm me down, then she gets depressed, and I wear myself out getting her to see that I'm trying to do the best I can for her.

Social Factors

The presence of social supports is critical to most people mourning a loss. Survivors of a loss often have powerful feelings of emotional isolation but have little energy to reach out to others; they may not even know which people might best be able to offer comfort at such a difficult time. The professional can help the client identify a support network of caring people willing to do concrete physical tasks, to serve as empathic listeners, and to offer diversions and distractions from the preoccupation with loss.

Depending on the nature of the loss and the social stigma associated with it, support groups may provide an environment of nonjudgmental listening that is highly validating of the loss and the survivors' efforts to cope. Support groups have some added benefits. Since their members often are at different stages in the process of coming to terms with their respective losses, a new member can take hope from realizing that people who work hard to resolve their losses can, indeed, gain a new perspective on life. Support groups also provide an important opportunity for the survivor to offer help as well as ask for it. Since most people grieving a recent loss feel that they are a burden to others, it can be reassuring for them to know that their sensitivity also enables them to perceive and respond to others' pain. Another value of a support group of people experiencing similar losses is that people are able to speak in an emotional shorthand. Their very presence in the group means that they share some special characteristics with other members, and that they can dispense with giving detailed explanations of their loss, knowing that others in the group will understand much without the need to ask questions. If the loss is a socially stigmatized one, such as AIDS or incest, the members of the group will value one another's support in a special way, since it is unlikely that they know anyone else who has experienced their particular loss.

The professional may find that a client would like to bring significant people in his life to some counseling sessions, as a way of acquainting them with his problems and, perhaps, in an effort to improve communication with someone whose relationship he values. The client might initiate such a request, but the professional also should feel flexible in offering to meet with significant others as an adjunct to ongoing therapeutic efforts. If, as is extremely likely, the client is not the only family member who has been affected by the loss, the professional should give careful consideration to seeing the family as a group (or referring them to a family therapist), both as a way of helping them in the grieving process and as a way of acknowledging the importance of the family as a support system for all its members.

Another aspect of social support has to do with the rituals that can offer solace and comfort at a time of loss. We are all familiar with funerals, wakes, and the Jewish tradition of sitting shiva after the death of a loved one. These rituals not only bring loved ones together to mourn but also give form, structure, and meaning to their feelings. Unfortunately, there are almost no rituals for people who are grieving sexual and reproductive losses. The ritual comfort available to mourners of someone who has died is denied to people whose loss is less visible or less socially validated.

Thus, it often falls to the professional to help clients consider what, if anything, they would like to do to memorialize their loss. Parents of a stillborn child may choose to have a funeral service or a memorial service, but prospective parents who experience a pregnancy loss will need to develop their own ritual, if they believe it would be comforting. People with terminal illnesses also may choose to develop their own rituals, either to celebrate their years or months of survival or to specify to loved ones the ways in which they would like their own memorial rituals to be carried out after their deaths. Sometimes an anniversary ritual can be therapeutic; for instance, one woman with a spinal cord injury commemorates the anniversary of her accident by recounting the progress and life satisfactions she has enjoyed in the intervening years. Other rituals help to bring about closure; for instance, an infertile couple who finally decided to remain child-free turned the room originally intended as a nursery into an indoor greenhouse.

Therapeutic Implications for the Professional

The professional has a unique opportunity to help clients who are struggling with a loss. As this chapter conveys, sexual and reproductive losses are rarely even acknowledged as losses that deserve emotional attention. Yet survivors of these losses emerge feeling vulnerable, depleted, bereft, and often emotionally isolated. They arrive in a professional's office saying, "I just don't know what's wrong with me." "I think I'm going crazy." "I should be over this by now." Some gentle probing reveals that they are trying to resume life as usual in spite of losing a significant part of themselves.

So the professional's challenge becomes threefold. First, the professional must give credit to the survivor for having sought out help at such a difficult time. This is important, since clients who are bereaved may question whether they are doing the right thing. A person who thinks she is going crazy will be especially reassured to know that seeking help is a healthy response to her emotional pain. Second, the professional needs to explain to the client that what is happening relates to the recent loss, even if the client has never defined it as a loss. By using a term that connotes a previous attachment and a recent disruption, the professional can encourage the client to perceive the experience from a perspective that is socially acceptable. Furthermore, the perspective of loss allows more latitude in behavior than the perspective the client originally presented ("I don't know what's wrong with me" or "I think I'm going crazy"). Thus, the client can begin to understand why he has been behaving in a way that had seemed foreign to him.

The third function of the professional is to speak with the client about the importance of mourning his loss. In fact, the client is probably already moving into this process, but without the social or therapeutic validation that is so important. If the professional is able to anticipate with the client some of the concepts discussed in the next chapter, both may move ahead in the important griefwork that needs to be done.

2

Grieving and Coping: Reconstructing One's Life After Loss

As we recognize the importance of attachments that we develop over the life cycle, we can also appreciate that there is little rehearsal or support for relinquishing attachments that are not developmental. Agemates have the company of their peers in developmental transitions, whether they be signaled by weaning, toilet training, beginning school, entering puberty, or the host of other developmental stages that are signified by giving up familiar and secure attachments in favor of new and more age-appropriate behaviors. On the other hand, attachments to body parts, to fetuses, and to vigor and good health are not expected to be rudely severed. When a part of the self is lost, the person feels invaded, betrayed, and, most significantly, profoundly alone.

Friends and family members, confused about how to offer support, often ignore the loss or deprecate its importance. In part, this reaction reflects our society's avoidance of unpleasant events and emotions, but it also reflects the fear by loved ones that: "if I get too close to these feelings of despair, I might realize how vulnerable and threatened I really feel about the unpredictability of life's events." Since most family members have no personal familiarity with the kind of loss that is being experienced, they may have a limited capacity for empathy and may concentrate instead on encouraging the grieving person to cope by "getting on with life."

What loved ones may fail to recognize is that "getting on with life" must first include some time for grieving over the loss of someone or something that can never again be a part of the person's life. If friends and family cannot provide the support needed, the bereft individual may seek comfort and guidance in a professional relationship. As mentioned in Chapter One, the professional's first task is to commend the individual for seeking help at such a difficult time. While gathering more information about the specific loss, the professional also will want to offer some reassurance, assuming it is warranted, that the behaviors and feelings of the bereaved person are normal and expectable during a time of grief. Finally, the professional will want to introduce an element of hopefulness into the relationship—perhaps by telling the client that, although working through grief takes time, the client already has made important strides in this direction and the professional is willing to continue to support him in this effort.

This chapter emphasizes the behavioral and emotional components of grieving and coping after losing a part of oneself. Here, and throughout the book, the terms *grief* and *grieving* refer to an intense emotional suffering caused by loss, disaster, or misfortune. *Mourning*, considered by some authors to be similar to grief, refers to those behaviors following a loss that are prescribed as acceptable by social customs and rituals. *Bereavement* is a process that encompasses both the emotion of grief and the socially acceptable display of a mourning response to the loss. Grief and mourning can take place simultaneously in circumstances where rituals offer support for the display of emotions generated by a loss. However, as we learned in the previous chapter, sexual and reproductive losses are rarely accompanied by rituals; in fact, most people do not even consider the loss a valid one, in spite of the grief demonstrated by the survivor. Therefore, many people who have lost an integral part of themselves are left to express their grief without the support of social rituals or the understanding of significant others. Thus, to a great extent, this book will focus on grief, rather than on mourning, since that is the experience that many clients will present. On the other hand, since one challenge faced by the professional is to encourage the client to develop necessary social supports, we will also give attention to ways of creating meaningful rituals to commemorate a loss that begs for a socially acceptable outlet of grief.

What Do We Know About Grief?

Many authors have contributed to the understanding we now have of grief and adaptation after a loss. Freud (1917/1961), who dealt with grief in the era of World War I, took the position that grieving is normal but that melancholia—in his view, a chronic, maladaptive kind of grief— is pathological.

Bowlby's studies (1961) provide heart-wrenching testimony to the visceral demonstration of grief shown by infant humans and baby monkeys deprived of their mothers.

Lindemann (1944), in his study of people grieving the deaths of loved ones in Boston's 1942 Coconut Grove nightclub fire, made a major contribution to our understanding of the bio-psycho-social responses involved in grief. He delineates the tasks of "griefwork" as (1) the withdrawal of emotional investment in the deceased and the detaching and modifying of emotional ties so that new relationships can be established; (2) readjustment to the environment from which the deceased is missing; and (3) the formation of new relationships.

Kübler-Ross's research (1969) on the responses of terminally ill patients to their impending death laid the groundwork for an appreciation of grief as a process consisting of stages. These stages, well known by professionals, are thought to be individual for each person; that is, not all people need to work on issues in each stage, and people work through the stages in sequences that have meaning for them, often reworking earlier stages even as they are nearing the end of the grieving process. In Kübler-Ross's framework, a person grappling with a loss first experiences the stage of denial, in which the full impact of the loss is not absorbed. During the next stage, the individual feels and expresses the anger associated with the loss. A stage of bargaining often follows; here the individual makes real or symbolic offers of good behavior, as if in an effort to delay a perceived punishment for unatoned bad deeds. When the period of bargaining passes, the individual enters a period of active grief, manifested by tears, sadness, and preoccupation with the lost object. Ultimately, most individuals progress to a stage of acceptance, in which they are able to reorder their lives around the loss they have sustained without being preoccupied with the loss. Although Kübler-Ross's stages have been applied to the reactions of people grieving losses other than their own impending deaths, most of the literature on grief focuses on the ultimate loss through death.

Simos (1979) broadens this perspective to define loss as a universal human experience, thereby honoring as valid those losses other than death that people experience at all stages of the life cycle. In an effort to normalize behavior that otherwise might be considered pathological, Simos elaborates on the phases that grievers go through. The initial stages include shock, alarm, and denial as the person tries unsuccessfully to absorb the full implications of the loss. Somatic distress, searching for the lost object, and feelings of anger, guilt, and shame are increasingly apparent as the reality of the loss becomes clear. Efforts to live without the lost object often are accompanied by psychological identification with the object, regression, hopelessness, and depression. Ultimately the grieving person begins to feel relief and the restoration of meaning accompanied by efforts at substitution or, failing successful griefwork, by feelings of depletion.

Worden (1982) specifies four main tasks of bereavement as he writes about grief counseling following a death: accepting the reality of the loss; experiencing the pain of grief; adjusting to an environment in which the deceased is no longer present; and withdrawing emotional energy and reinvesting it in another relationship.

Rando (1984, 1986), writing about the process of grief precipitated by terminal illness and death, suggests ways in which professionals, caregivers, and family members can use grief therapeutically, thereby maximizing one's capacity to move past a current loss and live life more fully.

The temporal dimension of grief requires that one consider a continuum. At the beginning point of the continuum is the awareness that a loss will occur; at the end point, which may occur long after the actual loss, feelings about the loss have been consolidated. Between these points on the continuum, we will find the ebb and flow of griefwork that provides an outlet for the powerful emotions stimulated by the loss.

Anticipatory Grief

It is not unusual for a warning to occur before an actual loss, thus giving those affected some time to grieve before life alters dramatically and forever. Rando (1986) defines anticipatory grief as the phenomenon encompassing the processes of mourning, coping, interaction, planning, and psychological reorganization—processes set in motion by the awareness of an impending loss and the recognition of associated losses in the past, present, and future.

In contrast to the unanticipated loss, an expected loss will make sense because it is part of a predicted process. Consequently, the bereaved person can prepare emotionally for the loss rather than experiencing it as an unexpected emotional assault. In this sense the person can get a head start on the process of mourning that may cushion the intensity of feelings following the finality of the actual loss. However, anticipatory grief is complicated in that there is a delicate balance between denial and acceptance as intensity waxes and wanes over time. The psychological exhaustion that results from this emotional roller coaster can lead the mourner to detach prematurely from the person or object being mourned. Premature detachment has the potential to disrupt and even sever relationships, to the pont where the ill person feels she is being treated like a corpse. Premature detachment in other situations could result in a devaluing of the part of the self to be lost, such as breast cancer survivors who "forget" to do regular breast exams or persons with AIDS who neglect their medication.

Too often, it is assumed that the anticipatory grief is associated only with the pending physical loss; in fact, much grief is actually focused on secondary and symbolic losses, such as the loss of previous functioning, health, and abilities; the loss of the future as it had once been envisioned; the loss of security, predictability, and control; and the loss of the sense of personal invulnerability. Thus, the time dimension of past, present, and future is highly relevant when one is speaking of the detachment that begins during anticipatory grief. A major component of anticipatory grief is concerned with the image of a future that must be endured despite the inevitable loss.

Grief Following a Loss

Responses to a loss can be grouped into three major phases. These phases do not predict an orderly passage through the griefwork that lies ahead but are, instead, markers for the professional to recognize as clients evidence certain behaviors that are normal in grieving but would be suspect in the absence of active grief. The phases of grief after a loss tend to overlap, and the feelings described in each phase will ebb and flow, depending on the vulnerability or the resilience of the survivor.

The first phase is that of *avoidance*, which includes shock, denial, and disbelief. During this time, the individual needs to avoid acknowledging the enormity of the loss and therefore will use denial as a defense mechanism. Such a response is normal and even therapeutic, since the effect of denial is to cushion the emotional blow and give the damaged psyche time to absorb the reality of the loss a little at a time. Feelings of confusion and disorganization are common and represent the unsuccessful effort to make sense out of a reality that has been devastated. Some individuals may dissolve in tears and seem completely unable to cope, whereas others may consciously put aside their grief for a time, especially if there are others affected by the loss who need solace and comfort.

Kathy spoke with a counselor a few days after being raped by an acquaintance:

> It's hard to believe that it happened, especially since I've only told a couple of my close friends. The rest of the world just keeps moving on, and here I am wanting to say, "Hey, wait a minute! What about me? Can't you see I'm hurting?" But people are just going on about their lives and I guess that's what I'll try to do too. My friends are sympathetic, but I can tell they're uncomfortable whenever I bring the subject up, so perhaps putting it behind me is the best thing to do.

The professional's role during this avoidance phase is to be supportive but not confrontational. The elements of denial that are present need to be respected as the client's defense against an unbearable reality. With enough support and the encouragement to talk, the normally grieving client will begin to acknowledge at least some aspects of the loss. However, even acknowledging the facts of the loss may represent some denial if there is no evidence of the accompanying feelings. Professionals need to be particularly watchful here, because at some level they themselves may wish to avoid the intensity of the pain that the client feels and may therefore accept the client's cognitive acknowledgment of the loss as a movement past denial—when, in fact, the client needs to get in touch with the feelings that the loss arouses. Professionals who have worked with grieving clients will attest to the recurrent dynamic of denial. Just when it seems that a client has grappled with the reality of the loss, she may retreat again to the comfort of denial, needing more time to replenish herself for the ongoing griefwork. The professional is probably best cautioned against believing that denial has an end point, since it is likely to crop up repeatedly throughout the later phases of grief following a loss. If the denial is respected, most clients will be able to find their own pace in accepting the enormity of the loss, both cognitively and affectively.

The second phase, *acute grief* or *confrontation*, consists of an intense display of emotions as the reality and irreversibility of the loss become apparent. The responses in this phase are reinforced by the daily experiences that remind one of the loss: the putting on of a prosthesis, the taking of medication, the irreversibility of physical decline, the dismantling of a nursery, the inability to engage in once-familiar hobbies or chores, and, more indirectly, the expression of concern by others that life should be getting back to "normal" soon. Denial and disbelief may occur from time to time, but these reactions are intermingled with the new reality, in which the loss cannot be ignored. Each reminder of the loss brings fresh anguish.

Expressions of feeling will vary with the individual. Some people express emotion easily and, even when such emotions provoke tears or angry outbursts, are comfortable with showing their feelings to others. In contrast, other individuals may be reluctant to express the emotions that they feel. This reluctance can stem from personal feelings of awkwardness, uncertainty about the reactions of others, or an unwillingness to burden others—especially if they also are grieving.

In addition to the affective response to the loss, there is also a cognitive response that has certain predictable components. The client often is preoccupied with thoughts of the loss, speaks incessantly about it, and, ultimately, begins to consider how to carry on life in spite of the loss. There may also be more abstract cognitive responses, such as a feeling of dread or impending doom, the belief that life can never be worthwhile again, and a feeling of being in limbo and removed from involvement in others' activities. Feelings of disorganization and confusion are common. Survivors often complain that they "can't seem to get organized," that they feel restless and jittery, that they are overwhelmed, and that they believe they are going crazy.

Physical symptoms also are identifiable during this phase: disruptions in patterns of eating and sleeping, the feeling of wanting to cry at unexpected times, constant sighing, tightness in the chest, physical exhaustion—not only because of the disruption in sleep patterns but also because of the amount of energy it takes to remain in control when one is assailed with feelings of disorientation and confusion.

In sum, the period of acute grief is confusing, emotionally intense, and frightening as the survivor attempts to live with the loss he has endured and to envision the life he will need to reconstruct in response to the loss.

The professional who is working with a client in the acute grief phase will need to be introspective regarding the feelings aroused by the client's emotional vulnerability. Professionals who have their own unresolved losses may find themselves confronting these losses as they witness their clients' pain and helplessness; professionals who have as a goal the independence of their clients may feel threatened or disconcerted by the dependence that clients demonstrate in the midst of their grief; and professionals who are more at home with the quietly introspective client may be frightened by the angry or anguished displays of emotion brought on by acknowledgment of the loss. In all these areas, the professional must be as attentive to her own internal signals as to the client's, so that she can keep pace with the client and not be therapeutically sidetracked by her own unacknowledged emotional responses. If the client's needs in the acute grief phase are difficult for the professional, then—for the sake of this client and all future clients who are grappling with the intense emotions generated by loss—the professional should seek supervision or consultation for herself.

A social worker recounts:

> Jon began coming to me for therapy a few weeks after his lover died of AIDS. His pain was so raw and his memories were so full of anguish that I could barely keep back the tears. When I asked myself why I felt so vulnerable to the emotions he evoked, I realized that I was getting back in touch with the feelings I had when my husband died of cancer eight years ago. I thought I had worked my own feelings through, but it's clear that I still have some emotional raw nerves. I'm finding it increasingly difficult to encourage Jon to share his sadness when I know his words will reawaken my own pain.

Clients in the acute grief phase are often bewildered and frightened by the intensity of their emotions. Some fear that they are going crazy; others fear that they will never be emotionally healed. The professional can reassure these clients by pointing our that their feelings, although painful, are both expectable and normal following a loss of such magnitude. Clients should be told that the professional will stay with them and support them in their grief; that, with careful attention to the loss and the emotions associated with it, they can expect the pain to diminish with the passage of time; and that, although their loss has changed them forever, they must now make choices about how to reconstruct their lives. In this sense, healing does not represent resuming the old life but, instead, finding new ways of living life after the loss. In general, however, clients should be discouraged from making any irreversible decisions in the first year after a loss. Decisions about changing jobs, moving, giving away possessions, and so on, should be delayed until the client can have a better perspective on them. The danger of creating secondary losses is great as bereaved people hasten to get their affairs in order, little appreciating the comfort of possessions, co-workers, and familiar surroundings.

Some clients may take comfort from reading books that relate to their particular kind of loss; others may benefit from talking with others who have survived a similar loss and who can assure them that their griefwork was also difficult and painful. At times, the professional will need to accept the client's dependency, perhaps assigning specific tasks to help put some small amount of order back into the client's life. The professional will also need to accept and encourage the client's expression of emotions—angry outbursts, tearful deluges, and cognitive confusion—that may have exhausted the patience of family and friends during the "ebb and flow" of griefwork. During this phase, clients can become discouraged and disconcerted by the periods of emotional expression, followed by quiescence, followed again by familiar emotions.

Nathan expressed his confusion at his emotional ups and downs:

> No sooner do I recover from a round of chemotherapy, and I begin to feel hopeful, when something coincidentally happens that knocks me completely off balance. Last month the after-effects of the chemo weren't too bad, and I began to think I could handle this. Then this month right before I was scheduled to go in for chemo I caught my daughter's strep throat and had to go on antibiotics. The doctor refused to do the next

> chemo treatment until I'm off the antibiotics, so now here I
> am, feeling out of control again. I'm afraid the delay in the
> chemo may cause the cancer to flare up again. I find myself
> facing all the old fears all over again, and I'm thinking more
> about dying than I have in a couple of months. I thought I was
> past all that!

What clients fear as regression or lack of progress must be interpreted by the professional as the client's unique pace, which requires some emotional rest between periods of intensity. Clients need to be reassured that repetition of issues and feelings is normal in the course of coming to terms with their loss, and that they will move ahead slowly, but that the passage of time is less important than their continued willingness to express the many feelings associated with the loss.

The professional must be especially sensitive to the client's physical health during the acute grief phase. Disruptions in patterns of eating and sleeping can compound the client's miseries, leaving her less resilient emotionally and more vulnerable to illnesses. If clients are experiencing troublesome physical symptoms, they should see a physician, in order to rule out a condition more complex than the physical effects of grieving. Antianxiety and antidepressant medications should be used, ideally, on a short-term basis; otherwise, clients run the risk of developing a dependence on such medication and, as a side effect, not being able to get sufficiently in touch with their emotions to do the painful griefwork that is necessary to work through the loss.

Professionals must be quite specific in their questioning of clients, who will tend to be forgetful about what they are eating and when they are sleeping. This is an important time to watch for overdependence on alcohol and drugs; the consumption of caffeine should be discouraged, because the client may be unaware of its tendency to exaggerate "the jitters" and to prolong periods of sleeplessness. It may seem an impossible burden for the client to consider getting regular exercise, even though such exercise is known to have antidepressant effects. However, the professional should offer firm encouragement for daily walks, assuming the client is ambulatory, if only to get the client in touch with an environment beyond the four walls of a familiar office or home.

Clients who are grieving may need to be seen at more frequent intervals than other clients. The professional will want to discuss with the client how much time he or she can tolerate between appointments. Certain periods are especially painful for a bereaved person. Anniversaries that remind her of the loss, weekends, holidays, and unstructured time are all difficult for someone who is struggling to find some meaning in a world that has been turned upside down from the loss.

In addition to the previously mentioned expressions of fear and bewilderment, some clients in the acute grief phase will say flatly that life is not worth living. It is amazing to me that a great many of the books on grief and loss contain not a single reference to suicidal thoughts and behavior. And, yet, it is unusual to find a bereaved client who has not considered that death would be a welcome release from life after his loss. Chapter Twelve contains detailed information about assessing the lethality of a client; however, it is my belief that one should not wait for a bereaved client to raise the warning signals of suicidal thoughts. Some professionals fear that any question from them about suicide might provoke that very behavior. But I routinely ask all bereaved clients if they have felt despondent enough in their grief to consider killing themselves, and I have never had a client say, "No, not at all, but come to think of it, that sounds like something I should think about more seriously!" I do not want to make light of a very serious subject, but I believe strongly that getting the topic of suicide out in the open between client and professional means that either can come back to it in the future as the struggle becomes more exhausting.

In the third phase, *reestablishment* or *consolidation*, the intense symptoms of acute grief gradually decline. This phase is an outgrowth of the confrontation phase, and feelings of that earlier phase coexist with the efforts to adjust as one accommodates to life with the loss. The loss is not forgotten, but it is becoming more integrated into the client's acceptance of her current reality and is no longer a total source of preoccupation. Memories of the loss are now accompanied by feelings of poignancy and caring instead of anguish. The client's self-esteem will increase as she becomes more able to cope with the challenges of life, to focus on the present and future rather than on the past, and to go on to new attachments. Depending on the loss, the client may have made an effort to define a new identity that incorporates the loss, and may even have feelings of satisfaction when she recognizes the personal growth that has come from the pain of loss.

Gina had a double mastectomy six months ago and speaks of ways that she has consolidated her grief:

> For a while after the surgery I didn't think I'd ever feel attractive again. I was withdrawn and kind of depressed. The thought of putting on a bathing suit really freaked me out, and even the idea of wearing a form-fitting sweater was pretty intimidating. But eventually I decided to stop letting the absence of my breasts rule my life. I bought a prosthesis to wear in my bra, I took my husband with me when I shopped for some skimpy negligees, and I decided to make the best of my good health today. Sure, I worry about the future, but in a way that is why I can't waste the good times in the present.

With the resumption of some new aspects of life may come feelings of guilt and ambivalence. Sometimes the client feels amazed that life can go on in spite of the loss that once seemed overwhelming; this realization may give rise to questions about the worth of the loss in the first place if one can, in fact, accommodate to it. Sometimes the client feels that his ability to enjoy life, to laugh and smile again, amounts to a betrayal. In situations of pregnancy loss, for example, prospective parents are caught between wanting to get on with their lives and holding on to their grief out of fear of "losing" their barely tangible memories of their unborn baby. Some people are conflicted about consolidating their loss because they fear that others will not give them support and attention when their grief is no longer outwardly apparent.

Martha, with a four-year history of infertility, was devastated when she lost a pregnancy at five months:

> My depression after my miscarriage lasted so long that I almost forgot what it felt like to be happy. When I finally began to return to my old self, I realized that I didn't want to give up all the support and attention my family had extended. I have eight brothers and sisters, plus my parents, and all of them live nearby. Usually I've been sort of lost in the crowd of the family, but everyone was so concerned about my misery that they really made me feel special. Now that I'm feeling better, I really want to keep getting their attention, and I'm afraid I won't get it if they stop thinking of me as "poor Martha."

Simos (1979, p. 55) articulates the different forms that the ambivalence of grief can take:

> The bereaved show both a desire to be alone and a craving for companionship. There is an attempt to avoid reminders of the past, yet a compulsion or urgency to talk and dwell on the loss exists. There is a conflict between being passive and active, dependent and independent, regressive and moving forward, and between being supersensitive to the least slight from others and rebuffing overtures of help and sympathy when offered. The conflict shows in the insistence that life has lost all meaning coupled with the simultaneous competent attention to the daily routines of living. The bereaved alternate between despair and hope. They are torn between wanting to be helpless and to be exploitative of others and the fear that they will lose all their friends if they are. They may compulsively seek distractions only to discover they have no interest in these very distractions.

Marris (1974) says that during normal grief the individual works out his feelings of ambivalence by recognizing the conflicting impulses, suffering the pain of the awareness, and eventually mastering the feelings. The struggle and pain that accompany this process drain the bereaved of energy for other routine tasks of living. In the dysfunctional conditions that substitute for normal grief and mourning, the conflict may never be admitted, or the process of going through the pain may be avoided, so that the ambivalence is never resolved.

Not all grievers will be able to consolidate their loss successfully. If the magnitude of the loss is great, and if they lack emotional resilience, social support systems, and good physical health, some people may enter into chronic grief. Unable to relinquish memories of life as it was before the loss, or consumed with anger that such a loss could occur, chronic mourners have a lingering sense of depression and a lowered self-esteem. For these clients, the development of a new identity consists of preoccupation with the loss, diminished resiliency in personality functioning, constricted social involvement, and vulnerability to other separations and losses.

Coping

Coping and consolidation represent an effort to come to terms with the meaning of the loss in relation to one's objective reality. The grieving person is now able to look at the loss squarely and to integrate it into other aspects of his life, although he still will continue to experience periodic upsurges of sadness as he moves ahead in forging a new identity. Rando (1988, p. 225) maintains that successful consolidation after a loss involves completing three sets of processes: acknowledging and understanding the loss; experiencing the pain and reacting to the loss; and, finally, moving adaptively into the new life without forgetting the old.

Acknowledging and Understanding the Loss

As Marris (1974) points out, any event that destroys one's understanding of the meaning of life can be experienced as a loss. Yet many individuals are reluctant or unable to perceive a particular experience as a loss; as a result, they attempt to forge ahead with their lives as if nothing momentous had occurred—especially if the losses have to do with sexual and reproductive health. Since the areas of sexuality and reproduction are often considered private and also are intertwined with self-esteem, losses in these areas may seem particularly threatening and, therefore, difficult to grieve openly.

Acknowledging an intensely private event as a loss may require the gentle prodding of a professional, who can remind the individual that the meaning of life has changed dramatically. As they both explore the ways in which such change is perceived, the professional can begin to portray the change as a series of losses emanating from the private event, ultimately encouraging the individual to feel entitled to mourn those losses. In effect, the professional is encouraging the client to acknowledge the event as momentous and deserving of careful emotional attention in order to understand the full ramifications of the loss.

For Elaine, the "event" was actually a series of events.

> Her father's incestuous relationship with her began when she was eight years old and ended when she turned twelve and her parents were divorced. At sixteen, Elaine sought counseling because she felt lonely and isolated, whereas her peers seemed to be enjoying their friendships and social lives. Her therapist helped Elaine remember back to the time when she was eight years old, and together they explored the ways in which she began to feel different and isolated from her peers. Remembering the years that she endured her father's sexual advances, Elaine was able to identify her feelings of being damaged and powerless, different from other girls her age, and alienated from her siblings. Her therapist was then able to help Elaine recognize the series of losses she had sustained in childhood—losses in self-esteem and in social relationships. Mourning these losses and moving forward to develop trust in new relationships became the next task of Elaine's therapy.

It is not only the client who needs to conceptualize the event as a loss worthy of grief. The client's significant others, who may have been touched by her loss and who may be feeling their own grief, must support her in her grief. Friends and relatives who are eager to see the client "get back to normal" and "get on with her life" may prove to be a source of resistance to the important work of acknowledging and understanding the loss. However, if the client can be clear about what she needs in the way of support and understanding in the weeks and months that follow, and if she widens her sources of support enough so that no one person feels overburdened with the role of sympathetic listener, it may be possible for even reluctant loved ones to support the client as she works toward emotional recovery.

There is a difference between *acknowledging* and *understanding* a loss. Acknowledging the loss has to do with accepting the reality of the event and being able to conceptualize and legitimize it as a loss. Understanding the loss has to do with defining the loss in the context of one's life and assigning a meaning to the loss over time. Thus, coping and consolidation may have their origins in the very early phases of grieving; with the passage of time, the client can be helped to refine his understanding of the loss as it is integrated into his new identity.

Understanding the loss is a process that evolves as clients try to make sense out of the events that have dramatically changed their expectations of how life would progress. Clients need to develop an explanation that makes sense to them intellectually and that answers whatever questions they have about the loss. The explanation that a client evolves may be different from that of others in his environment, but the accuracy of the explanation is less important than the satisfaction and security derived from it.

A person with prostate cancer, in reflecting on its impact, no longer feels the resentment that characterized the months immediately following his diagnosis:

> I finally realized that my anger wasn't getting me anywhere. It was alienating medical staff, irritating my wife, and constantly making me feel more ill than I really was. So I looked for the silver lining and decided to focus on the support that everyone was trying to convey to me. I'm a pretty fast-paced guy, and

> this cancer has forced me to slow down and smell the roses a
> bit. I'm getting closer to my friends and family, perhaps
> because I don't know how much longer I'll be around to enjoy
> them. So, in its own way, by threatening my life, the cancer
> has actually helped me to enjoy life.

A variety of behaviors may accompany the client's efforts to make sense of the loss. For clients with chronic or terminal illnesses, the efforts at consolidation must encompass attention to past losses and anticipation of losses yet to be experienced. Intellectual mastery has long been understood as a way of coming to terms with some aspects of loss. The client who reads voraciously about her medical condition and seeks out others who share her diagnosis would be an example of someone who empowers herself through education for the struggles that may lie ahead.

Many individuals demonstrate what is known as searching behavior, first described by Lindemann (1944) as part of the symptomatology of normal grief. Searching behavior could consist of a preoccupation with thoughts or images of the loss, a compulsion to speak of the loss or to retrieve the lost object, and a feeling of going through the motions of living.

Sandra, who had experienced two stillbirths in three years, entered therapy with many unresolved feelings about the loss of her babies:

> I find myself visiting their graves two or three times a week.
> Whenever I'm in the mall or the grocery store and I see a baby,
> I feel compelled to stare at it and to think whether one of my
> daughters would be the age of that baby if she had lived. It
> breaks my heart in a clothing store to pass a rack of dainty ruf-
> fled dresses. I have to force myself to go out of the house,
> because everywhere there are reminders of my babies who
> died.

Clients who manifest searching behavior should be encouraged to talk about their loss, to acknowledge their attachment to what has been lost and their sadness at resuming life with the loss still a poignant memory, and to try to find a patient listener among close family and friends. It can be devastating for an individual to search her memories, only to be told that she should "get on with her life and forget the troubles of the past." Reassurance from the professional that a review of memories is a healthy aspect of working through grief will be perceived supportively by clients, especially those who do not feel free to talk openly with others in their lives.

During the period of consolidation, clients are ready to look more openly at how their sexuality has been affected by the loss. The energy once consumed by their grieving is beginning to return; their need to talk about the loss no longer predominates in interpersonal relationships; friends and loved ones have demonstrated their capacity for caring, so that the client now can assess more realistically what he can expect from others; and sexual feelings may be emerging as the client begins to recover some of his old zest for life and seeks to reaffirm the new identity that has emerged from the loss experience. The energy level of clients with chronic illnesses will need to be taken into account as the issue of their sexuality is explored. And safe sexual practices will need to be emphasized for all clients, especially those who have AIDS, are HIV positive, or are in a nonmonogamous relationship.

Wendy, diagnosed with AIDS three months ago, has absorbed the initial shock, has joined a support group, and is beginning to confront her own mortality:

> Now that I know my time on this earth is limited, I want to live life to the fullest, and that includes being sexual. I know that unsafe sex is what caused me to contract AIDS, and I would never want to put another person at that risk, but I don't want to live out my final months and years as a sexual hermit.

Since most individuals are reluctant to initiate discussion of sexuality, the professional must not assume such needs are absent simply because they are not mentioned. Rather, the professional should say straightforwardly to clients that discussions of sexual needs are an important aspect of the recovery process, thereby encouraging the client not to ignore or discount this dimension of his new identity.

Experiencing the Pain and Reacting to the Loss

Clients who are successful in the phase of consolidation are ones who have not shied away from feeling the full intensity of the emotional pain associated with their loss. Whether the grief has been expressed through talking with others, crying, spending long periods contemplating the sadness of the loss, exploding in anger, regressing, expressing strong dependency needs, or trying to make sense of life in the midst of the loss, the client will need to have given himself permission to feel deeply the anguish of the loss in order to be in a position to accept it and move ahead with his life. Professionals must pay careful attention to clients who think they are grieving when they are focusing on others who are affected by the loss; they must be wary of clients who keep so busy with the demands of daily life that they take no time for their own griefwork; and, in spite of some positive aspects of intellectual mastery, professionals should not allow clients to believe that cognitive awareness substitutes for emotional openness.

It is important, too, to recognize that few clients will allow themselves to feel emotional pain on a constant basis. Taking "breaks" from grief is important, and as the phase of consolidation becomes more prominent, those breaks will stretch into longer and longer periods until the client realizes that he is spending more time coping with the loss than he is grieving for it. The restlessness that characterizes clients' grief can be mitigated if they have some diversions that take their minds off of the burden of sadness and enable them to feel glimmers of energy and "the old self."

Ted and Maria, both of whom were being treated for their infertility, were advised by their therapist to take a two-month "vacation" from their treatments. Maria recounts:

> I can't believe how caught up we had become in organizing our lives around doctors' appointments, taking temperatures, dealing with the side effects of medication, and generally being completely preoccupied with making a baby. It's hard to put infertility treatments on hold, because each month seems so potentially precious, and we're not getting any younger. But

> the pace of treatment we had been on was emotionally exhausting and took a real toll on our relationship. We know that we have to go back to that awful routine in a couple of weeks, but these two months of distance from our infertility have replenished us.

Clients may need help from the professional in thinking of ways to channel their feelings of restlessness, and they may also need support in believing that they are entitled to engage in an activity that seems incompatible with their feelings of sadness. The professional will want to explain that, important though griefwork is, such activities can give the psyche a respite from pain and can provide structure during a period that might otherwise seem disorganized and mired in sadness. They also enable the client to reconnect with the vital, growing aspects of herself, to be reenergized and replenished, and to reassure herself that there can be life activities in which she can take pleasure as the pain begins to diminish.

Moving Adaptively into the New Life

The final task in consolidating one's grief is to shape a new life that incorporates the loss without discounting or dwelling on life before the loss. In a sense, the professional is asking the client to recognize that the loss has provided new and unanticipated dimensions to the life that stretches ahead. Even though she would not have asked for the loss, the client has at least responded to the several challenges that the loss posed and has emerged from her grief with a fuller understanding of herself and what aspects of life she values.

One challenge posed by the loss is to adjust to the new world that exists. The natural inclination of most people, as well as their support network, is to assume that the world is the same and that the individual who has sustained the loss must fit back in. However, that point of view actually invalidates the belief in the loss and makes it harder for the client, who is bound to feel like a misfit or a freak. Rather, the client who has accepted the loss, and whose views of himself have undergone a transformation, needs to view himself as a traveler in somewhat unfamiliar territory, looking for reassuring landmarks and shaping his actions in new ways, depending upon the curves in the road. He will need to give up or modify certain hopes, plans, or expectations and to develop new ones to fit in their place, perhaps expanding roles or activities in some areas and contracting them in other areas. Learning new communication skills is often an invaluable asset for the individual who has sustained a loss. That person must be able to tell medical personnel, employers, family, and loved ones exactly what her new needs are and how these individuals can best support her ongoing recovery from the loss.

Implications for the Professional

Losing a part of the self is an experience for which few people have any preparation. And yet, during the life cycle, we all sustain constant losses as we grow, some of them more momentous than others. Why, then, do losses of part of the self—specifically, sexual or reproductive losses—loom so ominously to client and professional alike? I would suggest that, in large part, such losses are not only discounted as losses but are also "invisible" or "unspeakable" losses. Unable to garner social support after such losses, clients feel emotionally isolated. Professionals also feel isolated, since they probably know few of their counterparts who have faced the challenge of helping clients heal emotionally from such losses. Professionals who seek out reading material will not find much; most of what is written on loss concerns emotional recovery after the death of a loved one. Yet, for clients who have sustained a sexual or reproductive loss, recovery is particularly challenging because they feel intrinsically diminished by the loss of a piece of themselves.

Clients who have coped by denying that the loss was important or clients who have become depressed or withdrawn following the loss need the gentle encouragement of a professional to help them speak openly of their very private loss and to encourage them to rethink how they might incorporate this loss into their ongoing personal growth. For some, this will mean consolidating the loss and moving forward; for others, it will mean acknowledging the impact of the loss and anticipating how to cope with future losses that will come as a chronic illness worsens or as a serious illness progresses.

Yet, since we all know that life brings its share of losses, whether a client knows the specific nature of future losses or not, the coping skills detailed in this chapter have the potential to be utilized time after time as clients seek emotional respite and recovery from their grief. In some situations, a professional will be the most appropriate person to help with this challenge; in other circumstances, loved ones can be a sturdy source of solace; in still others, a support group may be a welcome haven from the tensions of battling a loss alone. In times of crisis or devastating grief, all three of these supports may be necessary to shore up the flagging resources of the bereaved individual.

After successful griefwork, an individual is able to make the loss seem meaningful and to gain a renewed sense of purpose and personal identity. As a client progresses in consolidating her grief, she will detect a rebalancing of her energies. Effort earlier spent on sadness and regrets ultimately will be rechanneled in new directions. As the client is ready to move ahead in her life without the professional relationship, she and the professional together should assess her progress: the work she has done, the effort she has expended, and the gains she has made in the process of recovery. This very focus on forward movement will help the client put her recovery into the perspective of the gains and losses that continually ebb and flow throughout life, and will strengthen her to meet future challenges that will contain elements of loss in the months and years ahead.

PART 2

Sexual and Reproductive
Losses

3

Struggling with Chronic
Health Problems

In this chapter, we will examine the sexual ramifications of a variety of chronic health conditions and the treatments associated with them: diabetes, endometriosis, hysterectomy, enterostomy, and paraplegia. By examining these health conditions from a bio-psycho-social perspective, we can take into account the needs of the ill clients and those of their sexual partners. This perspective is a crucial one for the professional, who must help both partners communicate their sexual satisfactions and difficulties in adapting to the changing health situation of the ill client. In addition, since many of the sexual difficulties of clients come from an incomplete understanding of their illness, the professional can play a pivotal role in providing educational information that will dispel myths and misconceptions about sexual functioning during illness.

The Impact of Chronic Illness

One of the most difficult challenges for the person with a chronic illness is to surrender the previous identity of robust good health and to incorporate a new identity that includes the restrictions of the illness. Wu (1973) emphasizes the differences between the "sick role," where individuals occupy a position accorded by society to those defined as sick, and the "impaired role," where individuals must assume role responsibilities that are compatible with their maximum potential. Similarly, Strauss (1976) maintains that the primary task of the chronically ill person is to "normalize"; no longer preoccupied with symptom control and staying alive, the chronically ill individual now must lead as normal a life as possible within the limitations of the illness. Difficult questions must be answered: What will be the effect of the illness on the person's life? What new coping skills will she need to learn? How will it affect plans and relationships?

Sheridan (1984) points out that adaptation is an ongoing task for the person with a chronic condition, since the course of the illlness is constantly changing, and there is little opportunity for planning and considerable scope for depression. The person may also have undergone a period of progressive illness and deterioration prior to diagnosis, and therefore may attribute sexual problems to personal failure rather than to the effects of the disease.

Unless the client introduces the topic as an area of concern, most professionals tend to assume that their clients have no sexual problems. However, it is the rare client who will bring up the subject of his or her sexual satisfaction for discussion or examination. Furthermore, many clients assume that such discussion is "off-limits" in their relationship with professionals, even though sexual functioning may be a primary area of concern, especially when they are grappling with unanticipated health problems. The professional can unwittingly reinforce this "off-limits" perspective by avoiding the area of sexual adjustments while exploring other areas of health in detail. Some professionals avoid discussion about sexual satisfaction because of their own discomfort or inexperience with issues that relate to sexuality. In addition, many professionals consider such discussions private and therefore are reluctant to intrude uninvited into this area of a client's life, especially when the client is recovering from health problems that may have many other adjustments associated with them. So an unwitting conspiracy can evolve, with the client assuming that sexual needs are not legitimate areas of concern to discuss and the professional assuming that the client's sexual adjustment is fine, since the client has not said anything to the contrary.

Transition from Health to Illness

For most clients with the unanticipated health problems covered in this chapter and the next, the transition from health to illness has been a sudden one, heralded either by a physician's pronouncement of a diagnosis or by the experience of physical trauma and immediate hospitalization. In none of these conditions is there time for anticipatory grief, which can often cushion the impact of the loss of robust health. Even those clients who have been in ill health—for instance, those with digestive tract difficulties—have always had hope that recovery was possible and that following the doctor's orders might result in a reprieve from illness. So clients and their families usually regard the onset of illness as a crisis, whether or not there have been warning signals.

Just as people need physiological homeostasis, they also need a sense of social and psychological equilibrium (Marris, 1974; Moos & Tsu, 1977). When illness strikes and families try to employ familiar problem-solving strategies, they often find that the novelty and the severity of the illness or diagnosis prevent the old strategies from working effectively. The failure of familiar coping mechanisms constitutes a crisis and leads to a state of disorganization, which is often accompanied by anxiety, fear, guilt, or other aversive feelings that contribute further to the disorganization. Crisis theorists (Caplan, 1964) maintain that the period of active crisis is time-limited and that some resolution is achieved in about six or eight weeks. Depending on the effectiveness of the new coping mechanisms used to meet the current crisis, the new equilibrium may be a healthy adaptation, promoting growth and maturation, or a maladaptive response, characterized by psychological deterioration and decline. Thus, the period of crisis is a transitional one that has implications for the person's capacity to meet future crises.

During the crisis period, an ill person experiences numerous losses, and the professional must try to understand the significance of each loss. Expectable losses that may occur include separation from family and friends; the loss or diminution of key roles in the ill person's life; permanent changes in appearance or in bodily functions; assaults on self-image and self-esteem; distressing feelings of anxiety, guilt, anger, or helplessness; and an uncertain, unpredictable future (Moos & Tsu, 1977). Patients also may lose confidence in their bodies as pain and physical discomfort set in. According to crisis theory, the period of disequilibrium causes individuals and families to be especially receptive to support and input from professionals. During this period in particular, the professional must be able to initiate discussions about loss, including the loss of sexual functioning.

The Hospitalization Experience

Every person who has one of the conditions discussed in this chapter and the next is likely to be hospitalized at some point in the periods of diagnosis or treatment. Although doctors, nurses, medical social workers, and others familiar with the hospital may be comfortable working in that environment, the patient and his family rarely adapt easily to the medical routines, procedures, and vocabulary that are commonplace in the hospital setting. The medical world seems strange and unfamiliar to them. However, a more significant deterrent to adaptation has to do with the losses experienced by a patient in the hospital environment—especially the losses involving sexual integrity.

At the time of admission, the person (referred to by hospital staff as a "patient" or a "case," and not—one hopes—as "the prostate in room 206") is asked a number of questions, some of which will seem personally intrusive. People who are being treated at the hospital for medical or surgical problems involving the sex organs may feel awkward divulging information about their condition to a stranger.

Also at the time of admission, valuable personal effects are removed from the individual: wedding bands, engagement rings, and other jewelry given by loved ones. As a result, the person loses the sense of security and comfort that she derived from these possessions. This symbolic stripping of identity is continued in the hospital room, where the individual often is expected to don a skimpy hospital gown. Split up the back and of a unisex design, these gowns lack any resemblance to the distinctive attire usually worn by men and women.

Once settled into the hospital routine, the individual is expected to assume a passive and accepting role as he is subjected to an array of procedures and tests designed to diagnose and treat the problem for which he was admitted. Many of these procedures involve intrusions into physical and psychological aspects of sexual privacy. In addition to a detailed medical history that may involve confusing medical terminology around sexual functions, the individual also is subjected to a thorough physical examination, in which the examiner's eyes and hands come into contact with areas of the body traditionally reserved for sexual intimacy. The rectal examination for the male may be embarrassing, particularly when prostatic stimulation precipitates emission of semen. Procedures such as catheterization or enemas may be compromising simply because they invade body territory in the vicinity of the genitalia (Woods, 1979a).

The hospitalized individual no longer assumes a familiar sex role. Males may feel stripped of their masculinity and adulthood. Placed in a passive position, either in bed or wheeled from place to place in a wheelchair, the individual feels acutely the lack of autonomy introduced by hospital procedures. The male patient becomes dependent on females to respond to his requests and to make him comfortable. He may fear both responding to female staff sexually and not responding. For males who are uncomfortable in dependency roles with women, the hospitalization experience may evoke both anger and anxiety. Even taking directions from a male physician or nurse may cause him to feel compromised. Under the duress of illness, the adult male feels as though he is expected to submit to medical authorities with childlike accommodation.

The female experiences many of the same losses as the male. In addition to the loss of her autonomy, she may feel an

alteration in her familial role as she, usually the comforter during times of illness, now needs the support of others. Women
tend to feel more comfortable than men in accepting care
from other females, although, in the understaffed hospital
environment, many women may have difficulty being assertive
about their needs with medical staff. Separation from family
may be especially hard for the woman with small children; worries about her own health are compounded by her concern for
her children's welfare in her absence.

Separation from one's sexual partner, combined with
the lack of privacy in the hospital environment, requires that
the patient abstain from sex or use masturbation as a sexual
outlet. Individuals who are seriously ill will be concerned
mainly with surviving and seeking relief from pain. But when a
more stable recovery period ensues, seeking comfort from
one's partner through lovemaking is a natural recourse for
many patients, who feel stifled by the lack of privacy and the
unspoken message that patients ought not to feel sexual. The
presence of a roommate further inhibits sexual expression,
either with a partner or through masturbation. Gay and lesbian
patients face a particularly trying time during their hospitalization. Not only may the hospital be reluctant to extend visiting
privileges to their lovers, since they are not technically "next of
kin," but any display of affection and sexual expression may
provoke disapproving glances from hospital staff. Thus, both
heterosexual and homosexual individuals find that they must
deny an integral part of their personalities by virtue of their
patient status.

The effects of illness on one's sexuality are multifaceted
and will depend to some extent on the particular health problem of the individual. Certain disease processes, such as those
found in chronic illnesses or paraplegia, may interfere with
sexual function as a result of bodily changes or tissue damage.
Certain treatments, such as enterostomal surgery, may create
changes in body image that are considered incompatible with
maintaining a sexual relationship. Medication or therapies
used to treat disease states may interfere with sexual function.
Physical fatigue or pain may render a person unable to per-

form sexually. Anxiety related to an illness may interfere with sexual response. Finally, depression or grief may be associated with diminished or impaired sex drive.

Diabetes

Diabetes can have a significant impact on sexual and reproductive functioning of adult males and females. Studies of diabetic males repeatedly find a high incidence of impotence associated with diabetes. Recovery of sexual function tends to be poor once erectile dysfunction becomes severe. In women, orgasmic dysfunction and accompanying loss of libido are significantly more prevalent when diabetes is present. Diabetic women, especially those who are nonorgasmic, may have difficulty with vaginal lubrication.

Although there are no known effects of diabetes on the testes, certain complications of the disease appear to interfere with reproduction. In males, a gradual decrease in volume of semen has been noted during the years they are treated for diabetes, and diminished sperm motility and sperm count are present in some diabetic males. Androgen deficiency and abnormal spermatogenesis have been noted as well. Woods and Herbert (1979) report that varying degrees of atrophy of the ovaries and uterus may occur in diabetic women, largely proportional to the duration and severity of the diabetes. Since diabetes is genetically determined and since diabetic women have a greater frequency of spontaneous abortions, stillbirths, malformed infants, and high-birthweight infants, their pregnancies are considered to be high risk. It is thought that the diabetes has an adverse effect on the mother's blood and blood vessels, which in turn affects the baby's supply of nourishment and oxygen.

Many genetics counselors believe that diabetic individuals or couples should be informed about the odds of their having a child who will develop diabetes. Woods and Herbert (1979) offer the following information. Two known diabetic persons theoretically could have children who were all diabetic—although in reality the incidence of diabetic offspring is usually only about 60 percent. If a diabetic individual and a carrier have a child, diabetes probably will occur in about 50 percent of their offspring. If a nondiabetic person with no family history of diabetes and a diabetic person have children, all the children will probably be carriers. Counseling for diabetic individuals and their partners is essential to permit the couple to recognize and deal with problems of transmission of the disease.

Assessment of biological factors that affect the sexual functioning of the diabetic man or woman would include information about the person's present level of sexual functioning, the duration of the disease, and the extent to which the diabetes is well controlled. For women, additional questions about vaginitis and presence of vaginal lubrication will enable the professional to assess the extent to which these factors are interfering with sexual pleasure. With regard to plans for a pregnancy, the couple might be asked whether they are trying to conceive and, if so, whether there have been any fertility problems, including pregnancy losses.

With regard to psychological factors, the professional will want to keep in mind that sexual dysfunction may be the result of nonorganic problems. The presence of morning erections is helpful in determining whether the male is physiologically capable of an erection. The often unnerving emotional impact of one episode of impotence can cause a diabetic male to become so anxious about sexual performance that the anxiety, not the diabetes, interferes with his ability to achieve or maintain an erection.

Bob relates his concerns about possible impotence:

> You know, I've lived with my diabetes for the past ten years, so I'm pretty tuned into my body and how it responds. But three weeks ago something happened that really threw me. My wife and I were making love, and I just couldn't get an erection. I wasn't tired, I wasn't sick, and I was trying for all I was worth! Nothing. My wife made light of it, but each time I've thought of initiating sex, I've backed off because I'm afraid it will happen again. I guess she is too, because she hasn't given me any of our usual signals about wanting to make love. I just don't know how to get back on track again.

In addition to exploring the psychological tensions, the professional will want to assess whether ejaculatory dysfunction is a problem. He will also want to assess the diabetic woman's sexual self-image and to determine how she has adjusted to the chronicity of the diabetes.

In assessing the relationship between the diabetic individual and his or her partner, the professional will want to ascertain that both understand the disease and its management, as well as the role it may play in any areas of current sexual dysfunction. She should encourage the couple to communicate openly with each other about their sexual needs, keeping in mind that orgasm and ejaculation are not the only measures of achieving intimacy and sexual fulfillment. She should also determine whether the couple are aware of the genetic transmission of diabetes. If infertility has been diagnosed, she will need to know whether it has presented interpersonal problems for them. The professional will want to extend her services to the couple at whatever point concerns in the relationship emerge, since the chronicity of diabetes and the potential for deterioration of sexual functioning could pose a threat both to individual self-esteem and to the relationship itself.

Endometriosis

Endometriosis is an often painful condition in which tissue from the uterine lining is present in such abnormal locations as the tubes, ovaries, and peritoneal cavity. In these locations, the endometrial tissue develops into nodules, tumors, lesions, implants, or growths. Because the endometrial growths usually respond to the hormones of the menstrual cycle, they accumulate tissue, break down, and bleed each month. In addition to the internal bleeding, there may also be degeneration of the blood and tissue shed from the growths, inflammation of the surrounding areas, and formation of scar tissue. Other complications, depending on the location of the growths, include rupture of growths (which can spread the endometriosis to new areas), the formation of adhesions, intestinal bleeding or obstruction, interference with bladder function, and pain associated with these complications.

Endometriosis tends to worsen over the years, often causing infertility. Women with endometriosis, therefore, are placed at double jeopardy: they not only must cope with the sorrow of their infertility, but many also must endure very real physical pain and the frustration that there is yet no definitive cure, other than hysterectomy and removal of the ovaries. Some physicians prescribe hormonal treatment, but the side effects of these medications can also present problems. In addition to the grief associated with her infertility, the woman is also likely to grieve because she is different from the ideal adult whom she envisioned during her growing years. Instead of this ideal figure, she has become a woman who inconveniences her family by not functioning optimally, and she must now depend on her family in areas where she would prefer to be independent. Because of the often unpredictable nature of the pain from endometriosis, the woman and her family often live in uncertainty regarding her feelings of health and capacity to participate in family activities.

Susan speaks of her ten-year battle with endometriosis:

> I was pursuing an infertility workup when the doctor diagnosed my endometriosis. On the one hand, I was glad to know there was a medical reason that I hadn't been able to conceive, but the next few years were frustrating because I remained infertile in spite of several surgeries for my endometriosis. So my husband and I adopted two children in the next eight years, and I had all sorts of hopes that now I could enjoy being a mother. No such luck! The endometriosis got much worse, causing lots of pain and emotional exhaustion. And our sex life has really taken a downward plunge. We have to be in certain positions that can't put pressure on my tender spots, and by the time we've orchestrated that, it puts a real damper on our spontaneity!

Inasmuch as one's sexual relationship often mirrors other stresses or satisfactions in the relationship, one can anticipate that endometriosis robs couples of the full sexual pleasure in their relationship. Hysterectomy, although an answer to the problem of pain, presents its own problems as well.

Hysterectomy

Each year, some 650,000 women in the United States undergo a hysterectomy, the removal of the uterus. According to a recent article in *Consumer Reports*, at least one out of every three women eventually has the operation, most commonly in her thirties or forties ("Hysterectomy and Its Alternatives," 1990). Reasons for the operation vary from the presence of fibroid tumors to endometriosis to cancer. The removal of the uterus affects a woman most during her childbearing years and can be devastating if she has not been able to have children or has not had as many as she had hoped for. The emotional response to the resultant infertility is discussed in greater detail in Chapter Five. Even for women who have completed their families, there may be other ramifications to the hysterectomy. Some women experience a decline in sexual desire, while others do not. *Consumer Reports* cites a 1981 study by the U.S. Centers for Disease Control that reviews some 1,400 hysterectomy patients. More than half the sample reported no change in sexual desire, 9 percent noticed a slackening in desire, and 9 percent said they were more interested in sex after the operation.

Some women feel a sense of relief after the hysterectomy, especially if the operation has put an end to painful endometriosis, heavy bleeding, or the discomfort of a prolapsed uterus. In addition to removing the uterus, many physicians advocate also removing the ovaries, thus precipitating premature menopause in women whose ovaries were still producing estrogen. Ovaries have a role that is broader than reproduction alone, and the woman who faces premature menopause will need to familiarize herself with the pros and cons of estrogen replacement therapy. While doing so, she may also have to contend with some of the effects of estrogen reduction: changes in breast tissue, skin, bones, and vaginal mucous membranes. These bodily changes may affect her physical and psychological sense of well-being and, in turn, her sense of herself as a desirable sexual person.

Enterostomy

In the treatment of some digestive tract diseases, such as cancer of the large intestine, diverticulitis, and ulcerative colitis, part of the digestive tract may have to be removed. When it is not feasible to sew the two cut ends of the digestive tract together, an opening called a "stoma" is made in the abdominal wall, through which undigested materials can pass into a bag. This operation is called a colostomy when the colon opens through the stoma, and an ileostomy when the lower part of the small intestine (the ileum) opens through the stoma.

Thousands of Americans have had a colostomy or an ileostomy, and it is estimated that over 100,000 persons will undergo this procedure each year. The change in body image that is faced by the person with an enterostomy (ostomate) can be perceived as a loss, since the person is no longer physically the same as before the surgery and life is now complicated by attention to an external function that previously was internal and required little thought. Orbach and Tallent (1965) found that men and women had strong reactions to the surgery, which they perceived as mutilation. Some men reacted to the surgery as if it represented castration; some women equated the surgery with being sexually violated. The creation of an ileostomy or a colostomy requires an adjustment for the sexual partner as well as the ostomate. Woods (1979b) suggests that the response of loved ones to a disfiguring injury or loss of an organ exerts a significant influence on the injured person's ability to reintegrate his or her body image.

The literature dealing with adaptation to ostomies is largely based on studies of married heterosexuals; thus, little information is available on the coping skills of single and homosexual ostomates. In a literature review of sexuality following ileostomy and colostomy, Woods (1979b) found that sexual function and interest appear slightly to moderately depressed after creation of the ostomy, although some people report improved sexual interest and performance. Both males and females reported more interference in their sexual functioning with a colostomy than with an ileostomy. Burnham, Lennard-Jones, and Brooke (1977) report that only a minority of men and women indicate that a stoma physically makes intercourse difficult. Both men and women fear damage to the stoma or problems with the appliance, such as displacement or leakage, and noise or odor from flatus. These fears can lead to social restrictions, as well as to awkwardness in sexual relationships. Some ostomates conceal the bag with a garment during sexual activity. Many find that their anxieties are eased if they empty the bag prior to intercourse, and others restrict their dietary intake somewhat before having sex.

Dlin and Perlman (1971) studied 160 ostomates over the age of fifty and found that most of them maintained an active and interested sex life after surgery. The frequency of intercourse per month did decrease after surgery, as did the ability to attain orgasm and interest in sex. However, as the authors point out, the high interest in sex in a population over the age of fifty who have experienced surgical mutilation strongly suggests that aging people still have a significant investment in life.

For some ostomates, life before surgery was characterized by chronic pain, preoccupation with dietary restrictions, and feelings of bodily betrayal. Their reaction to the surgery and their subsequent adjustment are likely to be affected by their coping patterns during the time of their illness. Ostomates who feel out of control, exhausted by their physical symptoms, and mutilated by surgery may be at risk of depression. They will need help in assessing realistic restrictions on their activities, as opposed to the restrictions that their depression may cause them to impose.

Counseling can focus on changes that the ostomate has experienced: the losses to be grieved, as well as new opportunities for healthy functioning that can now occur. This counseling ideally should include the sexual partner and other loved ones at various times, so that the ostomate can express concerns and receive reassurance from his available support network and so that the loved ones can learn how to be supportive and caring without encouraging inappropriate dependence of the recovering ostomate.

Paraplegia

For the thousands of people who sustain spinal cord injuries, the losses can be massive, and the professionals who work with them must be aware of the many changes in body image and functioning caused by the injury. Initially, the individual may be preoccupied with intense rehabilitation programs that focus on recovery from spinal shock and the stabilizing of vital physiological functions. The losses that paraplegic clients must face as they proceed with rehabilitation may include mobility, bladder and bowel control, and resumption of the pretrauma role in society and within the family. Issues of sexuality may not surface until later, as the client is perceiving the far-reaching impact of the injury on his or her future functioning.

Paraplegic clients may give subtle or direct indications that they are concerned about their future as sexual human beings. Comments such as "I guess I'll never be attractive again" or "What kind of a husband can I be to my wife?" are cues to the professional that the client may be ready to discuss future sexual functioning. The professional must respond to these tentative cues, since a failure to respond may reinforce the client's fear that sexual functioning will never return.

A complete neurological evaluation emphasizing sacral segments will help to assess the likelihood of sexual potential. A person's sexual function after cord injury is dependent on two biological variables: the number of fibers that were severed (complete versus incomplete lesions) and the level of the injury (cervical, thoracic, lumbar, or sacral). In general, the higher the lesion, the more likely the male is to be able to experience an erection (Woods, 1979c). That is, those men with cervical lesions are able to achieve erections in a greater percentage of cases than those with lumbar or sacral lesions. Besides the lack of sexual sensation experienced by some paraplegic people, other physiological factors also may interfere with the capacity for sexual arousal or enjoyment. Comarr (1971) cites a low level of muscular strength, inability to support one's body weight, and incontinence as potential complications. In addition, pressure sores, spasticity, and muscle contractures may interfere with coitus, although spasticity of the lower extremities may bring on erection in some men.

Women with spinal cord injuries can experience orgasm if there is some residual pelvic innervation. Even with complete denervation of their pelvic structures, some women experience orgasm by using fantasy as a major stimulant. Both males and females can use a technique known as sensory amplification (Mooney, Cole, & Chilgren, 1975), whereby the individual concentrates on a physical stimulus and mentally amplifies that sensation to an intense degree. Another technique is developing sensation in another area of the body that is innervated.

Paraplegic clients also may be concerned about their fertility. Traumatic spinal cord injury does not, of necessity, preclude fertility, although artificial means of obtaining semen may be necessary for some male clients hoping to impregnate their partners. Electroejaculation has been used as a means of obtaining semen for the artificial insemination of wives of paraplegic men. Sterility may be caused by loss of temperature regulation of the testes, as a result of autonomic denervation or hormonal aberrations, or by retrograde ejaculation. In some cases, the projectile power of ejaculation may be insufficient to maximize chances of conception, although artificial insemination may be a satisfactory solution in such cases. In females with spinal cord injuries, there is no apparent permanent interference with the menstrual cycle or fertility, although women who are in or near menopause will probably not menstruate again after their injury (Comarr, 1966). Pregnancy, labor, and delivery have the potential to proceed without complication, although, depending on the location of the lesion, some women may not be able to feel labor pains and therefore will not know that labor has begun. One problem that can complicate labor in paraplegic women is a profound cardiovascular reaction known as autonomic dysreflexia, which results in hypertension, bradycardia, and headaches, and which occurs during the final stage of labor (Woods, 1979c).

Sexual functioning may be affected by the paraplegic person's reaction to the other losses caused by the spinal cord injury. The potential effect of loss of body functions on self-image and ego is obvious. Woods (1979c) states that the altered role of the paraplegic person within the family and society may decidedly influence his or her perception of gender-role performance and sense of worth. These feelings may engender performance anxieties, which can further limit sexual function. In addition, if the losses associated with the spinal cord injury precipitate feelings of depression, the paraplegic person may demonstrate a lack of energy for meeting life's challenges, including sexual expression and gratification.

Tom, a twenty-three-year-old paraplegic following a swimming accident six months ago, communicates his despair about his future:

> Who is going to want to spend the rest of her life with someone like me? I'm not kidding when I say it would be easier to be dead than to face the stares and the pity I see on everyone's faces. What do I have to offer anyone? A life of taking care of me? Forget it! I'm no prize.

In addition to giving the client ample time to grieve the losses precipitated by the spinal cord injury, the professional will need to collect data from the client, family members, and other members of the health care team. By doing so, the professonal hopes to be able to place into context the potential sexual problems to be faced by the client in the midst of the other losses and adjustments caused by the injury. The professional also should consult with the neurologist to determine the level of the cord lesion and its degree of completeness. Lack of this information could lead to incorrect explanations, raising or dashing the client's hopes unrealistically or providing inappropriate reassurance.

Woods (1979c, p. 357) suggests that the professional should seek answers to the following questions: Is libido present? Does the person desire sexual gratification? Has it been an important part of pretrauma life? Does the client have a current sex partner? What is his or her sex role in society? Do occupational requirements place constraints on people with physical handicaps, necessitating a change in job or a cut in income? What was the pretrauma role in the family? Will the person face dramatic alterations in role performance, including sexual function? Is the partner supportive, in general, of the paraplegic person? What are the expectations of the partner? After collecting this information, the professional can assess the strengths and limitations of the client and the sexual partner, thereby better understanding the client's concept of himself as a sexual being.

Therapeutic Implications for the Professional

Depression is a common accompaniment to chronic conditions. With diminished role functioning, heightened dependence on others, loss of body integrity, and impaired hopes for the future, the individual is highly vulnerable to feelings of helplessness that can result in depression. The feelings of physical frailty, including pain, and the depressive effect of some medications further contribute to psychological vulnerability. Any resulting depression will have an impact on self-esteem, sexual functioning, and intimate relationships.

Chronic illness places a stress on the entire family system. Family roles must be reallocated, plans often become highly dependent on the health of the chronically ill person, family finances are strained, relationships take on new twists, and favorite activities may need to be modified or discarded. Exhaustion of other family members may limit their patience and willingness to accommodate to the new balance of family roles. If other family members are accustomed to being dependent on the ill person, they may feel resentment that the ill person is no longer able to meet their needs. If, on the other hand, family members are moving away from the family or becoming autonomous, they will feel resentful because the person's illness beckons them back into the family for caretaking activities. Reciprocally, the ill person will be likely to detect the often unspoken feelings of resentment, and will feel both burdensome and guilty.

In adults, the relationship between sexual partners is dramatically affected by the illness of one of them. The healthy partner may have physical or emotional needs that the ill partner cannot meet in ways that have been mutually gratifying to them both in the past. The ill partner, struggling to find a role that is acceptable to him and to his partner, is grieving the loss of his former self and all the capabilities that went with his previous good health. Unlike the professional, who understands that denial, anger, bargaining, and grief are normal phases of griefwork, one's partner is not likely to be tolerant of emotional ups and downs when she is already feeling overburdened. Thus, the chronic illness of one person must truly be understood in the context of the family and the delicate balance of relationships that has been upset by the illness.

Sheridan (1984) asserts that the sexual arena will be a place where this whole experience is acted out, so that problems more related to illness may appear to be sexual problems. At the same time, the sexual arena can be a place where bonds with one's partner are reaffirmed, where the sick person provides gratification to the well partner, and where the healing process begins.

4

Confronting the Challenges
of Cancer and AIDS

The mention of cancer evokes terror in almost anyone whose doctor delivers this dreaded diagnosis. In spite of years of medical progress, many forms of cancer do not have impressive cure rates, and the treatment for cancer is disruptive to one's life and to one's health. Most adults know people who have died lingering deaths from cancer, and those are the people they tend to remember when contemplating the disease, instead of other acquaintances who have lived many years in remission.

Most persons diagnosed with cancer are reluctant to consume a professional's time with their many questions, doubts, and anxieties. Yet many decisions need to be made, not only about the immediate medical recommendations but also about future prospects for recovery. The Cancer Information Service (CIS) is a nationwide toll-free telephone program sponsored by the National Cancer Institute. Trained information specialists are available to answer questions about follow-up care and to provide information about other aspects of cancer. The toll-free telephone number for CIS is 1–800–4–CANCER. In Alaska, call 1–800–638–6070; in Washington, D.C., and its suburbs, call 363–5700; on Oahu, call 524–1234 (call collect from neighboring islands). Spanish-speaking staff members are available to callers from the following areas (daytime hours only): California (area codes 213, 310, 818, 714, 619, and 805),

Florida, Georgia, Illinois, northern New Jersey, New York City, and Texas.

The losses associated with cancer will depend on the individual's emotional, familial, medical, and financial resources. Many of the emotional reactions of a person diagnosed with cancer mirror the classical symptoms of being in crisis. In the early stages after diagnosis, the central concern is with one's survival. Persons who have been in good health and have tended to view themselves as invulnerable to catastrophe suddenly are seriously shaken as they realize the limits of their own mortality. Some people lose their self-image as a robust and vigorous person, although others use this self-image to sustain their defense of denial about the potential seriousness of the cancer diagnosis. Another loss that may occur is an offshoot of the cognitive confusion that often accompanies a crisis. The person with cancer will receive a great deal of medical input and will be asked to make decisions, sign release forms, and anticipate the impact of various treatments. At such an emotionally vulnerable time, the overload of unfamiliar information can be overwhelming. The loss of cognitive functioning may be manifested as the individual asks for material to be repeated, misunderstands information communicated earlier, or makes decisions that seem disjointed. The professional who is aware that the crisis of cancer diagnosis can cause cognitive confusion is in the best possible position to help the individual and concerned loved ones sort out and review the options available.

The diagnosis of cancer may evoke other losses as well. Depending on the medical services available to the person, he may feel a loss of his familiar family doctor as he is transferred to an oncologist for future health planning. If the person lives in a rural community, this change of physicians may also involve travel of significant distances to medical facilities that are best prepared to offer quality care. Hospitalization or treatment in a city far from one's own community can increase one's cognitive confusion. The costs associated with travel, time lost from work, surgery, and treatment may present significant losses for the individual and her family, necessitating sacrifices in personal and family expenditures, as well as changes in plans for the future. Some cancer patients may make decisions on their medical treatment based primarily on their efforts not to diminish familial financial reserves set aside for other priorities.

Although all forms of cancer, especially in their most terminal stages, are likely to impair one's capacity to participate in sexual activities, some forms of cancer are more closely tied than others to one's view of oneself as a sexual person. Breast cancer, prostate cancer, testicular cancer, uterine cancer, and ovarian cancer all involve sexual and reproductive organs, and ultimately have an impact on a person's feelings about sexuality.

Breast Cancer

Breast cancer (which occurs primarily in women) is treated by several different methods. The decisions regarding the extent of the surgical procedure, the use of radiation therapy, chemotherapy, or hormonal manipulation are individualized for each woman. Lumpectomy or mastectomy will be performed to remove the tumor and any affected axillary lymph nodes. Follow-up therapy, such as radiation and chemical and hormonal therapies, is usually accomplished on an outpatient basis. Physicians are likely to focus on the woman's medical progress and may emphasize the hopes for her recovery. The woman herself may find that her experience with breast cancer has caused her to reevaluate her priorities in life, to be more closely connected to loved ones, and to contemplate the meaning of her life in new ways.

However, in spite of realistic assessments of hopefulness and a new appreciation of life, the woman must be allowed to acknowledge the losses that she has experienced in the brief period of time between diagnosis and surgery. Dealing openly with these losses will enable her to feel open about her emotions, rather than to be privately preoccupied with the ways in which her life has changed forever. She has had an operation that has reminded her of her mortality, has changed her appearance, and may have affected her self-image. She is likely to be uncertain of how the mastectomy will affect her life-style and her personal relationships with family, co-workers, and friends.

The loss of a breast can mean many different things to a woman. If she is still in her childbearing years, she may need to confront the loss of capacity to nurse any future babies. If she is not in a committed sexual relationship, she must consider how and when to tell a prospective partner about her mastectomy or lumpectomy. This loss of spontaneity about sexuality is matched by another loss: the perceived loss of sexual attractiveness and the associated risk that her partner will find her unattractive once the information about the breast surgery is shared. Women in committed, long-term relationships have similar fears of being perceived as sexually incomplete and mutilated. These women's partners undoubtedly also have anxieties and concerns associated with the changes in physical appearance. The woman who has just faced breast cancer and surgery may feel overwhelmed because she must consider not only her own emotional needs but also her partner's difficulty in coping. The professional can be particularly helpful at this time, when both partners are grappling with feelings and fears that they are reluctant to communicate to one another.

By her willingness to let her partner see her body soon after the surgery, the woman enables both of them to share together their feelings about the loss of her breast and their hopes that the surgery has been successful in getting all of the cancer. The partner may feel anxious about touching the mastectomy incision, and the woman may need to be encouraged to communicate clearly what is physically and emotionally comfortable for her in this regard.

Linda shares her frustrations with her Reach to Recovery volunteer:

> The dressing has been off for three weeks now and the incision isn't too tender any more. But I haven't told my husband that it's healing because I really don't want to see his face the first time he sees me with no breast. And I'm not so sure he even wants to have sex with me any more. When we snuggle in bed

together, he's always so concerned about touching the incision and hurting me accidentally—I can't imagine we'll ever
get to a point where we can make love and forget that I have a
scar where my breast should be.

The woman will need to talk openly about her readiness
for lovemaking; even before she is ready for sexual activity, she
will want to let her partner know ways in which physical closeness and intimacy can be comforting. Unless the woman initi-
ates communication about her sexual preferences following
her surgery, her partner may assume that she prefers to delay
lovemaking until some time after surgery. The woman, on the
other hand, may interpret her partner's lack of sexual initiative
as rejection. Seltzer (1987) reports that male partners occasion-
ally have their own sexual problems, including difficulty having
or maintaining an erection. These problems often are related
to the enormous stress that the cancer provokes in the couple.
The male's difficulties usually will disappear as other tensions
in the relationship diminish. If difficulties in sexual responsiveness persist for either the male or the female, a referral for
short-term sexual counseling is highly appropriate.

Some women are not interested in having a sexual relationship after a mastectomy. If she and her partner have come
to this decision mutually, there is nothing inherently problematic with this perspective. Possibly they had had little or no sexual activity prior to the surgery and did not find the sexual
aspect of their relationship meaningful. Frequently, however, a
woman's interest in sexuality is only temporarily diminished by
her feelings of anxiety and depression after breast surgery. The
professional will want to ascertain whether these emotional
issues are disrupting an otherwise fulfilling sexual relationship
and therefore require further attention.

Virginia remembers the early months following her
lumpectomy:

I felt so vulnerable. The diagnosis of my breast cancer was a
total surprise, and the surgery was less of a trauma than the
realization that this cancer could come back and kill me. I'm
only thirty-five and I have always lived my life looking forward
to the next adventure. Suddenly I found myself dwelling on

the past, and when I had any positive experiences I would
wonder, "Is this the last chance I'll have to enjoy this?" When
my boyfriend and I made love, I had a hard time feeling connected to the whole experience.

Helpful questions to explore include whether the
woman feels a sense of hopelessness about her condition,
whether there are emotional stresses in other parts of her life,
and whether she and her partner are communicating clearly
and openly about her health and their fears for her complete
recovery.

The quality of a woman's physical and emotional relationship with her partner after surgery depends to a great
extent on the quality of their relationship before the surgery. A
relationship that was already fragile may not be able to with-
stand the additional stress of the surgery and the recovery
period. Some couples respond to the crisis of diagnosis and
surgery by reevaluating the priorities in their relationship. This
reevaluation can lead to resolutions to recommit themselves to
one another or, conversely, to a recognition that the relationship cannot be sustained. The termination of a relationship
during recovery from cancer is an immense loss for the
woman, and the professional who works with her will want to
help the woman identify other loved ones who will stand by her
emotionally as her physical and emotional scars heal.

If the woman is not in a committed sexual relationship,
she is likely to be concerned about the impact of her cancer
diagnosis and surgery on future sexual relationships. Seltzer
(1987) reports that most single women who have had breast
cancer prefer not to tell a date about their condition until they
have developed a warm and caring relationship. Even then,
women are likely to fear this disclosure because of the potential
for rejection. Some women may shy away from relationships in
order to avoid the tension that comes with wondering whether
to allow oneself to become attached to a person who may ultimately decide that the cancer is a condition too burdensome
for their relationship.

These are realistic concerns, but the professional also
will want to assess the woman's self-image and self-esteem. If

she feels diminished and defeated by her ordeal with breast cancer, she may communicate these feelings along with the factual information about her current medical situation. A potential partner may feel overwhelmed, not by the cancer and the mastectomy but by the woman's other unresolved issues: dependency needs, depression, or desperation. Professional counseling on issues of self-esteem will not guarantee that a woman will develop a relationship with a companion who can accept her cancer, but such counseling should help the woman understand that she is a worthwhile person in spite of her ordeal with breast cancer.

When medical treatment has been terminated, the woman may also face some unexpected losses. During the treatment period, she had a focus for her need to *do something* to combat the cancer. Afterward, she may feel as if she is no longer taking any action to fight the disease. Another loss may involve termination of relationships with medical professionals associated with her treatment and care. During treatment, the woman has had regular contact with professionals whose concern and caring had a strong impact on her. These associations may have been powerful, especially if the woman's family and friends had been reluctant to speak with her about the breast cancer that had recently threatened her life. When treatment ends, the woman may feel a profound sense of loss because she no longer has contact with people who accepted and cared for her in spite of her incision, in spite of difficult side effects, and because of their belief that their treatment would improve her chances for recovery. The professional will want to help the woman acknowledge how important these lost relationships were to her.

In the midst of her transition from treatment to recovery, the woman may be receptive to being involved in community support groups for breast cancer patients. She has very likely already been visited by a Reach to Recovery volunteer in her community. ENCORE (Encouragement, Normalcy, Counseling, Opportunity, Reaching Out, Energies Revived), a national YWCA program for postoperative breast cancer patients, offers exercise to music, water exercise, and a discussion period. Some communities may have cancer support groups for people who want to find out how other cancer patients cope with the disease and the ongoing uncertainty of its potential recurrence. Since few older people have participated in a support group, the prospect of joining one may seem especially threatening at the very time the person is feeling vulnerable. Professionals who are sensitive to the reluctance of older people to share their feelings in a group setting can respond supportively in several ways: by arranging for a support group member to visit the cancer patient to familiarize her with what to expect from the support group experience; by encouraging the support group to set up a buddy system that pairs new members with experienced members; or by offering to accompany the client to the first meeting as a way of easing the awkwardness of the situation.

Uterine Cancer

Women with uterine cancer, in addition to losing bodily organs that may have strong symbolic significance for them, may also face the loss of hopes for future childbearing. If the woman is premenopausal, and if surgery involves removal of her ovaries, she will enter menopause prematurely. The adjustment of her body to synthetic hormones, or to the absence of hormones if estrogen replacement therapy is contraindicated, can pose difficulties, and can serve as an ongoing reminder of the precarious balance of bodily health.

Rachel, age forty, recounts the emotional turmoil she has faced since her diagnosis of uterine cancer:

> It was bad enough to have the surgery and then the radiation. But I was completely unprepared for coping with premature menopause. I never realized how delicate the estrogen balance must have been before my ovaries were removed. Let me tell you, I've been on a real roller coaster ever since, and the doctor is having quite a time deciding on a dosage that will work for me. I barely have the energy to worry about this cancer killing me—I'm too preoccupied with hot flashes, dizzy spells, and feeling disoriented. You can imagine the toll it has

> taken on our sex life! Right now I feel as if sex is just one more
> chore as I try to cope with just getting through the day.

Women with uterine cancer are treated by either surgery
or radiation alone. Radiation alone may be the treatment of
choice for those considered poor surgical risks: elderly and diabetic patients and those in poor health because of other diseases. Side effects of radiation include skin reactions, nausea
and vomiting, and fatigue. The surgical procedure is hysterectomy—removal of the uterus. The ovaries and the Fallopian
tubes that connect the ovaries to the uterus may also be
removed. For selected cases of very fast-moving cancers, nearby
lymph nodes may also be removed and biopsied; afterward, the
patient receives radiation treatments.

The use of chemotherapy in the treatment of uterine
cancer is generally limited to those whose cancers have spread,
recurred, or not responded to other treatments. Common side
effects of chemotherapy include nausea and vomiting, hair
loss, anemia, reduced ability of blood to clot, and an increased
likelihood of developing infections and mouth sores. Most side
effects disappear once treatment is stopped. However, at the
time of treatment, the losses can seem profound. The woman
may feel that her body is betraying her, that she is losing control over her physical well-being, and that her autonomy is
diminished as her loss of stamina and energy cause her to be
dependent on others.

In addition to the losses associated with the cancer, its
treatment, and the prognosis for continued recovery, women
of childbearing age must now acknowledge that they are bar-
ren. For some women, the loss of childbearing capacity is far
more devastating than the threat to their lives that the cancer
has posed. The woman may feel that she is sexually incomplete,
so that her sexuality no longer seems to be a fulfilling aspect of
her total identity. If the woman had viewed lovemaking in the
context of procreation, her inability to have children may
cause her to ask "What's the point?" when contemplating her
sexual relationship with her partner. Technically, she and her
partner are now infertile, with all the emotional ramifications

that occur with that condition (see Chapter Five). Although the professional may be tempted to view adoption as a viable alternative for the couple, he must first be aware of the losses that infertility had imposed on them and not use adoption as a means of bypassing the grief that they may feel at not being able to give birth to a child who is genetically linked to both of them.

If the woman is past her childbearing years, there will be other losses associated with her diagnosis and treatment for uterine cancer. If she has previously been in good health, the cancer may be her first brush with acknowledging her own mortality. The stress of the illness may have left her more vulnerable to subsequent illnesses, so that her health may seem to be in a constant state of decline and her body less reliable than it was before her cancer diagnosis. Realistically, if treatment does not eradicate the cancer, she *will* feel out of control, and she *will* feel as if her body is deteriorating. These feelings, often accompanied by depression, are likely to have a significant impact on her interactions with her partner and on their readiness to be expressive in their sexual relationship.

Ovarian Cancer

Since there is no simple screening test for ovarian cancer, and since this cancer often shows no symptoms until it is in an advanced stage, it is usually not detected early.

Elaine, diagnosed with ovarian cancer after visits to six different doctors, ventilates her anger:

> I am furious that *I* knew something was wrong with my body and no one took me seriously. I wasted precious months thinking that my symptoms were all in my head as I watched my abdomen become distended. Now the prognosis isn't good, I'm consumed with fury that I'm going to die, and I feel sick all the time. My husband alternates between being supportive and retreating. We almost can't bear the intimacy of being sexual because we know our time together is running out. It's just too painful.

Ovarian cancer is almost always first treated by surgery. Treatment usually involves the removal of both ovaries (oophorectomy), both Fallopian tubes (salpingectomy), and the uterus (hysterectomy). If other nearby organs are affected, more extensive surgery may be performed, since removal of as much of the cancer as possible will improve the effectiveness of later treatment. When the cancer is limited to one ovary and is detected early, only the affected ovary may be removed, especially in women who want to remain fertile.

As with uterine cancer, the removal of affected organs is undetectable to others, but the organs may be symbolically important to the woman's view of herself as a sexual being. The impact of surgery and chemotherapy or radiation will also mirror the experience of the woman with uterine cancer.

Prostate Cancer

Cancer of the prostate is the second most common type of cancer among American men and the third leading cause of death among them. The risk of developing prostate cancer increases with age. This type of cancer rarely occurs among men under fifty. The average age is seventy-three. Thus, many men with prostate cancer are at an age when they may already have sustained other losses in their lives, including those related to their physical well-being.

The prostate is a male genital gland about the size of a chestnut. It secretes a milky fluid that is part of the semen needed for ejaculation. Removal of the prostate gland (total prostatectomy) is the surgical procedure used when the cancer is confined to the prostate. During this procedure, some of the nerves may be unavoidably damaged and some degree of erectile impotency usually results. Five to 15 percent of patients also have urinary incontinence. Both of these aftereffects of surgery are likely to be perceived as losses by the male.

If he and his partner have had a rewarding sexual relationship, the loss of erectile capacity will cause them to reevaluate ways in which they can maintain a positive view of their sexuality. Men with more advanced cancer may be treated with radiation, which, within two years of treatment, causes impotence in 30 to 50 percent of patients. A third form of treatment, hormone therapy, is used primarily with metastatic and recurring prostate cancers causing symptoms such as bone pain and bladder obstruction. In one type of hormone therapy, the testes—the major producer of testosterone, the hormone that stimulates the growth of prostatic cancer—are surgically removed. In another type, the female hormone estrogen is administered to counteract the testosterone. Diethylstilbestrol (DES) is a synthetic form of estrogen whose side effects in men can include breast enlargement (sometimes painful), water retention, and impotence. When chemotherapy is used to reduce pain and other symptoms of advanced disease, patients may experience the common side effects of nausea and vomiting, hair loss, anemia, reduced ability of blood to clot, and increased likelihood of developing infections and mouth sores.

Rick speaks of his experiences following surgery and chemotherapy for prostate cancer:

> I know I'm no spring chicken, but ever since my wife died a few years ago I've led a pretty active social life. But now I'm embarrassed to ask a woman out to dinner, let alone into my bedroom. Look at me! Would you believe six months ago I had a full head of hair, a dashing moustache, and plenty of get-up-and-go? I look and feel like an old man.

For males in the advanced stages of prostate cancer, the losses that are important may relate less to their sexual potency than to their sexual self-image. The decline in physical health, the increased dependence on others, and the feelings of fatigue and depression that often come with advanced cancer are a source of tension for the man and others with whom he interacts.

Testicular Cancer

Cancer of the testes is a relatively rare form of cancer, accounting for approximately 1 percent of cancers in American men, usually occurring between the ages of twenty and forty-four. Since this is a time when a man may be most concerned with his sexual fertility and plans for having children, testicular cancer will threaten his image as a fertile male and as a healthy person. The testes are the male reproductive glands that produce the sperm cells necessary to fertilize female egg cells. The testes also produce the male hormone testosterone, which is responsible for deepening of the voice at puberty, a more muscular body build, pubic and facial hair, and other male traits.

If diagnostic tests confirm the presence of a tumor in a testis, the affected testis is removed, both as part of the diagnostic process and as the first step in treatment of the disease. Testicular cancer rarely occurs in both testes, so the remaining testicle can enable the male to maintain his fertility. In cases where the cancer has metastasized to other parts of the body, treatment with further surgery, chemotherapy, or radiation may be recommended. The side effects from these treatments are similar to those discussed in other sections of this chapter.

The male who has had one testis removed will carry the anxiety that all cancer patients have regarding the prognosis for their return to good health. However, unless anxiety or declining health interferes, the man should not experience any problems with his capacity to be sexually active. His fertility, assuming that he has one testis that was not affected by the cancer, should return to previous levels within several months after the ending of treatment.

AIDS

In the literature, AIDS is only recently emerging as a chronic disease. The United States has now observed a decade of transmission of the human immunodeficiency virus (HIV), the cause of acquired immune deficiency syndrome (AIDS). With the increased awareness of drugs that can delay the onset or slow the course of AIDS, many infected individuals are living for years as they grapple with the chronicity of AIDS and their altered health. During the period between the diagnosis of being HIV positive and their ultimate death from AIDS, these individuals sustain a number of losses, in areas that affect sexuality directly and indirectly.

A diagnosis that one is HIV positive has a dramatic effect on one's view of the future. Suddenly, one's life script, with all its hopes and dreams, has to be rewritten. These hopes—for loving relationships, sexual fulfillment, parenthood, good health, and economic security—enable most people to surmount current difficulties and strive for the best that life may offer. For the HIV-positive individual, many of these hopes for the future no longer seem realistic. Although there are potential positives, as loved ones rally, as medication prolongs periods of good health, and as one tries to live life as fully as the remaining months and years will allow, the HIV-positive individual also will experience many losses. The professional working with this person will need to be sensitive to the range of losses that may occur, beginning with the awareness that HIV is a highly stigmatized condition.

The stigma associated with HIV infection was initially accorded when the virus was thought to be transmitted primarily through unprotected homosexual intercourse or contaminated needles shared in intravenous drug use. Walsh and McGoldrick (1991) and Gochros (1992) point out that too often distinctions are made between "innocent victims," such as children born with HIV or individuals infected through blood transfusions, and those who "brought it on themselves" through homosexual acts or drug use. In fact, AIDS is a condition that defies easy categorization, as demographic trends show an ever-changing shift in populations at risk. Although most early cases of AIDS were restricted to males, women, originally considered to be at low risk for AIDS, are now becoming infected at catastrophic rates. According to the Centers for Disease Control, heterosexual transmission is the fastest-growing category of AIDS cases in the United States. In New York City, AIDS is now the leading cause of death for women aged twenty-five to thirty-four. For females, as for males, HIV is linked with race and social class; nationally, 84 percent of the women who have died of AIDS have been women of color—50 percent of them African American and 23 percent Latina. Rochman (1990) contends that over the past decade of the AIDS epidemic, the medical establishment, the media, and public information campaigns have ignored the extent to which AIDS is a women's disease, thus contributing to the widespread belief that women are not at risk of acquiring HIV.

Although not specified as a separate category by the Centers for Disease Control, lesbians, once believed to be protected from the virus because of their lack of sexual contact with males, are at risk just as heterosexual women are. Lesbians may have slept with men in the past or may sleep with men currently for money, for drugs, to get pregnant, or for other reasons. In addition, intravenous drug use could place lesbians at risk of acquiring the virus, as could contact with bodily fluids of infected males or females. If lesbian and heterosexual women believe that they are at low risk, there is less likelihood that they will emphasize "safer sex" practices with their partners or bring suspicious symptoms to the attention of health care professionals.

Whether the infected individual is male or female, gay or straight, one of the most painful concerns associated with being HIV positive is the fear of losing precious relationships after others learn of the diagnosis. The individual who tells loved ones risks rejection at the very time he most needs the support of family and friends. Gay or bisexual men diagnosed HIV positive may decide, as a result of the diagnosis, to reveal their sexual orientation to family and friends. That news, coupled with the knowledge of the HIV diagnosis, will cause family members to do some careful thinking about their changed perception of their loved one and their capacity to stand by this person as his health deteriorates.

Gary recounts his family's response to the news that he had been diagnosed with AIDS:

> My parents have always had a hard time accepting that I am gay, and we usually avoid the issue as much as possible when I'm home on visits. That has worked fine so far, but now that I have to make plans for having someone take care of me when I get sick, my life-style can't stay in the family closet. Jeff, my lover, is prepared to do all he can for me, but I'm going to want my parents to visit me in our apartment or in the hospital, and they'll need to interact with Jeff. I just know it's going to

be awkward, and I don't know if I can be strong enough to
stand their disapproval.

Just when the infected individual needs to rely most on
others for comfort, he now must deal with their biases, their
misinformation about the transmission of the virus, and their
attempts to ignore the impact of the recent news. Even if the
loved ones have been aware of the individual's gay life-style,
they may find it hard to extend their acceptance to him now
that he has a virus they fear they may contract. Thus, the
infected individual faces a risk of losing the emotional support
of persons who fear for their own health. Some friends or family may justify their rejection by maintaining that he could have
avoided the virus if only he had abstained from unsafe sexual
activity.

A significant loss for gay or bisexual individuals is that
their lovers are not regarded by the legal system as next of kin.
Thus, blood relatives, rather than lovers, are given priority
when hospital visits are limited and are consulted when legal
and medical decisions must be made. Ultimately, the lover may
be completely excluded during the last stages of the disease,
when the gay person is most in need of comfort and solace.
Such treatment results in an infuriating loss for both partners;
but the gay person is now too weak to fight the system or the
family members who exclude his lover, and his lover has no
legal rights to treasure and consolidate the relationship in its
most fragile weeks and months.

A medical social worker relates:

A challenge that I often face is to help mothers of gay men
with AIDS find a way of being nurturing without intruding on
the special relationship between the patient and his lover.
Often the mother will want to move into her son's hospital
room, bring him favorite foods, and offer lots of comfort.
When the patient's lover enters this scene and tries to establish
his position as primary caretaker, the mother and he have
some real work to do. I try to help them both give the patient
enough space so that he can ask for help from whomever he
pleases, set his boundaries, establish some independence, and
be clear about how both the mother and the lover are very

much needed, but in different ways. That's a pretty delicate balancing act.

The professional at this time must keep in mind that the ill partner is the primary client and that advocacy on behalf of his needs may necessitate skillful communication with family members and hospital staff in order to be responsive to the ill man's emotional needs.

Since gay men are by no means the only persons who contract the virus, heterosexuals, too, face the dilemma of whom to tell. Despite the amount of publicity about AIDS in recent years, most people remain ill informed about the way in which the virus is transmitted. Inaccurate beliefs—for instance, that the virus is transmitted by sneezes, by touching, and by food handled by an HIV-positive person—are pervasive even among educated persons. Consequently, an infected person's family and friends will probably spend the initial days after learning the news trying to reconcile their need to stay healthy and their desire to extend comfort to their loved one. If their fears of contracting the virus outweigh their empathy for the infected person, they may engage in scapegoating as a means of justifying to themselves their decision to cut off relations with him or her. Others, less certain of their feelings initially, may simply minimize contact until the infected person no longer tries to overcome the feelings of rejection that are communicated. In either case, the experience of rejection by a loved one can make it that much more difficult for the infected person to decide to take a similar risk in telling others and asking for their support.

The individual who is diagnosed with HIV and who is not in a committed relationship with a partner will be confronted with different losses. That person must decide whether, or at what point, to reveal in a relationship that he or she is HIV positive. This disclosure can precipitate a number of losses: the loss of potential sexual partners; the ultimate loss of participation in a committed sexual relationship, with its potential joys of mutual exploration and pleasuring; and the loss of future roles as spouse and parent, which the individual had imagined would come with a committed relationship.

In addition to the loss of roles that the person had projected into the future, persons involved in sexually intimate relationships face a major loss: the loss of sexual spontaneity that accompanies the awareness that one has HIV. Since the HIV virus is known to be transmitted through the exchange of bodily fluids, persons infected with the virus are at risk of infecting their sexual partners. To minimize the danger of infecting a partner, many infected persons practice "safer sex." But that is accomplished at considerable sacrifice: no longer can the HIV-positive individual enjoy the spontaneous expression of sexuality that had been a source of pleasure in earlier months.

Mike, a gay man who is not in a committed relationship, comments:

> I've tried to be pretty up-front with my sexual partners about being HIV positive. For some of them it's a real turnoff, but even with those who agree to use condoms there are usually problems. By the time I've handled my own worries about rejection and discussed how we can protect my partner, the mood is pretty subdued. What I wouldn't give for some good, old-fashioned spontaneity!

If the person with HIV has been living with a partner on a long-term basis, the change in their sexual relationship will affect both partners. Their uncertainty about the course of the infected person's illness and about the continued health of the noninfected partner are likely to produce stress in their relationship.

Gochros (1992) reports that most HIV-infected gay men maintain continued sexual interest after the HIV diagnosis and throughout much of the course of their illness. There is no reason to believe that the need for sexual expression is different for heterosexuals, given the periods of general good health that occur intermittently with this chronic condition. The professional will need to be open in discussing with couples the options that are available for them to express their sexuality while preventing the spread of the virus. Continued safe sexual expression can offer many positive emotional advantages, such

as maintaining a sense of security and mutuality in the relationship, affirming one's sense of normalcy in spite of illness, con-
firming that one is still viewed as being sexually desirable, and
signifying that one is still capable of celebrating life through
sexual expression.

As Gochros points out, professionals who work with people with AIDS must be able to accept differences in sexual
expression and a spectrum of responsible, fulfilling sexual
choices and life-styles, including monogamous and nonmonogamous homosexuality and the sexuality of gay men with
HIV infection. Gochros suggests a number of unorthodox but
safe sexual activities that might suit people with HIV infection:
telephone sex, sexual role playing, masturbation with pornog-
raphy, consensual exhibitionism and voyeurism, erotic massage, safe use of sexual appliances, mutual masturbation, and
protected oral sex with condoms. Professionals who believe
that HIV-positive individuals are entitled to safe sexual expression can help them explore various opportunities for celebrating some continuing joys in life, despite the losses that are also
present.

What are the implications of the HIV-positive diagnosis
for reproductive decisions? In this area also, the infected individual and the healthy partner face massive losses. Clearly, the
likelihood of declining health would cause any couple to think
carefully before they try to conceive. But when the woman is
infected, the odds are between 30 and 65 percent that the
infant will test positive for HIV at birth. Few prospective parents would choose to take this risk; as a result, one of the losses
with which a couple may grapple is their inability to become
parents.

HIV-positive individuals who have children bear the special anguish of knowing that they probably will not live to see
their children grow to adulthood. In addition, AIDS will bring
about a number of changes in the family, all of which can be
understood in the context of losses: the change in roles as the
illness causes the HIV-positive person to relinquish responsibilities and other family members to shoulder them; the loss of
financial security; the precautions taken to prevent others in

the family from contracting the virus; and the anger, often unspoken but probably expressed in more subtle ways, at the uncertainty that the future holds for all family members.

If the ill parent is a single parent, the anguish is compounded by worries about the children's well-being during the progression of the illness and after the parent's death.

Ruby, an African American woman with AIDS, tells of her worries:

> My two kids are real scared about what will happen to them when I die. I'm trying to make plans for my parents to take them, but Mom and Dad aren't in good health and I just don't know how they'd keep up with my two. The social workers I've talked to say that black kids don't get adopted very easily, and the last thing I want is for my children to be separated or to be moved from one foster home to another. It's so hard to try to work all this out when I feel so tired and sick every day. I almost can't bear the sadness.

It is not unusual, as with any loss, for denial to be a powerful coping mechanism. Persons with AIDS will cling tenaciously to what they have of their good health for as long as possible, in part because to acknowledge such losses is to admit that life is slipping away. The professional working with someone who has AIDS will want to respect his need to see himself as healthier than he actually is, realizing that such respect will ultimately enable the ill person to acknowledge certain limitations when they can no longer be denied. If some advance planning is necessary—for instance, if decisions must be made about the children's future or if the person must get on the waiting lists of already crowded services and facilities—the professional still can respect the ill individual's right to self-determination. She can encourage the person to apply for some services, at the same time emphasizing that these plans can be revised and that the person can remove his name from the waiting list once he becomes eligible for services.

As the disease progresses, the losses in physical energy, sexual desire, physical functioning, and physical appearance will have an impact on the emotional well-being of the individual and his or her loved ones. Depression is often a response to other losses that a person with AIDS may experience: loss of employment, loss of income and social status, loss of friends and social supports, loss of privacy, and loss of hope. The change in physical appearance that comes with the progress of the disease may take away the last shred of denial that the person had been able to muster.

Grieving the loss of one's familiar appearance and the health that was once taken for granted, the individual may retreat from all but the most intimate and secure relationships, fearing that he is no longer an attractive person and seeking to fend off experiences of rejection. This retreat is both emotional and physical. At the same time that the individual seeks emotional seclusion from relationships, there is often a physical seclusion that restricts the person's opportunity for exercise, nutritious food, and stimulation of the outside world. Gochros (1992, p. 106) quotes a gay man with AIDS who formerly had taken considerable pride in his physical appearance: "I would never have sex with someone who would be willing to have sex with someone who looks like me!"

The professional will need not only to demonstrate continued caring and concern for the person with AIDS but also to bolster the flagging resources of family members and loved ones, who must cope with the emotional impact of their own fears while caring for the ill person and helping him to live as productive a life as possible. The following hotlines are available for persons with AIDS, their families, and their loved ones:

AIDS Testing and Counseling: 1–800–872–2777
AIDS Drug Assistance Program: 1–800–542–2437
Confidentiality Law: 1–800–962–5065
General Information: 1–800–541–AIDS
National AIDS Hotline: 1–800–342–AIDS

Even in the medically caring environment of the hospital, the person with AIDS can be made to feel like a pariah. In spite of an increased need for comfort, including a need to be touched, he is likely to be touched only when medically necessary—and then by health care professionals decked out in gloves, masks, and sterile gowns. Even friends may stop offering the familiar comforting gestures of the past:

> I went to visit George in the hospital last week. I hadn't seen
> him in six months, and I was shocked by the whole experi-
> ence. He was on a ward of only AIDS patients, and as I
> observed all the nurses and doctors wearing their protective
> clothing, I kept wondering if I was safe to be coming in with
> just my street clothes. Then I saw George and I tried to cover
> my shock at how much he had changed. His face was covered
> with lesions, his eyes were sunken, and he looked so shriv-
> eled. As I approached his bedside, I realized I couldn't bring
> myself to give him our familiar hello kiss. I was too afraid of
> those lesions.

The HIV-positive diagnosis and the ultimate appearance of AIDS are challenges that few persons are prepared to meet. This disease, so recent and so devastating, has been over-whelming to individuals, family members, professionals, and health care facilities. The early lack of clarity about its transmis-sion, the absence of a cure, and the terminal nature of this ill-ness have left healthy adults in fear of contracting it. Profes-sionals also carry this fear and may be extremely reluctant to work with clients who are HIV positive. Yet, while others debate the biomedical issues or the urgency of preventing HIV infec-tion from a distance, helping professionals are desperately needed to work with AIDS clients and their loved ones around the concerns that others are too busy (or too emotionally guarded) to raise: the losses that come with the disease, the continuing need for safe sexual expression, and the social stigma associated with AIDS that affects the quality of life of all people.

Therapeutic Implications for the Professional

Although there are many differences between the medical con-ditions of cancer and AIDS, both present special challenges for the professional. In both conditions, the specter of terminal ill-ness looms large, in spite of the client's hopefulness that aggressive treatment will slow the course of the disease. So in the inital stages following diagnosis, the client usually is more preoccupied with survival than with sexual expression.

However, as treatments are undertaken, as the disease is better understood, and as family or community supports are developed, the client will want to enhance the quality of his life, including the quality of sexual expression. Although side effects from chemotherapy, radiation, and medications are likely to have an impact on libido, the professional still can encourage the client to engage in comforting forms of sexual expression that do not require the exertion of coitus. Clients with AIDS will also need to be encouraged to assess the extent to which an active sex life may enable them to feel healthy in spite of having AIDS. The professional will want to discuss with each client the importance of practicing safe sex, including the use of new and creative forms of sexual exploration and expression.

Questions about sexual matters are important for the professional to raise periodically, although they should be kept in the broad perspective of the client's overall physical and emotional condition. Sheridan (1984) maintains that professionals dealing with sexual and gender problems of ill clients can make use of certain familiar counseling techniques that enable the professional and the client to share information and emotions. By showing comfort with the subject of sexuality, beginning where the client is, respecting individual differences, asking open-ended questions, and encouraging reflective discussion, the professional can communicate to the client that sexuality is a valid area for concern and exploration.

Professionals must be careful to respect the client's values and beliefs and should strive to present a range of options for the client and partner to consider. Discussions of sexuality should be kept as broad as possible, especially since clients may tend to focus on specific genital activities that present problems. The professional also will need to differentiate between sexuality and genital function, emphasizing that one is no less of a man or a woman because of difficulties in intercourse or, in the case of a client with AIDS, a need to find a substitute for intercourse as a sexual outlet. At the same time, professionals must allow clients to experience the grief associated with the losses that have occurred as physical health deteriorates, including sexual losses.

By emphasizing intimacy and sensuality, the professional can enable the client to gain a broader perspective on sexuality, thereby placing coitus as only one in a range of pleasurable sexual activities. At times, the relief from stress that this approach provides will aid in the eventual reestablishment of genital sexuality, as well as enlarging the couple's repertoire of sexually gratifying activities. Careful timing and probing on the part of the professional can facilitate open communication, tolerance of trial and error, and a new view of sensuality and sexuality as clients learn of their capacity to give and receive warmth, affection, and pleasure.

As the person's condition deteriorates and hospitalization becomes necessary, the professional will want to be especially sensitive to the behavior of medical staff. Health care professionals may emotionally withdraw and spend only the necessary amount of time in the room of the dying patient—particularly the patient with AIDS, because of the fear of contagion and because of the time-consuming efforts to protect oneself from becoming infected. The message the patient takes from this is that she is not deserving of staff time, since staff seem to prefer spending energy on patients with a more hopeful prognosis. The professional should think of ways to bring these concerns broadly to the attention of staff, so that there can be some collective owning of the problem and some steps taken to work on the issues of alienation that are involved.

5

Mourning the Many Losses of Infertility

Infertility has been described as an experience of *biographical disruption* (Bury, 1982). For individuals or couples who have made careful and conscious decisions about their desire to have children, the inability to proceed according to plan is initially annoying, then anxiety producing, and ultimately disruptive as couples find their lives revolving increasingly around infertility treatments and the emotions aroused by them.

Couples who cope with infertility often speak of its intrusiveness into many areas of their lives. They must contend not only with disruptive medical diagnosis and treatment but also with the personal psychological pain of being an infertile person in a predominantly fertile world. Added to the personal struggle are the various social relationships affected by infertility—relationships with parents, in-laws, siblings, friends, relatives, neighbors, and co-workers, most of whom are unaware of the emotional pain the infertile person is trying to overcome. And most important is the couple's own relationship, which can serve both as a buttress against the insensitivity of the fertile world and also as a source of stress when partners cannot understand or reach out and comfort each other.

Infertility is the inability to conceive a pregnancy after a year or more of regular sexual relations without contraception or the incapacity to carry pregnancies to a live birth. In 1982, on the basis of data collected for the National Survey of Family

Growth, Mosher estimated that 2.4 million married couples were infertile. This figure represents 13.9 percent of all married couples who have not chosen to undergo surgical intervention (such as a vasectomy or a tubal ligation) to prevent conception. However, as Greil (1991) has pointed out, Mosher's estimate is almost certainly too low, because he does not account for the existence of hidden infertility; that is, some women, especially those in lower age brackets, have never had intercourse unprotected by contraceptive devices and therefore never have tested their fertility.

Not all infertile couples are childless. Those without children are referred to as having "primary infertility," whereas the couples who already have at least one child but are unsuccessful in having more are considered to have "secondary infertility." Hirsch and Mosher (1987) estimate that only 30 percent of infertile American couples have primary infertility. The remaining 70 percent, couples with secondary infertility, tend to feel particularly misunderstood by fertile acquaintances, who often discount their infertility and remind them that they are, in fact, already parents and should be thankful for the child they have.

Stress as a cause of infertility is very much misunderstood by professionals—including, unfortunately, some medical professionals. There is no question that the experience of infertility *produces* stress in the couple, but that must not be confused with stress as a contributing factor to the couple's medical inability to conceive or carry a pregnancy to term. Only twenty-five years ago, it was believed that as many as 40 percent of all infertility problems had a psychological origin (Mazor, 1984). Over the past two decades, less and less emphasis has been placed on psychogenic factors as causes of infertility. As elaborate theories about the psychodynamics of infertile people remained unconfirmed by rigorous research, and as advances in medical technology have led to improved diagnostic techniques and a better understanding of reproductive physiology, it is now possible to discover a clear medical reason (or reasons) for a couple's infertility in approximately 80 to 90 percent of couples who present themselves for specialized infertility treatment.

Salzer (1991) points out that blaming stress for a couple's infertility has been problematic in several respects. First, it creates additional guilt and depression in infertile individuals, who are already facing significant stress. Second, it misleads the public and encourages negative perceptions and comments. Third, it makes people hesitant to seek counseling for the normal stresses of infertility because they fear that they will be blamed for their difficulties. Professionals who counsel infertile couples will need to bolster their diminished self-esteem by emphasizing the areas of their lives in which they are functioning well *despite* the toll taken by their infertility.

Misunderstanding about the causes of infertility also contributes to the couple's feeling of being stigmatized. Although the popular misconception holds the woman responsible for her incapacity to conceive, either or both partners may have a reproductive impairment. According to Mazor (1984, p. 25), about 50 percent of all infertility problems are related to factors in the female (mainly problems in tubal patence or problems in ovulation). Approximately 20–40 percent of the problems can be traced to the male partner (Greil, 1991). For about 20 percent of infertile couples, the diagnostic workup reveals that both partners contribute to the infertility problem (Menning, 1977). Therefore, both partners must be involved in the diagnostic investigation of the couple's infertility.

Of couples who submit to a proper investigation of their problem, 50 percent will respond to treatment and can be helped to conceive (Collins et al., 1984; Insler, Potashnik, & Glassner, 1981; Kliger, 1984; Verkauf, 1983). In contrast, only 5 percent of infertile couples who do not seek medical intervention will subsequently conceive (Menning, 1977, p. 5). The impression that adoption will enhance a couple's chances of subsequently conceiving is not based in fact; adoptive parents achieve a pregnancy at the same 5 percent rate as those couples who do not seek medical intervention for their infertility (Lamb & Leurgans, 1979).

All the media attention devoted to infertility makes it appear to be a growing problem in American society. In fact, the incidence of infertility actually declined from 3 million in 1965 to 2.4 million in 1982. The number of couples with *primary infertility*, however, doubled from 0.5 million to 1 million during the same time period (Mosher, 1987). And, given the awareness of advances in infertility treatments and the long waiting lists of adoption agencies, the number of couples seeking medical treatment for infertility has increased dramatically: office visits for infertility almost tripled between 1968 and 1984, rising from about 600,000 to 1.6 million over fourteen years (Greil, 1991).

Attachment and Loss

The concepts of attachment and loss are integral to the infertility struggle. Although most people think that one becomes attached only to another living person, one can also become attached to a fantasy baby or to a fetus in utero. Couples who decide to try to conceive a pregnancy become attached to a dream child as they contemplate the ways that the baby will alter their life-style, envision the physical attributes that their baby may have, and anticipate the special talents or interests that they will encourage their little one to develop. Prospective parents also begin to think about themselves differently. If this is their first child, they begin to think about themselves as parents, about their parents as grandparents, and about their siblings as aunts and uncles. If they already have children, they think about the shift in family relationships that the new baby will bring about. Parents anticipate how to balance their energy and attention, as well as how to cope with siblings' potential feelings of rivalry toward a new baby. All this before the baby is even conceived!

The infertility experience abruptly interrupts these forming attachments. Perhaps the couple have difficulty in conceiving the dream child; perhaps the pregnancy is lost through miscarriage, ectopic pregnancy, or stillbirth. The interruption of the emotional attachment to a dream child or to a developing baby can present a devastating blow to the couple and their family members who shared in the anticipation of the new baby.

One man recounts the emotional upheaval as he and his wife received the results of their infertility workup:

> We're still in a state of shock. When the doctor finished our tests and invited us to meet with him to discuss the results, we expected to learn what we could do to be more successful in conceiving. Instead, his news put us into a state of shock. I learned that I am sterile and that nothing can be done to correct my infertility. Frankly, I didn't hear a thing he said after that. I can remember struggling not to scream or cry or put my fist through a wall. After I got home, I couldn't even talk to Betsy, and I could tell she didn't know what to say to me. Even now, a week after the diagnosis, our conversation goes in circles. We cry, we lose our tempers, but we can't make any sense out of this awful news and what we're going to do with our lives now.

Yet the loss of fertility or the loss of an unborn child is, for the most part, an unrecognized event in society. There are no rituals to legitimize the grief of the infertile couple who mourn the baby they could not conceive or give birth to. In a sense, infertility is a silent and unrecognized loss, one that many couples struggle to resolve in lonely isolation. Friedman and Gradstein (1982) differentiate the mourning that accompanies infertility from the mourning that occurs after the death of a loved one. When a pregnancy is lost or a dream child not conceived, there is no tangible "outside" person to mourn, and grieving for someone who is not physically present is awkward. Also, because there are no memories or shared life experiences, the loss often has a feeling of unreality about it— especially since no one else seems to share the couple's attachment to the unconceived or unborn child. The loss of fertility or a pregnancy is often met with comments such as "It's important not to give up" or "You can try again"; both of these statements minimize the couple's feelings that the loss is very real.

With the realization that infertility is a serious problem, many couples begin a process of anticipatory grief for the child they fear they may never have. There is an ambivalence in this grief; for just as they are emotionally in touch with their sadness, they also may be actively involved in treatments that they hope will cure their infertility. Greil (1991) asserts that most infertile couples experience infertility as a condition that they can neither escape nor accept as inescapable. Therefore, at the very time they are engaging in anticipatory grief at some level, they are also hoping that the next month may bring a positive pregnancy test. This chronic uncertainty about the outcome of treatment leaves a couple in emotional limbo, often preferring to think of themselves as "not yet pregnant" rather than as "still childless."

If the initial experience with infertility leads into subsequent diagnostic workups and treatments, the couple may find themselves confronting a number of losses (Mahlstedt, 1985). The loss of their dream child often is the most frightening one, but the couple also may lose their role as birth parents, their trust in their reproductive capacities, their sense of control over life plans, and their feelings of normalcy in a predominantly fertile world.

Diagnosis

Most couples enter the diagnostic workup with high hopes. They may deny that the term *infertile* applies to them, are not interested in hearing about adoption or in vitro fertilization, and believe that their infertility will respond successfully to competent medical help.

Most couples begin their initial infertility inquiries by having the woman initiate a discussion with her gynecologist. In time, the male may be encouraged to see a urologist. If partners are unable to attend their mates' appointments, the resulting fragmentation of information and lack of coordination between the doctors treating the couple can cause frustration at this stage of the diagnostic process. This diagnostic division makes it difficult for the couple to view their infertility as a shared problem and intensifies the likelihood that one partner will carry an inordinate feeling of guilt or blame (Mahlstedt,

1985). If the couple are being evaluated in an infertility clinic, both partners probably will have been seen by specialists in the clinic and told together of the outcome of their infertility workup. These couples find it easier to share the burden of infertility, since both partners are informed about their own and the other's condition.

Since many females are accustomed to receiving reproductive health care (pelvic and breast examinations, Pap smears, and the like), they usually are able to tolerate the initial procedures of an infertility workup without undue psychological difficulty, although the procedures themselves may be uncomfortable. However, as the effort to reach a diagnosis requires more tests, additional expenses, and perhaps hospitalization, the woman's anxiety is likely to build. She may worry about being found defective and may harbor the fear that she does not deserve to have a child (Mazor, 1984; Mahlstedt, 1985). Since the diagnostic process involves a range of procedures, she also is likely to feel probed and manipulated physically. Psychologically, she may feel the stress associated with revealing intimate details of her sexual life, charting her basal body temperature daily, and having intercourse on a schedule that coincides with ovulation (Lalos, Lalos, Jacobson, & van Schoultz, 1985). Some women feel apprehensive when they ask their partner to participate in a diagnostic procedure, especially if they want children more than their partner does.

A diagnostic workup can continue for months and sometimes years, and the length of time the couple must spend in this process can be frustrating and anxiety provoking. The couple have moved past denial in large part and may now be clearly aware of their anger at the way that infertility is disrupting their hopes and dreams.

A husband speaks of the disruption that infertility has imposed on him and his wife:

> We can't even get on with our lives. I still hope each month that Brenda won't get her period. I know her cycle better than she does, it seems. But I can always tell when her period has begun because even now, after all these years, her eyes are red and puffy from crying. It seems that we can't go on like this.

Isn't there more to life than living from one menstrual period to
the next?

The woman feels anger and sadness each month as the
beginning of her period indicates that, once again, she is not
pregnant; the couple face decisions about the risks and costs
and intrusiveness of each new procedure; and, if the woman is
in her thirties or forties, she feels strong pressure to reach a
diagnosis, thereby not wasting precious months in her quest to
achieve a pregnancy.

Males are less accustomed than females to seeking routine medical care for their reproductive health; therefore,
many males feel highly apprehensive at the prospect of seeing
a physician. This apprehension is often exacerbated by the
need to produce a semen sample by masturbation, a process
that may arouse feelings of guilt, inadequacy, and anxiety in
the male (Lalos, Lalos, Jacobson, & van Schoultz, 1985). A
semen analysis must be made at an early stage of the diagnostic
workup. In contrast to many of the procedures used to diagnose infertility in the female, semen analysis is an inexpensive
and nonintrusive procedure. Since many males attach feelings
of virility and self-worth to the outcome of the semen analysis,
the results can have an impact on the male's self-esteem and
his general feelings of adequacy (Mahlstedt, 1985).

Performing on command is a dimension inherent in
other diagnostic procedures, such as the postcoital test (where
the woman comes to the office a short time after having intercourse, so that her cervical mucus can be examined for the
presence of her partner's sperm) and scheduled intercourse
(occurring when the woman ovulates, regardless of whether
the couple are inclined to make love at that time). A male may
experience temporary impotence under this stress and, as a
result, may begin to question some basic assumptions about his
virility. In addition, scheduled intercourse turns lovemaking
into babymaking, thus removing for the couple their options to
be spontaneous about sex. Sometimes, couples will avoid intercourse during times of the month when the woman is not ovulating, because their associations with intercourse are failure,
anxiety, and dashed hopes. Lovemaking, which once soothed

the tensions between partners, now becomes a source of tension. This loss of sexual intimacy rarely is labeled as a loss; yet it has a powerful impact on the couple's view of themselves as lovers.

At the conclusion of the diagnostic process, the couple may be told there is no medical cure for their problem, or that their problem can be treated, or that (as occurs in 10 percent of cases) their infertility is unexplained. The couples for whom there is no treatment will now have to reevaluate their options and, at some level, will grieve the loss of the birth child they cannot have. The couples whose infertility can be treated will feel both relief and apprehension as they try to decide whether to embark on what may become a costly, disruptive, and psychologically stressful undertaking. The couples who receive a diagnosis of unexplained infertility carry a special emotional burden. They are plunged into a psychological limbo, in which neither they nor their physicians know what more to do to enhance their chances of becoming birth parents. For some of these couples, the diagnosis will precipitate a series of visits to infertility specialists; for others, it will represent the beginning of a mourning process in which they experience denial, anger, bargaining, and chronic grief without being able to move into the final stage of acceptance.

Treatment

The beginning of treatment represents both a confirmation of infertility and the hope that the condition can be cured. In both the male and the female, the psychological impact of treatment will be affected by a variety of factors: how they feel about the intrusiveness of medical treatments, what potential side effects are associated with specific treatments, how flexible their personal and work lives are to the carefully timed nature of some treatments, and what level of success they have been led to associate with the particular treatments they have been undergoing.

Treatment is often given at infertility clinics many miles from the couple's home. In that case, the woman may be separated from family and friends just when they might be most helpful in offering emotional support. Even the male partner may be unable to remain at the infertility clinic beyond a few days, since the economic or professional strains of missing work may be more compelling than his partner's need for his physical presence. The period of waiting during recovery or during ongoing treatment procedures is often immensely stressful for the woman, who must find other sources of support if family and friends are not accessible.

During the months and years of treatment, both partners probably will need help in looking outside their relationship for the emotional support they need. If the couple have unexplained infertility or if both partners have problems contributing to their infertility, each partner may be undergoing a variety of treatments in a close time span. Thus, each partner may be so immersed in his or her own emotional problems that there is little support to extend to the other. By sharing the problem of infertility, the couple may come to have more empathy for each other and may grow closer through the experience of their infertility. However, infertility is a major focus of these couples' lives, and it is often very difficult for them to think of themselves except in their roles as infertile people (Mazor, 1984; Mahlstedt, 1985).

Adrienne speaks of her sense of being defined by her infertility:

> I'm so sick of being infertile! It's not enough that my infertility occupies all my waking hours, but even when I try to go out to have fun, my friends are forever asking me how the treatments are going, whether we've considered adoption, and how I'm feeling. I guess I should be glad to have friends who care, but these days it just reminds me that everyone relates to me as an infertile person.

Sexual Relationships

The strain that infertility introduces into the sexual relationship is common among infertile couples. Some will feel able to discuss this problem with a helping professional; others will prefer to have the professional initiate such a discussion. All couples are likely to feel reassured that this is not a unique problem for them but, rather, that most infertile couples experience sexual stress from several sources. One source of stress is the gradual recognition that procreation rather than sexual pleasure is the goal of most efforts at lovemaking. Therefore, the couple may abandon sexual relations except when the woman is ovulating; the male may feel such pressure to perform that he becomes temporarily impotent; and events that threaten to separate the couple when the woman will be ovulating may have to be canceled. It is understandable that resentment begins to build in subtle ways as sexual spontaneity is abandoned in favor of maximizing the possibilities of conception.

A second source of stress is the imagined presence of others in the bedroom. Since many couples keep charts that include basal body temperature, cervical mucus viscosity, and occasions on which intercourse is performed, they begin to feel as if their gynecologist is peering over the bedpost to make sure that they are attending to babymaking on schedule. Conscious of the exacting eye of their physician, couples may even chart occasions of intercourse when, in fact, no sex has occurred. During medical visits, the questions about body positions, frequency of intercourse, and female body posture after intercourse can cause the couple to feel that their capacity to make love is being scrutinized under a microscope—hardly a stimulus to passion!

A third source of stress for some couples is the demise of their sexual self-esteem as their infertility persists. This association of sexuality with fertility is rooted in earlier experiences— often memories carried over from adolescence, when sexual myths were taken seriously and never quite discarded, even though the individual knows better intellectually. Discussing sexual self-esteem openly can be a helpful experience for the couple, since they probably have kept these feelings carefully hidden during the tension of their infertility.

One couple, Jennifer and Dan, were encouraged by their therapist to discuss their mutual dissatisfactions with their sexual relationship.

Dan: Jennifer seems to get so moody and depressed at the end of the day that I try to hug her to comfort her, but I don't initiate sex because I don't want to put any demands on her while she's so sad.

Jennifer: When Dan treats me platonically night after night, I can't help thinking how unattractive I must have become in his eyes. Not only has infertility robbed me of a baby, but it's robbed me of good sex as well! Sure I'm sad, but I'm not asexual! If he would only be open to a sexual relationship, we might get some vitality back into our lives again.

Dan: Jen, I adore you, but I've been so confused about what I could do to comfort you. If making love would feel good to you, then I'm all for it!

The professional cannot banish all the threats that infertility presents to a fulfilling sexual relationship, but a number of efforts can be made to help the couple come to terms with their bedroom demons. First, simply the act of bringing sexual issues into the open can be immensely freeing for the couple. They need the professional's reassurance that they are not sexually maladjusted but, rather, are responding as many infertile couples do to the strains that infertility puts on sex. The professional may want to encourage the couple to acknowledge the very real pressure they feel when the woman is ovulating and to examine why they have difficulty giving and experiencing sexual pleasure at other times of the month. Perhaps they do not feel entitled to such pleasure as long as they are unsuccessful in conceiving a baby, or perhaps guilt over sexual enjoyment causes them to view procreation as the only valid purpose of lovemaking; sometimes the very act of making love is emotionally painful because it reminds the couple of their repeated failure to achieve a pregnancy. In any case, when these issues are explored, individuals can begin to understand their behavior more clearly and may be able to continue such discussions between themselves if sexual fulfillment becomes difficult.

The professional also may want to encourage the couple to be innovative about their sexual practices, as a way to offset the sexual monotony that can arise from purposeful lovemaking. In addition to encouraging the couple to introduce fun, humor, playfulness, renewed passion, and experimentation into their lovemaking, the professional also should remind the couple that orgasm and intercourse are not necessary components of lovemaking. Clearly, at the time of the woman's ovulation, the couple will feel compelled to have intercourse to maximize the possibilities of conceiving; but they need not feel this pressure during every sexual encounter. Instead, they can enjoy the intimacy that comes from cuddling, caressing, manual stimulation, and physical closeness as an extended dimension of their lovemaking and a valid end in itself, rather than as a prelude to more active sex.

Therapeutic Implications for the Professional

The professional who works with infertile people faces several challenges. First is how to help make life meaningful during the quest for a baby. Many infertile people deny themselves life's pleasures "until we have a baby" and thus face the double predicament of suffering with their infertility and having no daily enjoyments to sustain them during this difficult time. At some level, these people may believe that perhaps they do not deserve to have children and, therefore, are also undeserving of the other joys that life could hold. Aware of the battered self-esteem that infertility can inflict on otherwise confident people, the professional needs to determine how the infertility has affected these individuals' self-esteem and how their lives have changed since infertility was diagnosed. Only then can the professional begin to appreciate what was normal for them and, subsequently, help them look to past pleasures as models of what still can be possible. The professional can encourage the infertile couple to move beyond the identity of victim to that of survivor.

Sometimes one partner is caught up in the grieving process while the other is moving ahead with life despite the infertility that they share. In these circumstances, the person who has already adopted the survivor role may be able to help the

other partner regain a healthier perspective. The grieving partner, on the other hand, may feel a tremendous amount of
anger toward the mate who is coping. This anger stems from
the grieving person's belief that the partner does not want a
baby as much and does not understand the depth of the mate's
grief. Before the coping partner can help the grieving mate,
the professional must help them both communicate about
their different perceptions of the world and the effect of infertility on their lives, as individuals and as a couple. Then the
couple can begin to work together to restore some of the happier fragments of their times together before infertility perme-
ated their lives.

A second challenge is to explore what the quest for a
baby represents for the couple. It surely embodies their wish to
enlarge their family and to become parents, but it also may provide clues about why the couple persist in their efforts to
achieve a pregnancy, rather than considering other options.
Discovering what the baby means to the couple can be complicated and is likely to lead ultimately to some decisions about
how long to continue treatment. Prior to a decision, however,
the couple must communicate openly about what they hope a
baby will bring to their lives.

The professional can expect a range of responses: the
desire for a pregnancy, the wish to experience parenthood, the
need to be seen by the world (and especially by one's parents)
as an adult, the wish to relive one's childhood or to indulge in
childish pleasures, the need to provide a family experience better than one's own as a child, the desire to be loved by a little
person, the need for a child to carry on one's genetic lineage,
the need for a child as a confirmation of one's fertility, the
opportunity to consolidate one's relationship with one's mate
and, perhaps, the need to fill a void in the couple's relationship. It may be especially important to help the partners differentiate between realistic and unrealistic expectations that they
attach to having a baby. If achieving autonomy from one's parents, for example, is a strong motivation, the professional can
help the couple explore other ways to accomplish this goal.
Such exploration also provides the professional with an oppor-

tunity to discover how the couple's ideas about parenting were influenced by their parents.

A third challenge is to help the couple determine when they are ready to stop infertility treatment and explore other options. This is likely to be a time of great tension in the relationship, particularly if both partners do not agree that "enough is enough." Often the infertile partner, fueled by guilt for being the one responsible for the couple's incapacity to have a baby, needs to pursue doggedly every opportunity to achieve a pregnancy. In other cases, one partner will push to end treatment out of concern for what the treatment is doing to the mate, either emotionally or physically.

One or both partners may now be especially vulnerable to the encouragement of their doctors to pursue more aggressive medical treatment, including "high-tech" interventions. Sometimes the couple are apprehensive about letting down a physician who has been committed to treating their infertility and who may not appreciate the emotional toll the treatment has taken. The professional working with the infertile couple will need to encourage them to gather statistics on the success rate of the clinic where they would be pursuing treatment, to learn about the potential side effects of proposed medications, and to decide how much of their personal and financial resources they are willing to commit to the treatment. If the couple consider adoption a viable alternative, the professional will want to remind them that adoption can be costly and time consuming and, in some cases, will involve age restrictions for the parents.

An invaluable support service is available through RESOLVE, Inc., 1310 Broadway, Somerville, MA 02144–1731. By calling this organization at (617) 623–0744, the client or professional can learn about locations of support groups and availability of literature on various aspects of infertility.

The intrusion of infertility on the couple's sexual intimacy, financial resources, careers, education, family relationships, and self-esteem should ultimately be discussed, because each partner may ultimately be unaware of the other's experiences in many of these areas. There are several reasons why these matters are difficult to discuss. First, infertility hurts, and living with it is painful even without an open discussion about the specific sources of the pain. Second, ending treatment means "giving up" for some couples; and, because of the time and resources already invested in trying to achieve a pregnancy, giving up may make them feel like losers. Third, exploring what a baby represents is likely to serve as a poignant reminder of something that the couple desperately want but cannot have. Finally, any discussion of ending treatment implies that the couple will have to confront the profound grief that they have been holding in abeyance while they still had hope that they could have a birth child.

At this point, the couple have probably experienced many of the feelings associated with anticipatory mourning— the denial, anger, bargaining, and grief. Yet so far there has been no closure, just emotional exhaustion, since they have not yet acknowledged that their birth child will forever be a dream and never a reality. They are reluctant to accept this finality and move on with their lives, especially if they have been told by medical professionals that they deserve to cling to hope. When they finally let go of this hope, some couples choose to use birth control to emphasize the finality of their decision and to forge ahead with other ways of building their lives together. Ironic as the use of birth control will seem to them, many couples find that it is a welcome change from temperature charts, ovulation kits, medications, and all the other interventions that have consumed their energies over the years.

Acceptance does not necessarily mean giving up hope for a child, however; many couples will now choose to explore adoption. Such couples recognize that their dream of becoming birth parents will not come true, but they are ready to look forward to life's opportunities, despite the detour that infertility forced them to take on their path to enlarging their family.

Whatever choice infertile couples ultimately make, infertility presents numerous challenges to the professional working with infertile people. First is the challenge of inquiring about and acknowledging the intrusiveness of infertility into many areas of the individual's life. The complex interactions among medical disruptions, psychological pain, and social relationships can be difficult to sort out and work through. Second is the challenge of working with other professionals concerned with the well-being of the infertile partners; in addition to keeping channels of communication open among a variety of involved professionals, the professional may also need to help the infertile partners learn some assertive skills to employ in their interactions with these professionals. Third is the challenge of conceptualizing infertility as something that affects the *couple*, even though only one partner may be diagnosed as infertile. And last, and ever present, is the challenge to feel with the couple their pain and grief as the hope for parenthood eludes them. As individuals involve, blame, rage at, protect, withdraw from, and support their partners, their relationship alternately deepens and is strained by their efforts to come to terms with the impact of their infertility. The professional who recognizes this delicate balance is in the best position to help both partners articulate their needs and extend support to one another.

6

Coping with Reproductive Losses: Elective Abortion, Miscarriage, and Ectopic Pregnancy

Reproductive losses have always been hard for Americans to regard as losses. For, when we think of abortion, ectopic pregnancy, miscarriage, and stillbirth as losses to be mourned, we are challenging others to regard the unborn baby as a real entity; but the invisible emotional attachment between parents and their unborn baby is difficult for others to relate to. They often cannot appreciate the intensity of this attachment. Infertile couples may have a vivid picture of their fantasy baby—its physical attributes, its talents or skills, and the loving care they expect to give it. When conception has occurred and the fetus is growing in utero, the parents' attachment increases as the pregnancy develops and the movements and heartbeat of the baby can be observed.

Since most people are impatient with the grieving process associated with a concrete loss, it is not surprising that they accord even less attention to the need to grieve the loss of the baby who died before or during birth. In general, there are no rituals and no comforts for family members whose anticipations of a healthy birth have been interrupted by a pregnancy loss. Only recently have newspapers begun to include stillbirths in the obituary columns; some enlightened clergy are beginning to help couples create a service in memory of their baby who died during pregnancy. But in the midst of this immense sadness, couples are met with empty phrases that do more to discount their loss than to validate it: "It's for the best." "Another pregnancy will help you forget." "It's time to get on with your life." Such responses make it very difficult for family members to mourn the loss of the baby they had cherished in their fantasies, the baby whom they must mourn with no joyful memories to cushion their grief.

Elective Abortion

In 1973, the United States Supreme Court ruled that states could not interfere with women's rights to seek abortions during the first twenty-four weeks of pregnancy. This is the period of time that the fetus is considered not to be capable of life outside the mother's womb. Decisions about allowing the abortion of a fetus after the twenty-four-week potential viability period are left up to individual states, except when the mother's life is threatened by the pregnancy. In 1976, the Supreme Court further ruled that the right to choose or reject abortion belongs solely to the woman; sex partners or parents have no valid role in that decision.

Despite its legality, abortion is not an easy choice—partly because the right to abortion is relatively recent in our country's history and because opponents of abortion are so vocal. Therefore, some women who contemplate abortion find that they are uncertain whether to terminate their pregnancies. They will need help in sorting out their feelings about the pregnancy, their relationship with their partner, their readiness for parenting, and their ability to provide for a baby, both emotionally and financially. Ideally, such discussion should take place early in the pregnancy, so that the woman can have the time she needs to weigh her options. Realistically, many women do not seek counseling around their pregnancy options until very close to the twenty-fourth week. As a result, some women may proceed with an abortion before they have fully resolved their feelings about terminating the pregnancy. Since few clinics have follow-up services for women who have had medically uncomplicated abortions, women who have unresolved feelings of guilt or grief are often left to grieve alone, particularly if family and other loved ones had urged the woman to terminate the pregnancy.

The feelings of confusion and grief may ultimately cause the woman to seek counseling. If she does so relatively soon after the abortion, her feelings will be fairly accessible, and the professional can help her to identify the losses associated with her decision to have the abortion.

Fifteen-year-old Amy shared her residual feelings of sadness and ambivalence after her abortion:

> I thought he loved me! I thought when I told him I was pregnant that we'd get married and have the baby. I had all these great dreams and they just died when he told me I'd better get rid of it, that he had his own life to live. So now I've got no boyfriend, angry parents, kids whispering at school, and money that I owe my parents for the abortion. I'm beginning to wonder if it wouldn't have been easier to set up house with the baby and stop being a drag on other people's lives.

For many women, the primary loss is likely to be that of the pregnancy, but other losses should be explored as well. Does she feel a loss of autonomy, if family or loved ones pressured her to have the abortion? Does she feel a loss of support, if she had the abortion without sharing the news of her pregnancy with loved ones? Does she feel a loss of love, if relationships have changed since others learned of her unplanned pregnancy? Does she feel a loss of trust in herself and her capacities to make decisions? Does she feel a loss of a part of herself that would have loved to continue the pregnancy and to become a parent, in spite of the life circumstances that made the abortion decision more compelling?

Certainly, all these losses are likely to contribute to the complicated feelings of sadness and grief that may follow an abortion. As with any loss, the woman needs to feel accepted and understood, with ample time allowed for reviewing the regrets that are troubling her and for validating that she has sustained losses in the aftermath of the abortion. The woman must be helped to come to terms with these losses, since unresolved regrets over the abortion decision could cause her to become pregnant again, thereby having the opportunity to "replay" the abortion decision differently.

Some women carry the sadness and guilt of their abortions with them for many years. Infertile women in particular may believe that the aborted fetus represented their one opportunity to have a successful pregnancy. Whether the infertility is her partner's problem or her own, the woman may have great difficulty forgiving herself for having chosen an abortion over continuing a pregnancy many years before.

Patsy feels haunted by memories of an earlier abortion:

> Ten years ago, when we were first married, we weren't too conscientious about using birth control and I became pregnant. We both were still in school and we knew that to begin a family at that time would have cut off a lot of experiences we wanted to have. But the decision itself was really pretty hard on me—it felt selfish to have an abortion for our convenience. So I've always carried around a core of regret about that decision, and now that we're infertile I keep thinking this is our punishment for not being willing to have that first baby.

If complications associated with the abortion are in any way responsible for her infertility, then the guilt is likely to be even more pronounced and mingled with feelings that she is being punished, either for earlier sexual activity that led to the unplanned pregnancy or for the abortion itself. Some infertile women have not told their husbands about their earlier abortion, so they carry both the grief and the guilt alone. These women often fear that their husbands would leave them if they learned of the carefully kept secret.

In such circumstances, the woman often needs help in contemplating the reasons for her decision to have the abortion. She also needs help in remembering that her decision-making skills were less developed then than they are now and that she probably did the best she could under difficult circumstances. She may not have acknowledged other losses associated with the earlier abortion, and should be encouraged to remember the amount (or lack) of caring and support extended to her at that time by loved ones. Ultimately, the woman may need to forgive herself for a decision she regrets in view of her current infertility, even though years ago the decision seemed the best one to make. Sometimes an infertile woman will cling to grief over an earlier abortion as a way of avoiding the more pressing sadness in her life—her inability to conceive. As discussed in Chapter Five, facing the pain of infertility presents its own challenges to the client and to the professional.

The decision to terminate a pregnancy because of a prenatal diagnosis of a probable birth defect is particularly excruciating. Blumberg, Golbus, and Hanson (1975) report that abortions performed for genetic indications resulted in a higher rate of depression in both the mother (92 percent) and the father (86 percent) than other elective abortions did. Undoubtedly, there are a number of plausible explanations for this emotional reaction.

First, the parents were committed to the pregnancy and had entered into prenatal testing as a means of ascertaining that the fetus was healthy. Thus, the news of a probable birth defect presents itself as an unexpected intrusion into the couple's fantasy of a healthy pregnancy, a positive birth experience, and a healthy child. Second, although some prenatal diagnoses are quite straightforward, allowing the couple to know the consequences of carrying the pregnancy to term and bearing the child, most diagnoses have ranges of ambiguity that prevent the couple from knowing exactly how the defect would affect the life and health of the child. And third, although many couples have discussed in the abstract what they would do if an unfavorable prenatal diagnosis were associated with the pregnancy, few couples are really prepared for such a diagnosis.

In addition, the aftermath of the termination procedure is likely to be made more difficult by the lack of time the couple had in which to make this crucial decision. Genetic test results often are not available or confirmed until close to the twenty-fourth week of pregnancy, the time at which a fetus might be viable if delivered prematurely. Therefore, many couples feel pressured to make a hasty decision, with no time to contemplate the impact of this loss and rarely enough time to make peace with their decision.

Sandra remembers the days before her abortion as especially traumatic:

> The first sonogram was inconclusive, but it showed the possibility of some developmental abnormalities. Since we live in a rural area, we went to a teaching hospital in a city two hundred miles away for our second sonogram. The specialist who examined it couldn't be definitive, although she was concerned about the baby's uneven development. She called one of her colleagues, and my husband and I rushed over to his office with the sonogram pictures. He was more negative, although both he and the other doctor said that they could be more definitive with us if we had another sonogram done in three more weeks. But three weeks would put me into week twenty-six of my pregnancy, and if the baby had problems at that point, we wouldn't be able to get an abortion at all. We knew even then that finding a doctor to do such a late abortion wouldn't be easy, but the doctors at the teaching hospital were able to be helpful in suggesting someone, and the next day I had the procedure. "The procedure"—what a euphemism. I'll always feel as if I killed my baby.

Although most couples want to have tests for possible birth defects, few of them actually believe that the results will be anything other than routine—unless one or both of them may be carriers of a defective gene. For such a couple, the period of tension as they await the outcome of the prenatal diagnosis is anguishing. In fact, they may already have a child with a genetic defect, may have lost pregnancies as a result of the genetic defect, or may have decided to terminate earlier pregnancies following an unfavorable prenatal diagnosis. For these couples, the quest for a healthy baby may already be shadowed with grief over pregnancies doomed by genetic defects, and the hopefulness associated with each subsequent pregnancy is tainted with the memories of past losses.

The emotional issues that the professional elicits are likely to be similar to, yet different from, the issues associated with miscarriage, discussed in the next section of this chapter.

The feelings of loss will be prominent: anger, guilt, and grief are unlikely to have been satisfactorily worked through. Yet, even as women who have miscarriages wonder whether they should assume the blame for the loss of their baby, couples who have decided to terminate their pregnancy do not wonder; they know that their decision has ended their hopes for this baby, and the guilt from that decision is usually a significant emotional component in their grief. In a sense, these couples face a classic double bind: they know that either having or not having the child will result in pain, so that neither choice seems the right or correct one.

This issue of choice is compounded by the ambiguity of the prenatal diagnosis. Even though a diagnosis may be rendered, few couples can know in advance how severe the baby's handicap will be, how much sacrifice will be demanded of them, or how the handicap will affect the child or the family over time. The couple may feel that they have opted for the "safe" choice, rather than remaining open to the unknowns of having a baby with special needs. In retrospect, their decision seems to them a selfish one, and they may be plagued by the belief that they have needlessly killed their baby. These feelings are likely to be even more intense for the woman, since it was in her body that the baby grew and it was she who submitted to the procedure that removed the baby from her. The professional should encourage the couple to explore their emotions about these matters, since they probably have not had an opportunity to articulate their very private feelings of ambivalence and grief to many other people in their support network.

Margaret remembers feeling that she would be judged by others if they learned of her abortion:

> After we were told that our baby would be born with Down's syndrome, we anguished over the decision of whether to carry the pregnancy to term. Finally, we decided to have an abortion, but we told people that I had miscarried. We just couldn't bring ourselves to have others pass judgment on our choice. We needed lots of sympathy, and people were able to give it for my "miscarriage" more readily than they would have been able to for my abortion.

Ultimately, after the couple have experienced the professional's nonjudgmental acceptance of their decision and the reasons for it, they may come to realize that they made the only decision that seemed possible at the time. The professional can help them separate their own guilt about the decision from their very real grief for the baby who will never be born. The reassurance that the couple did the best they could under terrible constraints may permit them to move ahead in their valid efforts to mourn for their baby, for their lost roles as parents to this baby, and for their possible future losses as they face subsequent pregnancies without the hopefulness that most couples take for granted.

Miscarriage

A miscarriage—or *spontaneous abortion,* as it is known by medical professionals—is the unintended ending of a pregnancy before the fetus can survive outside the mother. A *missed abortion* occurs when the fetus dies in utero but there are no symptoms such as cramping, spotting, or bleeding. A pregnancy that aborts after the twenty-sixth week is called a *late abortion* or a premature birth, depending on the weight of the fetus.

The timing of a miscarriage gives the first clue to possible cause. Seventy-five percent of all miscarriages occur within the first twelve weeks, and about half of these early miscarriages are caused by an abnormality in the embryo or in the process of its implantation in the uterus. The fetus may be deformed because of genes inherited from the parents, but more often a chance mutation has occurred during fertilization or the early growth of the embryo (Borg & Lasker, 1981).

Late spontaneous abortions occur between the seventeenth and twenty-eighth week of pregnancy. In late miscarriages, the fetus is usually normal but there are problems in its attachment to the placenta or to the uterus. There also may be abnormalities in the structure of the uterus itself. Sometimes the cervix is too weak ("incompetent" is the medical term) and dilates too early.

Since the current rates of maternal and infant death in the United States are low among middle- and upper-income women, a couple often interpret a positive pregnancy test as a virtual guarantee that they will have a baby in nine months. Thus, when the woman begins to have cramps and to bleed, the experience is terrifying on several levels: first, she is frightened about the implications for the remainder of her pregnancy; second, she is afraid for herself, since she may be experiencing pain along with the unpredictable symptoms of an impending miscarriage.

What a miscarriage means for a particular couple may depend on whether the couple had planned and hoped for the pregnancy, had experienced previous pregnancy losses, had any difficulty in conceiving the baby, have negative feelings about hospitals and emergency medical care, and are familiar with what occurs during a miscarriage. The professional will want to explore these questions at least briefly, because they will suggest to what extent the miscarriage represents a disruption and a loss.

Unplanned Pregnancy

Sometimes the couple are not yet aware that the woman is pregnant, so her symptoms of bleeding and cramping will be frightening and bewildering. Moreover, the realization that they have lost the pregnancy before they were even aware of it can precipitate a variety of responses in the partners, ranging from lingering regret to wrenching grief.

If the pregnancy was unplanned but wanted, the couple may express feelings of loss in retrospect, since parenthood is something they might have welcomed. They might also begin to think more concretely about beginning a family and may express the wish to try actively to achieve a pregnancy in the near future. The professional, realizing that they are heavily influenced by the emotions of loss, can be most helpful by empathizing with these feelings and also by encouraging the couple to consider what, beyond emotional fulfillment, a baby would represent in their lives.

Planned Pregnancy

If this pregnancy represented the wish to have a baby, the couple will view the miscarriage as an interruption of their life plans and feel sadness as well as anger. If the miscarriage occurred so early in the pregnancy that they were unaware the woman was pregnant, confusion will be coupled with the feeling of loss. Some couples may express sadness that they did not even have an opportunity to rejoice in the pregnancy. Even though the couple did not know they had achieved a pregnancy, the professional must be sensitive to their feelings of attachment to the fantasy child they had hoped to conceive.

For the couple who had known of the pregnancy, rejoiced in the news, and perhaps shared it with some friends and relatives, the miscarriage represents an unanticipated emotional and physical jolt. Fantasies of the baby and prospective parenthood may already have been shaped and shared, involvement of others in the couple's life assumed a new dimension, and the remaining months of the pregnancy were anticipated with hope and joy. Now the couple are faced with dashed hopes, an end to the attachment to their developing baby, and the need to tell others of their loss at a time when they have not fully comprehended what this loss represents. In addition to helping them obtain medical information about the miscarriage, the professional should be certain that the couple have access to emotional support as well, since their emotional pain may continue for months, with its intensity related to poignant memories or anticipated events.

Several women tell of the ebb and flow of their sadness:

Jennifer: "Our baby would have been born in the spring, and before I miscarried, I had looked forward to pushing the baby carriage in the park, feeding the ducks, gathering bouquets of flowers, dressing the baby in cute sunsuits, and being a mother on Mother's Day! Now that it's April I almost can't bear to go outdoors because nothing has turned out the way I dreamed it would."

Dierdre: "We announced our pregnancy to our families at the Thanksgiving table last year. Three days later I miscarried. I thought I had gotten over my feelings pretty well until Thanksgiving came around again. I don't know how I ever got through the meal this year, but, worse still, I can't believe that no one else appreciated how difficult it would be for me."

Anne: "My sister and I became pregnant within a week of each other. Since she lives several hundred miles away, we followed each other's pregnancies by telephone conversations— until I had a miscarriage at four months. Our telephone conversations after that were pretty strained, and when she had her baby, I shed some tears for the baby I couldn't have. But what really caught me by surprise was my reaction when I held my new niece for the first time when she was several months old. I was overwhelmed with my feelings of loss as I realized that my own baby would have been just that size, and that I wouldn't have had to put her back into my sister's arms."

For couples with a history of infertility, including pregnancy loss, the miscarriage will be an anguishing blow. Many of these couples have tried for months or years to achieve a pregnancy, and all of them have had ample experience with mourning their reproductive unpredictability; therefore, the miscarriage represents many losses and a major setback. It not only means the loss of a cherished dream child but also threatens the couple's future roles as parents. They may regard the miscarriage as a final judgment that they will never have children, and this notion may precipitate significant depression in one or both partners. The need for ongoing emotional support after the miscarriage is especially crucial for the infertile couple, as they grapple with this latest blow to their hopes for a birth child.

Although the miscarriage is a loss for both partners, the male's emotions are often lost in the events that focus primarily on the female. The male is likely to feel helpless as he watches his partner in physical and emotional pain; he may also feel that he cannot indulge his own emotions but must be strong for his partner's sake. Many males, culturally accustomed to keeping their feelings inside, have difficulty recognizing that the miscarriage is an event that evokes strong feelings of loss; instead of acknowledging sadness, they may display other emotions, such as anger and resentment. Some males, in part because of their own inability to recognize their sorrow and in part because of the difficulty they experience in seeing their partners grieve, act cheerful and try to cheer up their emotionally bereft partner. Other males will feel responsible for causing the pain, because of their role in making the woman pregnant, and may vow never to put their partners through this again.

A man may become absorbed in work or hobbies as a way of defending against the painful feelings evoked by the miscarriage. Such preoccupation can cause feelings of friction and confusion if the woman expects a more direct expression of emotion from her partner.

> Aaron and I coped so differently! My energy was totally depleted for months, and Aaron somehow needed or wanted to take on one major project after another—perhaps to gain some perspective or perhaps because my grief was too painful for him to tolerate day after day.

Another response by the male may be relief that the miscarriage is over and that his partner is all right and no longer in physical pain. The woman may experience similar emotions, including relief that she has survived an awful ordeal. These emotions are common to survivors of accidents and disasters, and usually also include feelings of guilt that they survived while others did not. In an attempt to make sense out of their emotional confusion, the couple may feel compelled to review their behavior during the pregnancy and to absolve themselves of whatever guilt they feel.

Some couples, as a way of sharing their loss with others, will hold a "remembrance" service, with poems, prayers, and personal comments from the couple and from loved ones who shared the sadness of their loss. In a society that has no rituals for the often invisible loss of a pregnancy, a remembrance service can comfort the couple and validate their feelings of attachment to the baby they lost. Professionals will need to keep in mind that unresolved feelings of loss around a miscarriage will be likely to surface on the anniversary date of the miscarriage and perhaps on the anticipated due date when the baby would have been born; conversely, the individual who has been helped to mourn the loss of a pregnancy may be able to use those coping skills in coming to terms with any future losses.

Missed Abortion

A missed abortion will ultimately result in many of the same emotions as a miscarriage, but it includes some especially painful dimensions. Referring to the fetus that has died in utero, but has not been expelled, a missed abortion may occur at any time during the first twenty weeks of pregnancy. It will probably first be detected by the woman, who finds that the symptoms of her pregnancy have ceased. Her breasts are no longer tender, she may no longer feel the nausea and exhaustion of the early months of pregnancy, and she often feels that things are "not right." She may observe a brown vaginal discharge; and, if her pregnancy is more advanced, she no longer feels fetal movements.

If the woman mentions these observations to her gynecologist in the early weeks, blood levels can be drawn, and from the results the fetal death may be confirmed. In addition, an ultrasound can demonstrate whether or not the amniotic (fetal) sac is empty, which indicates that no fetus can be detected. If the fetus is developed enough so that a heartbeat can be detected, the absence of a heartbeat in combination with an empty amniotic sac will confirm the nonviability of the fetus.

Once the fetal death has been diagnosed, there are two possible courses of action: awaiting spontaneous labor, which usually occurs within a few weeks, or having labor induced. Some couples, feeling that they need some time to comprehend the diagnosis, choose to let labor begin naturally.

Karen speaks about waiting for labor to begin:

> When the doctor diagnosed my missed abortion, I knew I had
> hit the depths. Here was this baby I tried ten years to conceive,
> and suddenly she dies and a whole part of me dies with her.
> The doctor encouraged me to carry my dead baby until labor
> began spontaneously. I became a recluse. I couldn't even bear
> to go to the store for milk. And after the baby was delivered,
> the agony didn't stop. People who had known me while I was
> pregnant would inquire happily about the baby when it was
> obvious I was no longer pregnant.

Some women find it too painful emotionally to carry a dead fetus, especially if they are known to be pregnant and are constantly being asked questions about the pregnancy. For these women, to appear pregnant and not be able to rejoice in the joys of pregnancy that others expect is emotionally taxing, and they will decide to have labor induced. For women who had felt a strong sense of bonding with the fetus, induced labor is often a way to move ahead in the grieving process. Other women may decide to have labor induced as a way of getting on with their lives, especially if the fetal death is the end of a problematic pregnancy. Although much of the initial grieving will have occurred at the time of the diagnosis, a couple's sadness will peak again at the time the dead fetus is expelled, because many couples have held out a secret hope that the diagnosis was inaccurate, and these hopes must finally be abandoned at the time of delivery.

Ectopic Pregnancy

An ectopic pregnancy occurs when a fertilized egg is lodged in an abnormal location, usually in one of the two Fallopian tubes. The pregnancy cannot progress in such a restrictive environment, and if surgery to remove the embryo is not performed in time, the tube may rupture. Diagnosis of an ectopic pregnancy can be difficult, however, because the woman may not even know that she is pregnant.

The sense of being helpless and out of control is one of the most common elements that a woman and her partner experience during an ectopic pregnancy. The physical symptoms may have caused the woman to make several trips to her physician or to more than one physician to determine the cause of her symptoms. At the time that a diagnosis is confirmed, surgery is scheduled immediately, because of the danger to the woman's life if her Fallopian tube ruptures. The woman will be administered a general anesthetic and will awaken in the recovery room feeling groggy, nauseated, and in pain. She may also feel disoriented, in part because of the anesthetic and in part because her physician may not have had time prior to the surgery to explain the details of her condition.

An ectopic, or tubal, pregnancy is difficult on many levels for the woman and her partner. It is both a physical assault and an emotional shock. Such a pregnancy not only damages the woman's sense of bodily health and well-being but also leaves her feeling emotionally vulnerable as she contemplates the life-threatening nature of the pregnancy and the increased risk of a future ectopic pregnancy. If she has lost both of her tubes to ectopic pregnancies, or if the second tube is known to be damaged, the loss of her fertility will be an added source of pain and bodily betrayal. Her mate experiences fears about his partner's close brush with death and also mourns the lost pregnancy and what the baby would have represented in their lives. If one or both of his partner's tubes were damaged or removed, then he also must come to terms with his diminished chances of becoming a birth parent.

A pregnancy ending so abruptly leaves a couple feeling confused and vulnerable. They are relieved that it is over and that the woman is alive; at the same time, they are grieving over the loss of the baby they had hoped to have. Couples who had not planned the pregnancy will need to discuss whether it was a wanted pregnancy, so that they can come to terms with their mixed feelings of relief and sadness. Couples who had planned the pregnancy and who have a history of infertility will regard the loss of future fertility as a devastating blow. Many couples welcome literature on ectopic pregnancies and infertility at a time when it is hard to put emotions into words. Literature on the emotional aspects of their loss may help them feel less alone and may prod them to talk openly with one another about feelings that are connected with their losses.

The hope of achieving a future pregnancy will be clouded by the fear of another ectopic pregnancy, which not only would result in the loss of a hoped-for baby but also would seriously risk the mother's life and future fertility. The male may feel that he cannot face the possibility of causing his partner a potentially life-threatening pregnancy. These feelings will interfere with the couple's efforts to communicate and with their sexual relationship. Therefore, both must be encouraged to discuss their fears about pregnancy and attempt to overcome them.

Anger is a common element in the mourning process, but couples who have just coped with an ectopic pregnancy are unlikely to appreciate the normalcy of their anger unless the professional helps them understand its significance. In particular, they should be encouraged to express their anger that the ectopic pregnancy happened to them when they had done nothing to "deserve" it. If there are aspects of their history that they believe may have contributed to the ectopic pregnancy, guilt will be an expectable response. In particular, a woman may feel guilty about previous damage to her tubes as she contemplates her carelessness in contracting a sexually transmitted disease. Although an earlier abortion is unlikely to have contributed to the ectopic pregnancy, it may emerge now as a source of guilt. The woman recollects that she made a conscious choice to terminate an unintended pregnancy, never realizing how difficult it could ultimately be to have a healthy and wanted pregnancy.

The couple recovering from an ectopic pregnancy will face a variety of challenges. In addition to being an available source of support for the couple, the professional can help the partners communicate between themselves about the impact that the ectopic pregnancy has had on each of them. The couple initially will experience the pregnancy as a crisis, and at least one partner ultimately may mourn some losses associated with the pregnancy. If the ectopic pregnancy turns out to be

the beginning of a series of infertility problems, the professional will want to explore the chronic aspects of infertility with
one or both partners.

Therapeutic Implications for the Professional

Many elements of the mourning process may emerge as individuals and couples come to terms with losing a pregnancy. Clients will need support as they reach out for help from their
partners and other family members. One organization that
may be of help to couples is Compassionate Friends, P.O. Box
1347, Oak Brook, IL 60521. Compassionate Friends provides
support and information to couples who have experienced
pregnancy loss. It also has chapters in many states where couples can receive support and counseling.

The response of couples to a pregnancy loss will depend
on their backgrounds, their coping skills, their ambivalence
about the pregnancy, and the extent of their bonding with the
fetus in utero. In order to be most responsive to the couple's
immediate needs and to help them communicate with each
other about the impact of the experience, the professional
must understand the meaning that both the man and the
woman attach to the loss. Since the loss probably was not anticipated, many clients will feel that their lives are out of control.
The loss may represent a crisis for the couple as they struggle
to find coping skills appropriate for coming to terms with their
feelings of loss and grief. Although the greatest concentration
of professional help at the time of a pregnancy loss will be from
hospital personnel, all professionals in contact with the couple
must be highly sensitive to their emotional needs.

Grieving the Birth
of a Stillborn Baby

Stillbirth, defined as the death of the fetus between the twentieth week of pregnancy and birth, is always a tragic blow to prospective parents. Whether the baby dies prior to the onset of labor, during labor, or at delivery, the parents feel completely unprepared for this unanticipated outcome of the pregnancy. In the United States, one stillbirth occurs for every eighty live births (Friedman & Gradstein, 1982).

The news of an impending stillbirth comes to some couples when the woman has not felt fetal movement for a day or so, and the death is indicated by the lack of a fetal heartbeat. Sometimes bleeding may be an indication of problems with the pregnancy. Often a sonogram will be used as a final confirmation of the news that is devastating to parents: their baby has died. The finality of that pronouncement is usually too shocking for the couple to grasp as they struggle to reconcile their earlier happy anticipation with the realization that the baby they have not even met will not be theirs to cherish (DeFrain, 1986; Berezin, 1982).

As the couple wait for labor to begin spontaneously or to be induced, the time before delivery may allow them to make some important decisions in the process of mourning: whether to keep a lock of the baby's hair, the hospital wristband, the blanket the baby will be wrapped in, or a record of the weight and length; and whether to have a photograph taken of the

baby or of them holding the baby. They can also make decisions about having a baptism or a service, naming the baby,
and sending out announcements of the baby's birth and death.
They must also decide whether to have an autopsy performed.
They can find out whether the woman will be placed on the
maternity floor or in another section of the hospital (and they
should be supported in expressing their wishes not to be on
the maternity ward, in case hospital bureaucracy is not sensitive
to this need). Finally, they can make plans for the difficult time
when the woman leaves the hospital and returns home with
empty arms; they must decide, for instance, whether to dismantle the nursery and what to do with gifts and purchases for the
baby.

Although some couples must wait several days or weeks
for labor to begin once they know the baby is dead, many couples have little forewarning of one of the most tragic experiences they will ever have to face. The onset of labor may occur
soon after the fetal heartbeat is undetected, or fetal distress
during delivery may be the prelude to the delivery of their stillborn child. For these couples, the tension of childbirth gives
way to shock and disbelief as they try to comprehend the death
of their baby and the loss it represents in their world. The new-
ness of the unanticipated decisions that the parents must make
in the midst of their shock and grief lends an unreality to the
entire experience.

In the Hospital

Professionals can be enormously important during the time
the woman is in the hospital, both to be an advocate for the
needs of the couple and to help the couple anticipate how
opportunities in the hospital can serve to ease their grief once
they are home. Practically speaking, the couple need time to
grieve and to be comforted. The professional can advocate for
unrestricted visiting hours and for a room, preferably a single,
that is apart from the maternity ward. In the midst of the
couple's raw grief, the professional may present some options
that they will later find comforting. Memories associated with

the baby will ultimately help the couple come to terms with the loss. But memories must be consciously created, because the overwhelming recollection will be the horror of the stillbirth experience and the hushed sounds after the delivery. The professional will want to help the couple think of ways that they can create both memories and mementoes of the baby, not of the shock of the stillbirth.

If the parents did not see the baby after the delivery, they may benefit from having this option offered to them again. Any resistances they feel about seeing the baby should be explored, so that misperceptions about the baby's appearance can be clarified. The parents should not be pressured to see or hold their baby if they find it too difficult, but as many options as possible should be offered, so that they will have some memory of their baby to aid them in the mourning process. The professional can help the couple consider whether they would like a photograph of the baby, taken by themselves or by the hospital, if that service is provided to other parents. They may want a photograph of themselves holding the baby. If the couple do not want a picture, the professional may suggest that a photograph be kept in the hospital files in case the parents change their minds at any time.

Whether to name the baby is another important decision, although the couple can take as much time as they need for this decision. The professional might suggest that it will be easier to talk about their baby and its death if they are able to call the baby by name. Also, a name has a symbolic importance; it says to the world that this baby was born and carries a place in the family memories. Some parents may feel that naming their baby will make them become too attached, so that they will feel greater pain while mourning their loss. The professional will need to point out that the parents have already become attached, by virtue of having loved, wanted, and fantasized about their baby during the past months. The pain of loss will be there whether or not the baby has a name. ·

Parents who decide to name the baby must also decide what name to choose. Parents who had already chosen a name need to consider whether to use that name for their baby who has died. The professional might want to point out that, in a sense, the chosen name really does belong to this baby; if saved for a future child, it might carry memories of the baby for whom it was originally planned. A special name can be chosen for a future baby, just as the parents had chosen a particular name in anticipation of this baby.

Religious and personal beliefs will influence the couple's decision about having an autopsy performed. If the parents have a strong need to know what went wrong and whether the baby was healthy, an autopsy may provide some clues. Parents must be told, though, that an autopsy cannot always determine the cause of the stillbirth. If the parents plan to see the baby after the autopsy as part of a funeral service, they must be certain that the hospital and funeral director are both informed. The preliminary results of an autopsy may take one or two weeks; the full autopsy report will take several weeks longer. Once available, the results should be reviewed with a medical professional who can interpret the findings and answer the couple's questions. If the couple have questions after the autopsy conference, they should be encouraged to contact the medical professional for further clarification.

Whether to baptize the baby will depend on the couple's religious beliefs and need for personal comfort. The couple's religious leader or the hospital clergy may discuss this decision with the couple. Some denominations do not baptize children, while others baptize only the living. If religious comfort is important, however, the religious leader may suggest a range of options, including a prayer or a blessing for the baby.

Whether to have a service is also important to discuss. Again, this decision should not be rushed, except when the couple's religion encourages burial or cremation promptly after a death. Even then, the couple may decide to have a separate memorial service later. If possible, the service should be planned so that the mother can attend; perhaps it can be held in the hospital chapel, or perhaps it can be delayed until the mother has come home from the hospital. The professional will want to assist the couple in gathering information about burial and cremation and deciding which one is preferred. An important consideration may be whether the couple would like to have a memorial site to visit; if so, they will want to find out whether the cemetery in which the baby will be buried allows for individualized markers or whether it merely provides an anonymous plot in its infant section.

The service itself can be planned with the help of clergy, family, and close friends. The parents should be aware of the choices they can make, including what the baby will wear and whether they will take a part in dressing the baby or covering it with a blanket. Parents may want a special keepsake, doll, or other article placed in the casket or in the baby's hand. If the parents want to have some special involvement in the service, they should be encouraged to do so. The parents may wish to tape the service as one more way of preserving an important memory. If the baby will be viewed at the service, the couple may want to plan some private time with the baby before including loved ones in their expressions of shared sorrow. When family and close friends are included in the service, they will be better able to empathize with the couple's feelings in the months ahead. Many families find that sharing a meal with loved ones after the service can give emotional replenishment.

Regardless of the couple's choices about a service, some consideration will need to be given to notifying friends of the baby's birth and death. In some cases, the couple will prefer to call a few people and ask them to call others. For out-of-town friends and relatives, an announcement may be mailed. One such announcement, sent by parents of a stillborn son, was sensitively worded, "We are sad to tell you that our son [his name] was born and died on [date]. This baby meant so much to us. We hope you will understand and share in our sorrow and loss."

As they make plans for the mother to leave the hospital, both parents will have ambivalent feelings. On the one hand, the hospital, with all its reminders of the stillbirth and the intense feelings surrounding it, may have felt like a prison for the couple, who yearn to "get back to normal." On the other hand, the hospital offered something of a cushion against the realities of facing the world with empty arms, an empty nursery, and an ache in the heart. The mother may feel less bereft if she has a keepsake of the baby to carry out of the hospital with her as she leaves.

Common Issues Following a Pregnancy Loss

Once home, the woman still will be experiencing the physical aftermath of her delivery, whether it was vaginal or by cesarean section. The discomforts associated with recovery—engorged breasts, a still-pregnant appearance, and a lack of energy—will not be cushioned by the joy of having a newborn to cherish. In addition to the physical discomforts, the mother also must adjust to her body's hormonal changes. Such changes may make her feelings of depression even more intense. During this time, a professional can help both partners communicate about their sadness and their particular needs, since each will experience grief differently.

Returning Home

Arriving home with empty arms is painful, and this difficulty may be compounded by the appearance of the nursery or whatever area of the home had been set aside for the baby's homecoming. Some family members, wishing to spare the mother the pain of seeing the empty nursery, may have dismantled it and put away all reminders of preparations for the baby. If the mother was not consulted, she may feel robbed of the chance to make her own choices about how to deal with the baby's things; and the sight of the dismantled nursery may precipitate a fresh outburst of grief and anger.

> When I came home, I was shocked to find that all my careful preparations for the baby's arrival had been erased. It was as if I had never been pregnant. The nursery had been turned back into my sewing room; the booties and blankets I had knitted had been hidden away; the gifts for the baby shower were nowhere to be seen. It was as if people expected me to get back to normal and forget that we had organized not just our home but our whole lives to be ready for the baby's arrival.

Now our lives were shattered, and my relatives had robbed
me of the chance to begin picking up the pieces myself.

If the nursery has not been touched, the couple can take
time to decide what they want to do with the room. They need
not feel that they are abnormal if they want to leave it as it is for
a while; after all, they have a great deal of grief to absorb. When
the couple decide to make changes in the room, they may want
to ask a close friend or a relative to help or, perhaps, to do it for
them. Some couples choose to leave the room as it is, to
remind them that their hopes for another baby thrive, despite
the tragedy of losing the baby for whom the nursery was originally assembled.

The couple may be tempted initially to get rid of all
reminders of the nursery, as a way of banishing their pain. The
professional might want to caution them against making too
hasty a decision, especially if they may at some later time consider conceiving or adopting a baby. Their pain will be with
them regardless of the visual reminders of the nursery, and
even these reminders can be tucked away, either in their home
or in someone else's, until they can make a plan not influenced
by the haste of trying to restore normalcy to their lives.

The mother, who nurtured the baby in her body, will feel
a special emptiness—the loss of a part of herself. Because the
parents have had no opportunity to get acquainted with their
child as a person separate from the mother, the mother's associations with her baby are those of the baby in utero; and she
will feel the loss of her baby both as a bodily loss and as an emotional loss. There may also be feelings of shattered self-esteem,
as the mother wonders why she—unlike many other women—
was unable to give birth to a healthy baby. Such feelings are
common in the infertility experience, but to have come so
close to having a healthy baby and not to realize this dream
leaves the parents' self-esteem particularly vulnerable.

The mother will need to make choices about how to
spend the first days and weeks after the pregnancy loss. The
professional should help her understand that the early weeks
will be filled with an emptiness and a longing for the baby. She

may find herself daydreaming about the baby during the day, including some painful flashbacks to the birth and hospital experience. Night dreams, some of which may be painful, can also be expected as the mother slowly integrates the loss. Talking about the baby, both to her mate and to sympathetic loved ones, will probably be helpful; but she will also need some privacy for her grief. At this time, the helping professional might want to ask the woman what other losses she has sustained in her life and what methods of coping worked best for her during those difficult times. If the mother has not adequately mourned the earlier losses, she may need to grieve not only for her baby but also for the reawakened losses that the baby's death may represent for her.

The professional will also want to encourage the woman to pamper herself and not to expect too much of herself too soon, either emotionally or physically. Food and exercise may be especially important to discuss at this time. The woman may not have the energy or the inclination to prepare and eat nutritionally well-balanced meals. After all her concern about nutrition during pregnancy, she may not feel entitled to take care of herself alone. Perhaps this is a woman who tends to undereat or overeat during times of stress. If so, the professional can help her see that her current attitude toward food is interrelated with her grief. Together, they may explore ways in which needs can be met apart from food, putting nutrition in its proper perspective.

The woman may express anger about her physical appearance—her body "pulled out of shape all for nothing." Anger is a highly energizing emotion and may prompt her to consider how to begin getting her shape back. She should seek the approval of her physician or of a physical therapist before undertaking an exercise regimen, because it may be too taxing or inappropriate for the particular muscles that she hopes to tighten. She should be encouraged, however, to consider some form of moderate, regular exercise. The decision to exercise may enable the woman to get out of doors, join an exercise group, and think of something besides her sadness.

Rejoining the real world may hold special terrors for the woman who is recovering from a stillbirth. If she still looks pregnant, she may dread the questions from well-meaning strangers. She may be amazed at how the stillbirth experience has altered her perspective of the world: the sight of pregnant women and infants may stimulate feelings of anger and jealousy; seeing baby food and diapers in the grocery store may cause tears to well up in her eyes; even a picture or an article in a magazine or a newspaper may remind the woman of her dashed hopes and dreams.

The professional can help the woman with these problems in several ways. Some women may feel guilty about their anger toward expectant parents or parents of small children because, they believe, "Nice people don't feel that way." The professional should inform the woman that these feelings are normal for someone who has experienced her particular sadness and reassure her that she is not a bad person for having such thoughts. When the woman has these feelings toward close friends or relatives, the situation is more delicate. The woman may want to explain to them that being with them is difficult in these early weeks and months, because she is reminded of the joy she had hoped they could share as their families grew together. She may, on the other hand, want to see her friends without their infants and children. In addition, the woman may want to ask for her family's understanding if she avoids family reunions with other children, family christenings, baby showers, and other painful events.

The professional may want to explore with the woman how, or whether, to keep the lines of communication open with loved ones. She may need help in distinguishing which friends and relatives are not capable of understanding her particular needs—namely, those who tell her that she should be over her sadness by now, make her feel guilty for choosing to remain away from a family affair, tell her that she is wallowing in her grief, or feel awkward with her no matter what her mood. People who cannot be helpful to her as she recovers emotionally should be avoided as much as possible; when necessary, the woman's mate should help protect her from being pressured to participate in events she does not feel ready to handle.

Another problem that the woman may face has to do with structuring her time. If she has quit her job in anticipation of spending her days with her newborn, she may now feel unproductive and lacking in personal worth. In the first weeks, she may benefit from some time at home to pamper herself, absorb the shock of her loss, and gain physical strength and emotional equilibrium. If being at home is a difficult reminder of the infant who cannot share her days, however, reentering the work force may be highly therapeutic. The time away from her previous job may give her the flexibility she needs to consider taking some courses, either for fun or for educational advancement, doing volunteer work, or exploring new career directions.

Returning to Work

Whether in a familiar work setting or in a new undertaking, the woman will find unanticipated difficulties. Some colleagues will make insensitive remarks ("When are you going to try again?" "It's all for the best," "Glad to see you looking so cheerful"); some will avoid her out of feelings of awkwardness; and others will ignore altogether any references to the stillbirth, effectively communicating their view of it as a nonevent.

Diane recounts her hurt feelings:

> The worst recollection that I have as I think back was of people who knew of our son's stillbirth and said nothing. Nothing! Did they think that by ignoring our love for him they were shielding us from pain? Oh, we felt the pain, all right, but it was made so much worse by their inability to acknowledge our tremendous loss!

During the day, the woman may want to find a place where she can have the privacy to shed a few tears, as she will probably need to do. It may be difficult to encounter people whose lives are calm or who tend to complain about what seem like petty problems. The woman may feel out of place in the midst of the workplace gossip, which now seems irrelevant and unimportant compared with her own struggle to get through each day. If she has returned to work after originally planning to take some time off to be with her baby, she may sense a feeling of unreality because she is working rather than being where she thinks she should be—at home taking care of her baby.

Effects on Family Relationships

The sadness of having a stillborn baby will affect family relationships for a number of months. Family members will struggle with how to meet one another's needs at the same time they are seeking an outlet for their grief.

Other Children. If the couple are already parents, their need to grieve is complicated by other demands in their lives: the other child or children, the laundry, the shopping and cooking, and whatever other tasks at home need to be attended to regularly because of the needs of the other children. To the extent that they can, the parents should be encouraged to let their friends and relatives know in concrete ways how they can help. If money is not a problem, the couple should consider purchasing some of the services that would otherwise overburden them.

To combat any feelings of failure about the pregnancy loss, the woman may try to "do it all" on the home front, thereby tiring herself out and not leaving time for working through her grief. Much as she loves her other children, she will probably find herself becoming impatient more quickly. Concentration may be difficult, as may be any readiness to make decisions. The parents may need the professional's support as they help their children understand the loss and the feelings that have emerged in its aftermath. Parents may need to be reassured that they can share their tears with their children as they explain that they are sad about the baby's death and that their crying is one way of expressing their sadness. At the same time, parents should emphasize that, even though the loss has made them sad, they still love their remaining children very much. Parents may find helpful suggestions in books that explain a child's perspective on loss and death (Bernstein, 1983; Arnstein, 1978; Bluebond-Langner, 1977; Grollman, 1967; Jackson, 1965; Nagy, 1965; Ilse, Burns, & Erling, 1984).

The children's teachers should be told about the loss the family members are mourning, so that each teacher can be responsive to the child during this difficult time. The teachers should be asked to notify the parents if any problems arise in school that might benefit from being discussed in more detail at home. An older child may feel anger at the baby for causing grief in the family or for usurping the parents' time. The child may use negative behaviors as a way of telling the parents, "Here I am. I'm alive and I need you!" Regressive behaviors, school phobias, and general separation anxieties are common responses for children in a family where a death is being mourned. If parents feel drained and incapable of giving special attention to their children, they should consider other resource people—clergy, counselors, close relatives, favorite teachers, or parents of friends—who might be helpful at this time, either for them or for their children.

The Father. As the father begins to face the world outside the hospital, he may encounter special difficulties. Solicitous friends will inquire about his mate's condition, perhaps neglecting to recognize that he, too, has sustained a tremendous loss and deserves concern as well. A husband relates:

> People were forever asking how they could help or, worse still, suggesting things that I could do to make the experience less tormenting for Sally. Everyone seemed to assume that my role in all of this was to be the strong one. It would have meant so much for someone to have offered *me* a shoulder to lean on!

Just as the general subject of death is an awkward one for many people to respond to, the special nature of this death will cause both friends and acquaintances to be uncertain of the most supportive ways to extend themselves. Some people, in their awkwardness, will not even express their condolences, leaving the father to wonder whether these people view the pregnancy loss as a nonevent. The awkwardness of others can cause the father to wonder whether he is entitled to mourn. He may assume that his mate has sustained the greater loss, because she carried the baby in her body during the pregnancy, and that he should be emotionally strong to enable her to lean on him as she mourns. Yet, for the woman, this stoicism can feel like an emotional betrayal.

One woman speaks of the imbalance in emotional expression that occurred after their daughter was stillborn.

> John seemed so preoccupied with comforting me that I began to wonder where his feelings were. He seemed to be getting back to normal at the very time I was falling apart. I found myself feeling furious that he could absorb such a tremendous loss with so little reaction. I began to hate it when he comforted me. What I really needed was for him to share the sadness he was hiding so effectively.

The professional can help the father recognize that, even though he was not pregnant, he shared his wife's dreams for their child. He might be encouraged to discuss some of his fantasies about what the baby represented: the chance to be a parent; the opportunity to nurture a new life and to share it as the baby grew; the anticipation of birthday parties, developmental milestones, and sharing family traditions; the curiosity about family resemblances, inherited talents, and the investment in the name that he and his mate had selected for this special child. In addition to helping the father recognize the loss that his baby's death represents to him, the discussion of his attachment to the baby will help him put into words the ache that he may be stoically enduring.

Once the father has been encouraged to accept his stake in this baby, he may recognize that he has a right to grieve for all the losses represented by the baby's death. The helping professional may want to remind the father that neither he nor anyone else can protect his mate from the grief she will feel and that they might both be comforted if they share their sadness. Even though the parents may both be at different stages in the mourning process, keeping the channels of communication open between them is vitally important.

Because males in American society are often socialized to be stoic in the face of disaster, to ignore their feelings in favor of getting on with life, and to keep their emotions to themselves, the helping professional should reassure the father that crying is a normal response to the tragic emotional blow he has experienced. Males who believe that crying is a sign of weakness can be told that it takes a brave person indeed to be in touch with painful feelings and to express them through crying. Crying can also be described as an excellent tension release. These statements may help the father reframe his attitudes about his crying and recognize that crying can have a therapeutic effect on his mate.

The professional can also help the father think of other people with whom he can talk about his feelings—for example, a member of the clergy or another professional who is especially sensitive to the loss he has sustained. Since some men may be more inclined to take action as an expression of their grief than to use talking or crying as an outlet, the professional will want to discuss with the father whether certain efforts to memorialize his child would comfort him and other family members. Such efforts will be discussed later in this chapter.

The Couple. The strain of the loss on the couple's relationship will take a variety of forms. Initially, the couple will try to ascertain how much they can expect from each other by way of comfort, understanding, and responsibility for day-to-day tasks that now feel especially burdensome. The couple may benefit from concrete suggestions about ways to connect with geographically or emotionally distant family members. Perhaps they can ask family members to call more often than usual, even after the first weeks. Visits from some members of the family may be welcome, or perhaps the couple could travel to be with particularly supportive family members. The focus on the larger family network is appropriate at this time, because if the extended family is distant, the couple may find themselves totally dependent on each other for mutual comfort. When they are both so bereft, it is not reasonable to expect that either could have the emotional strength to meet the needs of the other.

In some instances, family members will not be the most helpful comforters for the couple. The couple will need to anticipate which friends, clergy, or community professionals they can reach out to for comfort. If the community has a support group composed of other parents who have suffered pregnancy loss or the death of a child, the couple might be encouraged to contact such a group. RESOLVE and Compassionate Friends are national groups concerned about parents grieving a stillborn child, and they have chapters in many communities as well as publications available to the public.

The couple's sexual intimacy is likely to be affected by the sadness they feel over the loss of their baby. Some couples find that intimacy offers them a special closeness at a time when life has little joy. Others find that the irritations and tensions of the day intrude on their sexual relationship and prevent them from enjoying sex. They may even feel that pleasure of any kind is disloyal while they mourn their baby, or they may associate sexual relationships with fear because of the prospect of a new pregnancy. Conversely, one or both partners may feel a desperate need to achieve another pregnancy as soon as possible, thereby turning sexual intimacy into a procreative effort at the possible expense of the comforting pleasures otherwise associated with lovemaking. For other couples, memories of how their dead child was conceived may overshadow their reawakening sexual interest.

The tensions associated with sexual intimacy vary; they include impotence, sobbing during lovemaking, physical pain during intercourse, and loss of desire. In addition, the two partners may have different feelings about their readiness to have intercourse. The woman's recuperation from childbirth will take about six weeks; and even after the six-week period, her vagina may not lubricate easily during lovemaking, so that she may feel pain during intercourse. The emotional readiness for intercourse may also be different for the partners. If one person is eager to resume lovemaking and the other is hesitant or opposed, the resulting tension can exacerbate the grieving process.

Open communication will be especially important at this time. The professional can encourage the couple to appreciate the many forms of sexual closeness and intimacy, since some couples tend to define sexual pleasure solely in terms of intercourse. The professional may also want to help the couple think of ways that they can separate their necessary grief from their efforts to be sexually intimate. They might, for instance, avoid discussing their baby in the bedroom or in whatever other part of the house they choose to make love; or they might set aside some time, long before lovemaking, to talk about their day and the way in which their grief has been helped or hurt by the events they have experienced. To begin lovemaking with these feelings unexpressed will make it difficult for them to focus on mutual pleasuring.

The helping professional may need to broach the subject of sexual intimacy with the couple, since many couples feel awkward about bringing up such a personal and sensitive subject. Once the couple understand that tensions around sexual intimacy are normal, they may feel comfortable about confiding any difficulties that they have been experiencing.

Memorializing the Baby

The word *memorialize* means "to commit to memory." Some parents who have experienced a pregnancy loss may want to have a lasting memorial to their child. Those who have buried their child may choose a small headstone for the grave. Those who did not have a service when their baby died may want to plan a service at a later date. Some parents have jewelry made, using their baby's birthstone, as a special keepsake. If the parents have a yard, they may want to plant a special flower or a tree.

Memorial gifts could include books for the public library, baby furniture for a day-care center, or a scholarship for a preschooler to attend a nursery school. A donation to an organization that helps parents to cope with the grief of a pregnancy loss may seem especially fitting.

At home, the parents may want to put in a special place all the keepsakes they brought home from the hospital, perhaps adding to them a favorite baby outfit, blanket, or toy that was made especially for this baby. Parents may want to collect or write a scrapbook of poems that are especially meaningful. It may be comforting to keep a diary of the weeks and months after the baby's death, both as an outlet for feelings and, later, as a measure of how far along the parents have come in resolving their sadness.

Future Pregnancies

The decision to become pregnant again is fraught with emotion for most parents who have experienced a pregnancy loss. These couples often have mixed feelings or change their minds several times. Assuming that the woman has her physician's approval to try to conceive again, the couple may fear that they will be unable to conceive or carry a pregnancy to term, particularly if there has been a history of infertility; they may worry about whether the baby will be healthy; and they may be besieged with emotional flashbacks of the earlier pregnancy.

The professional may be especially supportive by helping the couple examine whether their readiness to conceive again is based on the wish to replace the child who has died or whether it is an outgrowth of their resolution of their baby's death. The pregnancy should not represent an effort to erase the loss of the stillborn baby but, rather, to acknowledge the couple's desire to build a family, incorporating their loss as integral to the fabric of that family.

If, for medical reasons or personal choice, the couple will not have another pregnancy, the professional's assistance may be especially important, since the couple will be mourning not only their dead child but also all the other birth children that they will not have. The decisions that the couple must face include whether to expand their family through adoption or to remain child-free and find other ways to channel their nurturing capacities.

Therapeutic Implications for the Professional

The devastating emotions from surviving a stillbirth will touch the couple's lives for many months and years. The availability and support of a range of helping professionals may be very important during their period of mourning and, later, as they decide about their readiness to try to conceive again (Lewis & Page, 1978). Although the initial shock of the stillbirth may cause the couple to be highly dependent on professionals, these individuals will assume less significant roles for the couple as they leave the hospital experience behind, plan a funeral or memorial service, and begin to pick up the fragments of their lives and move forward.

All professionals who have interacted with the couple need to remember that time only gradually eases the pain of losing a baby. Therefore, even if the professional no longer has regular contact with the couple and sees them weeks or months after their pregnancy loss, he still should remember to ask them how life has been since they lost their baby; he can also offer soothing memories of what was a highly stressful period and determine whether there is any area in which they need help and support. Too often, friends and professionals forget that the mother and father may be silently struggling for months after medical visits end, friends visit less often, and neighbors stop bringing casseroles. An offer of help or support is especially welcome even months after the stillbirth.

The client or the professional may be interested in obtaining literature from the Pregnancy and Infant Loss Center, 1415 East Wayzata Blvd., Suite 22, Wayzata, MN 55391. This organization publishes a newsletter and other materials for professionals and families.

The professional who continues to work with one or both members of the couple must allow the clients to share their feelings of grief fully, since many friends and family members may be encouraging them to "get back to normal" before they feel psychologically ready to do so. These clients need to ventilate their feelings of sadness and to be reassured that such feelings are valid even months after the stillbirth. Anniversary reactions are expectable at several points in the first year: around the time the mother conceived the baby, when she first felt life inside of her, and, of course, on the date of its birth and death.

Some clients may feel as if they are betraying the still-born child by letting go of their grief too soon, so the professional will want to explore with these clients the many ways that they can create memories of this precious baby. Even with efforts to help the parents begin to take some pleasure in life again, they may find some events still painful: they may have particular trouble being in the company of infants and toddlers who are the age their child would have been if it had lived; the woman may find herself especially pensive at the time of her period, and both parents may have real difficulty finding an answer when new acquaintances ask them how many children they have.

However, as time goes on, it is likely that the couple are able to resume their lives with a growing acceptance of their baby's death and a gradual readiness to move forward, knowing that their lives have been forever changed. The professional will undoubtedly want to communicate that her door is always open to them, since the couple undoubtedly will feel that she has shared a particularly poignant experience in their lives and has a unique understanding of them and their needs.

8

Dealing with the Aftermath of Sexual Abuse: Children and Adolescents

For many people, the term *sexual assault* conjures up a vision of an adult woman victimized by a rapist. Certainly, rape is among the most serious sexual assaults, but other assaults as well can have life-shattering implications for their victims. This chapter and the next will discuss sexual assault and victimization from a life-span perspective, with an emphasis on the losses sustained and the therapeutic needs of individuals—young and old, male and female—who have experienced these losses.

Children, both boys and girls, are the victims of sexual abuse, which causes profound life disruptions during and for years after the abuse. Adolescents of both sexes also are victims of sexual assault, whether they are students on college campuses, runaways, or still living at home. Adult females experience sexual assaults both within and outside the marital relationship; and adult males, particularly prison inmates, are also the victims of sexual assaults. Elderly women, a much-neglected population in the literature on sexual assault, tend to underreport its incidence in their lives, thereby perpetuating the myth that only attractive young women are raped.

First, a word about the terminology in Chapters Eight and Nine. I have tended to use the term *victim* when referring to individuals who have sustained an assault but have not yet actively begun the emotional healing process that can enable the individual to shed the victim role and assume the more triumphant role and identity of survivor. I have also used the term *victim* when speaking of children who have sustained a sexual assault, since this term emphasizes both their emotional vulnerability and their physical powerlessness against their assailant. Certainly, some children who have been sexually victimized are more resilient than others and could be considered survivors even at a young age, but most children carry the legacy of their sexual abuse into their adolescent and adult years before they can feel like survivors. I have used the term *survivor* when referring to adults who have come to terms with their sexual victimization and reinvested their emotional energy in moving ahead with their lives rather than being preoccupied with the victimization experience. Some survivors are still actively engaged in the healing process, but their commitment is clearly to overcoming the victim role and all the devastation implied in that identity.

As McCarthy (1990) points out, the survivor of sexual abuse is aware of and responsible for her sexuality; clearly recognizes that she was not responsible for the sexual abuse; is assertive and maintains open channels of communication so that the assault cannot recur; acknowledges that she is a strong person and did survive the assault; and focuses her psychological energy on the present and future rather that allowing her life to be controlled by the past sexual trauma. I have used the terms *sexual assault, sexual abuse,* and *sexual victimization* somewhat interchangeably in this chapter, although I have tended to use the term *victimization* when referring to children and adolescents. *Victimization* refers to anal, oral, and vaginal penetration; in addition, since fondling and sexual stimulation are common ways of victimizing children, one's perception of sexual abuse should not be limited to acts that involve penetration. I have used the term *incest* sparingly, because I believe that a child who has been sexually victimized by an adored and trusted parental figure—whether or not this person is a blood relation—will perceive the abuse as a devastating betrayal even though the law may not define the relationship as incestuous.

In all sexual assaults, there is the danger that the victim may contract HIV. Professionals need to be aware of this key

area of concern, even though the victim may not recognize it as
a risk in the immediate aftermath of the assault or disclosure.
Professionals should encourage victims to be tested for the
presence of the human immunodeficiency virus (HIV). If there
is evidence of the virus, medical follow-up will be crucial, as will
psychological support for the victim, whose losses will be even
more profound than could have been anticipated.

Rape Trauma Syndrome

Although sexual assault is not limited to rape, much of the
research on rape is applicable to other forms of sexual assault
as well. In particular, an awareness of the rape trauma syndrome and the phenomenon of posttraumatic stress disorder
will be an important beginning point for any professional working with survivors of sexual assault, whether their assault
occurred recently or many years ago. Adult survivors of child
sexual abuse often show indications of the posttraumatic stress
disorder, even though years have elapsed since they experienced the abuse. And many children and adolescents who have
been sexually abused demonstrate behaviors compatible with
the rape trauma syndrome described on the following pages.

The rape trauma syndrome was first conceptualized in
1974 by Ann Burgess and Lynda Holmstrom following their
interviews with 109 children, adolescents, and adults, ages five
to seventy-three, who had been subjected to forced sexual penetration. They discovered that these individuals had similar
emotional and physical responses to the recent life-threatening
situation they had endured. Burgess and Holmstrom termed
this acute traumatic reaction the "rape trauma syndrome." This
syndrome has two phases, both of which can disrupt the physical, psychological, social, and/or sexual aspects of an individual's life.

The first phase, which typically lasts from days to weeks,
is labeled the acute phase. It is characterized by fear, anxiety,
and emotional turmoil. Some victims appear calm and controlled, but many experience free-floating anxiety; flashbacks;
phobias; sleep disturbances; mood swings; nonspecific physical

complaints, such as headaches or gastrointestinal disturbances; or trauma-specific symptoms, such as inability to swallow or pelvic pain. Feelings expressed during the acute phase include humiliation, embarrassment, anger, revenge, and self-blame, but primarily the fear of physical violence and death (Burgess & Holmstrom, 1974).

As the emotional turmoil of the first weeks begins to subside, the victim may experience a return to superficial normalcy. Routines are resumed, new efforts at security and vigilance are in place, and the individual wants above all to get on with her life and put the rape behind her. She uses the defense mechanism of denial to suppress anxiety and to demonstrate to herself and others that she has survived intact. This response may be reinforced by friends and loved ones, who may feel threatened by her experiences and may be reluctant to listen to her recollection of the trauma and feel inept in responding in a helpful way. If she has chosen to tell no one, or a limited number of authorities, about the assault, the return to a superficial normalcy may make her feel that she has not been damaged by the assault and deserves to be treated the same by others as she was prior to the assault.

However, victims' illusions of normalcy tend to be temporary. Their efforts at denial erode, and their difficulties become more apparent to themselves and others. Nadelson, Notman, Zackson, and Gornick (1982) interviewed a group of rape victims one to two and a half years after the attack. They found that 76 percent of these individuals were still suspicious of others; 61 percent restricted going out; 51 percent had sexual problems; 49 percent were afraid to be alone; and 41 percent described themselves as depressed. In 1978, four years after their original interviews with the rape survivors, Burgess and Holmstrom interviewed them again. None of them believed their lives were "back to normal," or back to where they were before the rape. Indeed, some victims bear devastating emotional scars for the rest of their lives, and many repress their feelings about the assault only to have them emerge at emotionally vulnerable times many years later (Burgess & Holmstrom, 1979a, 1979b).

The second phase of the rape trauma syndrome, the long-term process of reorganization, focuses on the efforts of the victims to regain control over the disruptions that the rape has wrought in their lives. Some authors (Rowan & Rowan, 1984; Burgess & Holmstrom, 1985; Patten, Gatz, Jones, & Thomas, 1989) conceptualize the resolution phase as a post-traumatic stress disorder (PTSD). According to the third revised edition of the *Diagnostic and Statistical Manual of Mental Disorders* (DSM III-R), this diagnostic category includes the following symptoms: "existence of a recognizable stressor; re-experiencing of the trauma (recurrent recollections or dreams or the sudden feeling of reoccurrence based on an association to an environmental or ideational stimulus); numbed responsiveness to or reduced involvement with the external world (diminished interest in activities, detachment, constricted affect); new symptoms such as hyperalertness or exaggerated startle response, sleep disturbance, guilt for survival, memory impairment, avoidance of activities that arouse recollection, or intensified symptoms when exposed to such activities" (American Psychiatric Association, 1987, p. 250).

Such reactions occur not only in victims of sexual assault but also in individuals exposed to battlefield experiences, accidents, and natural disasters. This phase of recovery can last from months to years. Therefore, although emphasis usually is placed on crisis services available in the acute stage, much adjustment work remains to be done after the acute stage has passed.

Child Sexual Victimization

Few occurrences in our society are as abhorrent as the abuse of a child. When the form of that abuse is sexual, adults—including professionals—are often unable to comprehend either the behavior of the assailant or its devastating impact on the child. They tend to react by denying the event or by elevating it to the level of an emergency. Both reactions run the risk of damaging the child further and reflect the lack of attention, both in professional education and in practice, to the importance of developing expertise and procedures to respond to reports of child sexual victimization.

Part of the difficulty in coordinating the efforts of professionals has to do with the competing professional and institutional aspects of the problem. Clearly, the sexual victimization of a child is a child welfare problem, but it is also a serious crime that must involve action by police and district attorneys, and it may also be a problem that involves medical professionals and mental health therapists. Either too much or the wrong kinds of attention focused on the child, or a total lack of recognition of the needs of the child victim, can perpetuate the damage that has already occurred. So, in order to serve the needs of both the child and the family members, professionals must understand the dimensions of the problem.

The early research on child sexual abuse focused on girls, many of whom were the victims of incest. Authorities now realize that boys also are subject to sexual abuse, although they are less likely to report it than girls are. Rogers and Terry (1984) found a number of differences in patterns of sexual victimization of boys and of girls. Eighty-three percent of boys seen were under the age of twelve, compared with 70 percent of the girls. Twenty-six percent of the boys were under six years of age. Boys and girls are almost equally likely to be abused over time (43 percent and 47 percent, respectively), but boys are more likely to be abused by multiple offenders (20 percent) than are girls (13 percent). Rogers and Terry also found that girls are more likely to be abused by a family member (52 percent), compared with 22 percent of boys. In these cases, 31 percent of girls and 8 percent of boys were abused by a parent or a parent surrogate. In contrast, boys are victimized primarily by nonfamily members who are known to the victim or his family (63 percent) or by strangers (15 percent), compared with 48 percent of girls abused by nonfamily members.

The abuse of girls by a family member results in a highly complex emotional situation. Research in this area reveals that male family members are the most frequent perpetrators of the abuse, but females are also known to have victimized girls in their families. At first, the girl may believe that the offender is simply expressing affection. Since young girls trust these adults and assume that a caretaker is interested in their well-being, the victimization can continue for months before the youngster begins to realize that the assailant's needs are being met at the expense of her own. At that point, her protestations may be met with threats or coercion to ensure her continuing silence and to intimidate the child into believing that she has no choice but to submit to continuing victimization.

Carol, sexually abused from ages eight to eleven, remembers her father's threats:

> He used to say that telling about us would make lots of trouble: he might go to jail or lose his job. He told me how angry and upset the family would be with me if I were the cause of his leaving and my mother having to find a job. Keeping the secret was a terrible burden, but he made me feel I had to do it for the good of the whole family.

If, in addition, the child has dropped veiled signals that her mother and others have ignored, the youngster may wonder whether she would be believed if she disclosed the truth in a straightforward way. Also complicating the decision of how or whether to disclose are the positive parental behaviors often displayed toward the girl by the caregiver. She may have been singled out for special attention, favors, or affection in exchange for her silence. If these favors result in feelings of sibling rivalry from other family members, or in jealousy from the mother, the girl may feel further isolated from a family support network and more tightly bound to her abuser.

Boys, too, face a number of conflicts when deciding whether to reveal that they have been sexually victimized. Finkelhor (1985, pp. 102, 103) suggests several factors that help explain why fewer abused boys than girls ever receive public attention. First, boys grow up with the male ethic of self-reliance. When they are victimized, it is generally harder for them to seek help. In his 1979 study of college students, Finkelhor found that 25 percent of sexually abused boys had sought help, as opposed to 33 percent of sexually abused girls. Second, since the preponderance of sexual abuse of boys is by males, boys have to grapple with the stigma of homosexuality surrounding their sexual abuse. Third, boys may have more to lose than girls by reporting their victimization experiences. Given that parents tend to be less protective of boys and more willing to extend permission for freedom and independence to their sons than to their daughters, boys may choose not to reveal sexual molestation out of concern that parents would revert to overprotective behavior.

Moreover, child protective agencies, because they deal predominantly with intrafamilial cases, tend to see more girls than boys. Hospitals, too, are more likely to see children who require medical attention. Because girls are more likely than boys to have sustained a physical injury associated with a forcible sexual assault, boys are less likely to be seen in hospitals. On the other hand, police are most likely to become involved with the extrafamilial child molester; consequently, boys tend to show up in larger proportions in police statistics than in records of social agencies.

The prevalence of sexual victimization of boys is difficult to measure, partly because of underreporting and partly because of methodological difficulties in the studies undertaken to date. Finkelhor's estimate, based on his review of existing studies, is that between 2.3 and 5 percent of boys under thirteen have been victims of sexual abuse.

The reactions of children to sexual victimization are both emotional and behavioral. They often feel guilt, which may be especially pronounced if they found the experience pleasurable, if they accepted bribes or gifts in exchange for their cooperation, if the victimization occurred while they were misbehaving (staying out late, going to places they had been forbidden to frequent), or if others blame or accuse the child victim. Guilt is also common when a child discloses the incident and fears the impact of disclosure on others.

Fear is also a common emotional reaction and may take the form of general anxiety or specific fears related to the victimization experience (fear of sleeping alone, fear of men, fear of specific situations). Another reaction of boy and girl victims is the difficulty in forming trusting relationships with adults.

Their victimization experience has taught them that the
offender's needs come first and that it is not safe to trust adults.
Trust may be further impaired by the response of others whom
the child may have tried to tell, especially if the disclosure did
not result in an end to the victimization.

Behaviorally, children demonstrate a variety of responses
to their experience of sexual victimization. In young children,
regressive behavior (thumb sucking, bed-wetting) is common,
as well as increased dependency on adults and demands for
comforting and nurturance. Preoccupation with sexuality is
common; this preoccupation in older children may take the
form of acting out sexually, whereas younger children may
manifest concern over genital body parts and may engage in
sex play with peers or dolls.

A mother relates how her daughter's behavior caused
her to suspect sexual abuse:

> When Cindy was four, I noticed that her play with dolls was
> becoming very sexual. Since my husband and I couldn't imag-
> ine where this was coming from, I began to ask Cindy some
> pretty direct questions like "Do you know anyone who does
> this?" and "Has anyone done this with you?" during the sexual
> part of her play with her dolls. Imagine my horror when she
> told me that a neighborhood teenager who baby-sits had
> brought over pornographic videos and had made Cindy act
> out certain scenes! I was overwhelmed, especially when I real-
> ized that Cindy had asked me not to invite that teenager to
> baby-sit any more and I had pooh-poohed it.

Sleeping disorders are common, taking the form of
night terrors or—especially in children who are sexually victimized in their own homes—a vigilant wakefulness or fear of
going to bed. Children who are in school may show a marked
decline in school performance and may feel depressed, different from other children, and unable to concentrate in the
classroom.

Boys experience some additional reactions to sexual victimization, apparently because of the messages they have inter-
nalized about being male in today's society. If they have been
forced to participate in a homosexual act, their understanding

of sexual relationships and of their own sexual identity can become confused (Rogers & Terry, 1984). Many boys worry that this experience may influence them to become homosexual. In addition, if the boy did not, or was not able to, resist the sexual assault, he may internalize feelings of weakness, which he subsequently identifies as a lack of masculinity. Or, in response to his own confusion, he may seek to reassert his masculinity through aggressive behavior: bullying other children, destroying property, and disobeying adult authority figures. He may commit these aggressive acts in part to persuade himself that he does not have homosexual preferences and in part to present himself as so strong that no one will victimize him again.

A less common, but not infrequent, reaction is the tendency for the boy to recapitulate his own victimization, with himself as the assailant and another child as the victim. Some professionals explain this behavior as an attempt by the boy to regain his masculinity through overidentifying with the aggressor. Others believe that his profound use of denial makes him unable to empathize with his victim as he reasserts his masculinity. Still others believe that the boy has developed a negative self-concept, and therefore acts out the most negative behavior that he can muster. Rogers and Terry (1984) maintain that these efforts to recapitulate the victimization experience are most common when the legal system fails to take appropriate steps against the original offender. Under those circumstances, the boy may perceive that he, rather than the offender, is to be blamed and that society tacitly condones such behavior.

Family members can aid or hinder the child's emotional healing from a victimization experience. At the most negative end of the continuum is the parent who blames the child for what has happened. The punishment and emotional rejection the child perceives in this response are likely to confirm the feelings of poor self-worth and loathing that are common in victimized children. The parent who refuses to believe the child's account of the victimization will further undermine the child's feelings of being unprotected and will confirm existing feelings of mistrust of adults. It takes a tremendous amount of courage for a child to tell of the abuse; the betrayal by parents who refuse to take action is compounded when the child realizes that the abuse may continue and that he remains vulnerable to retaliation by the assailant. If the child's father is the assailant, the mother may feel torn between comforting her child and protecting her partner from the authorities. In such instances, the child is likely to feel both guilty and betrayed because other people's needs continue to come before his own.

Helen relates her parents' response when she disclosed that her older brother had been sexually abusing her over a two-year period:

> They just didn't want to believe it. He had always been the kid in the family who could do no wrong and suddenly I'm expecting them to believe that he's been screwing me for the past two years? My mother just couldn't deal with it. She saw it as an issue of having to choose between me and my brother and she just couldn't do it. My dad wasn't much better, although I know he threatened my brother that there would be hell to pay if it ever happened again, which it never did. But then both my parents resumed life as usual, pretending that everything was all right again and never understanding my pain, my feelings of emotional abandonment, and my belief that the family actually blamed *me* for causing the trauma of strained relationships.

On the more positive end of the continuum, if one or both parents convey to the child that they believe the account, that they will seek retribution against the assailant, and that they will protect the child from further abuse, the child will have a broader range of feelings. On the one hand, especially if the child had some positive feelings for the perpetrator, she may feel apprehensive at the prospect of any retribution against this person. On the other hand, many children whose parents vow to stand beside them feel immense relief, some absolution from blame, and as if their childhood expectations of nurturance can once again be met.

If the protective and outraged parent is the mother and the father figure the assailant, the family can be thrown into structural (and perhaps economic) disarray. In such instances, the child may feel responsible for the splitting of the family and will need time to discuss the changes that have been wrought by the revelation of the sexual abuse. Nevertheless, the primary concern for the child is that someone has believed that the victimization occurred and is willing to make every effort to stop it. The emotional support itself conveys to the child that the assailant alone is to blame for the abuse.

Let us now summarize the losses that children subjected to sexual victimization are likely to experience. These boys and girls have lost their naiveté (perhaps their virginity), their self-esteem, their feelings of being safe and protected from harm, the opportunity to discover their own sexual feelings, the ability to take pleasure in their bodily sensations, the capacity to play and to enjoy life, the ability to trust (especially adults), and the belief that their needs deserve priority and that they are entitled to express anger. They also have lost educational opportunities (if daydreaming or lack of concentration has interfered with learning), normal peer relationships, and, in intrafamilial victimization, normal family relationships.

All these losses add up to the pervasive loss of the normal childhood experiences that most children take for granted. In some families, the child has been prevented from having social contacts with peers, either because the abusing parent figure demands the child's time and attention or because the perpetrator fears that the child will disclose the abuse. The child may be terrified to have visits from friends, because the abuser might behave inappropriately toward them, or because they might be made to feel unwelcome in the home, or because the child himself might unwittingly disclose information about the victimiztion. These children who have been forced to become prematurely sexually aware always feel out of synch with their peers and believe that the interests and concerns of their peers are irrelevant to their lives.

These losses will vary, depending on the experience of
the child, the response of the family, and the resilience of the
child to the victimization experience. Although much has been
written on therapeutic techniques for survivors of child sexual
abuse, the professional should remember that the child's family has the potential for creating the most powerful healing
experiences. Assuming that the parents are not the abusers and
that they are supportive of their child, the professional can
accomplish a great deal by letting them work through their
own feelings of guilt, remorse, and anger. Concurrently, the
parents can be encouraged to be supportive and comforting
toward their child, helping him or her reclaim lost areas of
childhood and getting in touch with emotions that had been
stifled during the period of victimization. The child also may
benefit from therapeutic counseling or play therapy, so that the
trauma of the victimization can be articulated and worked
through.

If the victimization has been intrafamilial, the therapeutic work will be more complex. Most experts on child sexual
victimization are opposed to removing the child from the
home, because such an action confirms the child's feelings that
she is bad and is to blame for the abuse. A preferred approach
is to remove the assailant from the home; to ensure that the
remaining parent and family members receive necessary financial, psychological, and medical services; and to reinforce the
remaining parent's efforts to support the family.

The professional should remember that the family members also have suffered some profound losses. Parents may feel
a loss of trust in their parenting abilities, a loss of their accurate
perception of events, and a loss of their ability ever again to
view the world as a safe place; siblings may feel the loss of parental attention because so much time and energy are focused
on the victim. The professional must be on guard to keep the
child from being blamed for these losses.

If the family member identified as the assailant was an
uncaring or a violent and abusive person, the other family
members probably will feel relief that he is out of the home
and can no longer bring sadness or terror to the family. Most

perpetrators, however, will evoke more ambivalent emotions. The family members may feel horrified and unable to understand how a trusted figure could have done what the assailant is accused of doing. If the perpetrator is a sibling, the parents will bear a heavy load of grief and conflict, as will the remaining members of the family. If the perpetrator goes to jail and can no longer contribute to the financial security of the family, the family's standard of living may be curtailed. Certainly, all family members will feel that the child's disclosure has forever changed the way the family views itself and its relationship to others in the community. If community members are punitive or rejecting, the entire family will feel a double loss.

Thus, in child sexual victimization, the losses encountered are biological, psychological, and social. The family members' sense of loss is further complicated by the efforts of many professionals (child welfare, medical, legal, and mental health) to work closely with the child, forgetting that the other family members are also in need of support.

Crisis intervention techniques are appropriate in the period immediately following disclosure, with care being taken to assess the needs of all family members for psychological support, concrete financial help, and ongoing community services. Sexual victimization of children covers a wide range of sexual behaviors. However, the older the victim, the more likely that vaginal or anal penetration has been a part of the sexual assault. Emotional responses to such an assault must be appreciated as losses of the self, as distinct from medical injuries.

A child who has been sexually abused and who has not received help and support specifically for this abuse is very likely to be affected emotionally during growth into adolescence and adulthood. The emotional trauma may lie dormant for years, yet the child may already have lost self-esteem, the capacity to form trusting relationships or intimate relationships that are supportive and mutual, and the readiness to accept sexuality as an integral part of oneself.

Sexual abuse experienced in childhood may reemerge as a primary issue during counseling at a later time in the person's life. The professional will need to be highly sensitive in uncovering hidden memories of damaged childhoods, so that those childhoods can be reclaimed and feelings of blame can be absolved.

Adolescents

Adolescents are at special risk for emotional complications following a sexual assault, in part because of delicate developmental tasks facing them at this age. Adolescents who have been sexually assaulted can be expected to demonstrate many of the responses typical of the rape trauma syndrome; in addition, the emotional ups and downs of this developmental period may make them particularly needy of patient and prolonged professional attention.

Adolescents face many stresses as they strive to meet the bio-psycho-social challenges that follow puberty. Garmezy (1981) specifies eight major developmental tasks for adolescents: to achieve the gender-appropriate social role; to accept one's body image; to achieve independence from parents; to find a responsible sexuality; to complete requisite academic goals; to prepare for an occupation; to develop a set of values necessary for filling later roles as partner and parent; and to evolve a set of values and a philosophy of life that will be compatible with successful passage into adulthood. These developmental tasks pose a serious challenge for the best-adjusted adolescent; for those who have experienced a sexual assault, the challenge is compounded by their efforts to come to terms with the assault experience. Professionals working with adolescent assault survivors must keep in mind the developmental vulnerability of this period, especially with regard to evolving self-image and self-esteem.

Adolescent victims of sexual abuse can be found in families, in homeless shelters, in foster homes, in residential institutions, and on the streets. Both boys and girls are vulnerable to sexual assault, sometimes because of their innocence and inexperience and sometimes because of life-styles that are fraught with risks. Although statistics about the incidence of sexual abuse in the teen years are not considered reliable (Burgess,

1985)—in part because adolescents often are extremely reluctant to report the abuse and in part because of confusion over what ages to include in defining a "minor," "adolescent," or "juvenile" (Schultz, 1980)—Burgess estimates that about 20 percent of all adolescents have experienced sexual victimization, and 50 percent of these adolescents have not disclosed this victimization to a responsible adult. The rates can be expected to be even higher for vulnerable adolescents— namely, those from dysfunctional families, those suffering from psychiatric illness or mental retardation, or those in institutions or foster homes. However, adolescents who are abused come from all strata of society and all family configurations.

Despite difficulties in defining the nature of the sexual assault and its incidence among adolescents, researchers agree that this age group is at risk for sexual victimization by various perpetrators, including peers (Ageton, 1981; Burgess & Holmstrom, 1979a, 1979b); adult acquaintances (Finkelhor, 1979; Geiser, 1979; Schultz, 1980); family members (Weinberg, 1968; Giarretto, 1976; Lystad, 1982); and strangers (National Crime Survey 1981; Federal Bureau of Investigation, 1980, 1981).

Adolescents are especially vulnerable to assault by a person who is known to them, whether a neighbor, a coach, a teacher, a family acquaintance, or a peer. Girls are especially vulnerable to exploitation by their male peers in dating relationships when both are engaging in gender-specific behaviors that can result in miscommunication about sexual expectations. Our society's emphasis on the woman as the passive and compliant partner, coupled with the image of the macho male as the sexual aggressor, causes adolescents to be unclear in their communication in heterosexual situations. Females are encouraged to flirt and to present themselves as sexually attractive, without realizing that many of their male peers have been socialized to view a woman's resistance to sexual overtures as symbolic and not genuine.

Further, many females feel confused about what they "owe" a date and may find themselves acceding to sexual pressure that eventuates in a date rape. Zellman, Johnson,

Giarrusso, and Goodchild (1979), in their study of 432 Los Angeles–area adolescents (ages fourteen to eighteen), found that societal attitudes had influenced adolescents' expectations for dating relationships. When asked whether force should be used to achieve sexual intercourse, 82 percent of the males and the females initially indicated that force was generally never acceptable. However, when they were provided with specific sexual scenarios involving force, the proportion of those saying "never" decreased to 34 percent. Male and female respondents articulated the belief that force is "all right" under certain conditions and is more acceptable when a girl leads a boy on or gets him sexually excited.

Incest by siblings has received little attention in the literature, yet this form of sexual assault by one's agemate is even more victimizing because of the complicating factor of family dynamics. The risk to children and adolescents may be increased because the parents have been led to think that sexual exploration between children is expectable and should be taken in stride. A more powerful older brother, who may earlier have inspired feelings of loyalty, may now demand that same loyalty in exchange for his sister's silence. Or he may draw on his knowledge of their mutual family to make intimidating threats, thereby placing his sister in the position of creating powerful family disruption if she reveals the incestuous activity. In addition to her fear that she may not be believed, the adolescent has other fears that may prolong her silence: her parents' anger that she was a participant, even though unwilling, in acts that result in family disruption; her own fear of being regarded as "damaged goods"; her fear that the parents may believe the brother's version and side with him against her; and her fear that she will not be protected from having her brother carry out his intimidating threats against her, now that she has revealed the incest.

Sexual victimization also is perpetrated by adults in the lives of vulnerable or intimidated adolescents. Incest, defined as the sexual assault or abuse of a child by a parent or other adult caretaker, is most commonly reported between a daughter and a male in a caretaking role, and is least reported between mother and son (Burgess, 1985). Herman (1985), in reviewing the literature on incest, found no data associating a particularly high or low prevalence of incest with any social class, racial, or ethnic group. Poor and disorganized families are heavily overrepresented among cases reported to public agencies, probably because they lack the resources to preserve secrecy. Giarretto (1976) reports that ten years is the average age of onset for an incestuous relationship involving the oldest daughter, whereas Herman states that incestuous abuse usually begins when the child is between the ages of six and twelve, although vaginal intercourse is not usually attempted until the child reaches puberty.

One of the most consistent findings is the unusually high rate of serious illness or disability of mothers of sexually abused daughters (Herman, 1985). In such family constellations, the daughter typically takes on many of the home responsibilities that the ill or absent mother is unable to perform; the adult male provider in the home adds sexual expectations and obligations to the role responsibilities already shouldered by the daughter, often under the initial guise of expressing his appreciation and affection for her.

Hillary relates:

> My mom is an alcoholic, and from the time I came home from school until I went to bed she was passed out on the couch. I got used to keeping the house picked up, and Dad and I would usually cook dinner and talk about our day together. The incest was pretty gradual. We used to sit together watching TV, and he would have his arm around me. Or after a long day he might ask me for a backrub. So it didn't seem all that strange one night when he said my mother was snoring too loud and he needed to sleep in my bed. At first we just snuggled, but gradually things got sexual and when I protested he told me that it was all right, that he wanted to teach me how to feel like a woman. I didn't feel right about it, but he was always so gentle that I wasn't quite sure what was wrong with it either. Except that I was pretty sure that none of my friends had their fathers with them in bed at night.

Certain high-risk situations place adolescent girls in a highly vulnerable sexual position. Herman (1985) asserts that father-daughter incest should be suspected in any family that includes a violent or domineering and suspicious father; a battered, chronically ill, or disabled mother; or a daughter who appears to have assumed major adult household responsibilities. Though the oldest daughter is particularly vulnerable, the perpetrator may turn his attention to younger children, who are less able to protest than their adolescent sister, and abuse each child in turn.

Girls who have been lured or intimidated into a sexually victimized relationship in their preadolescent years may find that, with the onset of puberty and other stresses in their lives, they are no longer willing to tolerate the vicimization when they reach adolescence. Whereas the sexual acts may not have included intercourse with the preadolescent child, her assailant may increase his sexual demands once she reaches puberty, while simultaneously restricting her social life outside the home (Herman, 1985). The resulting family conflict and distress may cause the victim to look for a means of escape. Runaway attempts, suicide attempts, drug and alcohol use, hysterical seizures, indiscriminate sexual activity, early pregnancy, and premature marriage are frequently seen in teenagers who have been sexually victimized (Benward & Densen-Gerber, 1976; Goodwin, 1982; Herman, 1981).

The losses faced by the adolescent victim of sexual abuse are the same as those faced by children, but added to those losses is the risk of pregnancy for the female and the inevitable losses that such a pregnancy would provoke: if it is terminated, the adolescent has lost her first child and has probably borne the stigma of being irresponsible about her sexual behavior. If she carries the pregnancy to term and places her child for adoption, she will face many losses, including the loss of the baby itself, loss of self-esteem, and the loss of the special attention she may have received due to her pregnancy. If the child is accepted into the family, the adolescent—who has already lost her childhood—will very likely be precipitated into premature parental roles. Even if the adolescent is fortunate enough not to become pregnant, she may channel her anger into self-destructive acts, thereby facing the loss of self-determination about her own behavior. Both male and female adolescents feel guilt and shame about these activities, because they *appear* to be voluntary, even though a sensitive professional understands that the roots of such behavior lie in the anger generated by the sexual abuse.

Therapeutic Implications for the Professional

Whenever a child discloses to a professional that he has been sexually abused, it is the adult's first responsibility to ensure the child's safety. Each state has mandatory reporting laws to which professionals should adhere carefully. If possible, the professional should keep the child in her office until appropriate authorities are contacted and arrangements are made for their intervention. Keeping the child informed throughout this process is imperative and will ultimately encourage him to maintain trust in the professional. If the abuse has been nonfamilial, the professional will need to inform the child's parents about the abuse, help them absorb the immediate impact of the news, and show them how they can be most supportive to their child.

If the professional plans to continue working with the child in a supportive relationship, coordination with other agencies—notably child protective services—probably will be necessary. When working in a therapeutic relationship with children and adolescents who have been sexually abused, the professional must attend to the needs of the family as well as the needs of the child. Each family will have its own unique attributes and its own therapeutic issues. If the sexual abuse has occurred within the family, the professional will need to formulate goals with the family. The goals should include, but not be limited to, stopping the sexual abuse, opening channels of communication, removing feelings of stigma associated with the sexual abuse, and helping the child see herself as a survivor rather than as a victim.

The professional will need to understand the child's own perception of the sexual abuse and the impact on his life. The loss of a sense of personal safety is pervasive for all victims. The professional must take steps, first of all, to make sure that the victimization will not occur again—specifically, by ascertaining that the perpetrator no longer has access to the child and that the child is being carefully supervised in his or her activities. Adolescents may need help in assessing the safety of the environments in which they carry out their daily activities, with an emphasis on ways of protecting themselves against threatening circumstances: unsafe neighborhoods that they may need to traverse, as well as potential difficulties in dating and social situations, where sex-role stereotypes often leave females unclear about how to communicate that they are not interested in becoming sexually involved.

At their first meeting, the professional should convey to the child that the perpetrator—and not the child—is responsible for the abuse. This communication should be offered in a way that feels supportive to the child without being perceived as an attack on the perpetrator, toward whom the child may have some positive feelings that will later need to be explored.

As trust builds with the professional, the child should be encouraged to express any feelings of confusion, mistrust, anger, helplessness, fear, and shame. Play therapy, group therapy, and family therapy may be useful therapeutic modalities for the child's long-range recovery. In addition, since the future holds many unknowns for a child survivor of sexual abuse, the professional should inform the child and the parents that they can always view therapy as an opportunity to work through any difficulties that may arise later in life—perhaps at delicate developmental stages connected with puberty, adolescence, separation from parents, and the social relationships of young adulthood. The professional should convey this information in the spirit of helping parents feel that they can be supportive if concerns surface, rather than making them feel as though the effects of the abuse will haunt their child for life. For, although the abusive act may have targeted the child, the parents have also been affected, and they too will need help in thinking of themselves as survivors.

9

Struggling to Come to Terms with Rape: Adults

The stereotypical adult victim of sexual assault is a female in her twenties or thirties and probably unmarried. It is in part this stereotype that causes an underreporting of several types of sexual assault: rapes of males, rapes of senior citizens, and rapes by husbands of their wives. In this chapter we will explore the broad occurrence of sexual assault, including those instances that fall outside one's usual perception.

Both the acute and the resolution phases of the rape trauma syndrome are replete with losses. Most survivors articulate feelings of diminished self-worth, heightened fear and anxiety, and depressed expectations for the future. Hilberman (1976) characterizes rape as the "ultimate violation of the self, short of homicide, with the invasion of one's inner and most private space, as well as loss of autonomy and control." Hilberman asserts that it is the person's self, not an orifice, that has been invaded and that the core meaning of rape is the same for a virgin, a housewife, a lesbian, and a prostitute.

For many survivors, feelings of vulnerability and fear replace their former sense of security, predictability, and protection. The central fears are ones that are reminiscent of the rape: the fear of being alone, of sex, of men, and, depending on where the rape occurred, of being at home or outdoors.

Many victims of sexual assault speak of the loss of control that remains with them long after the assault itself. The intrusion of flashbacks, sleep disturbances, fearfulness, and feelings of mistrust causes most individuals to feel that the assault now shapes their entire way of viewing their world and their interactions with others. Some will choose to change their living space (installing locks or security systems, taking in a roommate, moving to a different neighborhood); others try to regain lost control by engaging in time-consuming obsessive rituals: checking the locks on windows and doors, listening for noises, and anticipating potentially dangerous situations. All these changes and rituals are intrusive and unwelcome reminders that the survivor does not yet feel safe in an environment that previously had not posed a threat.

In addition to loss of control, survivors may face the loss of relationships. Parents, siblings, lovers, spouses, and even children of survivors may be experiencing their own private trauma as an aftereffect of the assault. The sexual aspect of a relationship is especially vulnerable to disruption—not only in the immediate aftermath of an assault but for many years afterward (Burgess & Holmstrom, 1979a, 1979b; Ellis, Calhoun, & Atkeson, 1980; Feldman-Summers, Gordon, & Meagher, 1979; Gager & Schurr, 1976; Hilberman, 1976; McGuire & Wagner, 1978). Such problems can result from the negative associations that the woman forms from the rape experience and generalizes more broadly to her sexual experience. Thus, a victim may inhibit her sexual feelings or withdraw entirely from all sexual behavior in order to avoid the fear and anxiety reminiscent of the rape. Other survivors may be able to resume sexual activity after the rape, but some specific sexual behaviors may be highly aversive because of the association with the assailant.

If the victim internalizes the societal message—sometimes conveyed by friends and loved ones—that she must have done something to invite the rape, she is also likely to have long-term sexual adjustment problems as a result. Husbands and lovers have several different reactions to an assault: some feel that they are to blame for not having protected the woman; others may believe that the woman herself could have prevented the rape.

The clinical observations of Miller and Williams (1984) indicate that the male identifies with his partner and, therefore, shares to some extent her pain and trauma. His rage derives from his sense of injustice and his powerlessness at altering the situation. Some partners become extremely possessive toward the victim, thereby altering the delicate balance of the emotional relationship. Miller and Williams report that many couples terminate their relationship shortly after the rape, while other victims refuse couple counseling because their partner "just doesn't understand."

Young Adult Women

The single woman between the ages of seventeen and twenty-four is the most frequently reported rape victim (Nadelson & Notman, 1984). Alone and often relatively sexually inexperienced, the woman may be vulnerable to date and acquaintance rape, especially if her earlier encounters with men were with caring figures from her childhood or with trusted male friends from school or work. She may blame herself after the assault for not having been more active in preventing the rape. If she was raped by someone she was dating, she may not even be sure whether to call the assault a rape, because it is different from her stereotyped ideas associated with stranger rape.

Losses experienced by the young woman who has been raped are most often in the psychological realm. Feelings of guilt and self-blame may dramatically affect the young woman's capacity for intimacy. Her feelings of mistrust against men may be heightened, and she may vow that she will never again place herself in a vulnerable situation with a male acquaintance. If the rape is the woman's first sexual experience, she will feel robbed of her virginity and of her right to choose the person with whom she would have had her first sexual experience; she also will feel as if sexual expression itself is poisoned by the violence and degradation of the assault. A woman who experiences an involuntary orgasm during the rape is even more likely to cut herself off from her feelings of sexuality, as she grapples with guilt and self-blame.

Some women, feeling like "damaged goods," may believe that the most major of their losses is the loss of self worth and the fear that no future person in their lives would see them as deserving of a warm and caring relationship. Some of these women may decide not to tell future lovers of their rape experience, fearing the rejection that such news may bring; other women may be tempted to disclose information about the rape at an early stage of a relationship, in order to avoid becoming emotionally involved with someone who may later reject them. In either case, the earlier spontaneity that these women had experienced in their relationships with men is likely to be permanently lost in the aftermath of the rape experience.

The young woman who has been raped also may lose her freedom to pursue the developmental tasks of separation and independence from parents. The rape may have threatened her belief in her ability to take care of herself, and her family may respond by being highly protective, offering to take care of her again. Welcome as these offers may be, especially in the acute phase of coming to terms with the crisis, the long-term effects can be more complicated. Rather than being reassured by her family's involvement, the woman may regress to levels of dependence that prevent mastery of the stress and conflict evoked by the rape.

Prostitutes, although they span a large age range, are predominantly women in their late adolescence or early adulthood. They are often neglected in the literature on rape, in part because they are perceived as unaffected when they are the survivors of a rape experience. Yet these women, a large proportion of whom have backgrounds that include childhood sexual abuse, experience sexual assault as a serious problem, both in and outside of their work as street prostitutes. In a study of two hundred female street prostitutes, Silbert (1984) found that 61 percent of these women were victims of incest and child sexual abuse and that 91 percent of these victims felt there was nothing they could do to stop the abuse; 70 percent of the women who had been victimized in childhood reported that their childhood sexual exploitation affected their decision to become prostitutes.

With this population, it is clear that massive losses have occurred in their childhood and adolescent years. Almost all the juvenile prostitutes in the Silbert study (96 percent) were runaways before they became prostitutes. The vast majority of the prostitutes in this study stated that they had no other options when they began prostitution. In addition to abuse that they suffered from customers and pimps, 73 percent of the women in the Silbert study were raped in a situation totally unrelated to the work situation. The vast majority of the rapes were committed by total strangers; most were violent; almost all the women reported serious physical injuries as a result of the rape; and all reported extremely negative emotional impact. Yet, in only 7 percent of the rapes did victims seek out services for any kind of assistance, support, counseling, or advocacy; only 7 percent of the rape cases were reported to the authorities.

According to Silbert, the losses experienced by street prostitutes relate primarily to their lost sense of control over their sexual activity. Not only does the informal street code of the prostitute preclude her from displaying feelings of hurt or emotional upset, but her poverty and lack of life skills compound the sense of powerlessness in her life. Since sexual activity is one of the few areas in which she has power, the prostitute suffers a significant loss when this power is taken from her in the rape experience.

Thus, the prostitute can be seen as a woman who has suffered many losses in childhood and adolescence that now leave her diminished in her capacity to recover emotionally from the rapes she experiences, since seeking help and receiving support are opportunities that she has never perceived as available to her. Professionals must be extremely careful to attend to the emotional ramifications following the rape of a prostitute, since the emphasis for this population often is on concrete services such as AIDS prevention and rehabilitation for substance abuse.

Lesbians who have been raped are likely to face complex emotional dilemmas. For some, the rape will represent their first heterosexual contact, and thus will seem to be a double violation. When she is examined at the hospital, a lesbian will be asked to answer questions about her recent sexual behavior. If she has not come out as a lesbian, answering these questions may cause her to reveal information that is intensely private. The presence of male police and male health care professionals may add to her feelings of alienation, as is common with any woman who has been raped.

Any communication of disapproval of her sexual preference will make the woman feel even more isolated and victimized. Such homophobic attitudes may be communicated in subtle or direct ways by males or females in the aftermath of the rape and will be even more repugnant to the victim at this vulnerable time. If she needs to be hospitalized, she may face another difficulty—namely, that her lover will not be considered a family member and may be excluded from visiting and discussing medical decisions with her. If her lover does visit her, they will have more difficulty than heterosexual couples in giving comfort to each other, since physical expression of emotion may evoke the disapproval of roommates, medical staff, and other health care professionals. At a time when a woman most needs the comfort and support of loved ones, a lesbian may find that the hospital environment increases her sense of isolation as she and her lover are discouraged from expressing their feelings openly.

The single woman in late adolescence or young adulthood is struggling with a number of developmental tasks that will be thrown into disequilibrium by the experience of rape. Differentiation from parents and the resolution of dependency issues; development of mature sexuality and intimate relationships; the acquisition of a vocation and a personal value system—all overlap and weigh heavily upon the individual attempting to achieve an equilibrium (Rowan & Rowan, 1984). In addition, women who have few social supports face a lonely healing process if they feel unable to reach out to others as they strive to recover from the rape. Professionals must take these developmental tasks and other complicating life circumstances into consideration when helping the young woman assess the extent of her recovery from the losses inherent in her traumatic experience of the rape.

Adult Women

The adult woman between the ages of twenty-five and fifty will perceive a rape as both an invasion against her self and an intrusion against her efforts to cope with the challenges of life. She also will feel a loss of control as she acknowledges her inability to prevent the rape. The subsequent feelings of vulnerability may extend beyond herself to fears for her family members and doubts that she will be able to protect them from danger. If she has functioned in the role of family nurturer, she and her family may feel a loss as she abandons that role out of her own need for others to comfort her. If she has children, she must decide how much to tell them about the assault and its effect on her. If the event is known in the community, the woman and her loved ones must face the loss of their privacy and, perhaps, the inability of others to be supportive and comforting.

If the woman is a single parent, people are likely to blame her for what happened, because they may regard divorced or separated women as sexually available (Nadelson & Notman, 1984). If she is forced to leave her job while she recovers from the rape, she may be—at least temporarily—unable to support herself and her children. Suddenly she is reminded how precarious the psychosocial balance is for herself and her family at the very time that she is feeling least able to be resilient.

Many people have tended to discount marital rape as a significant form of sexual assault by claiming that it is a rare phenomenon. Research in the past decade (Russell, 1982; Finkelhor & Yllö, 1983; Doron, 1980; Frieze, 1983; Giles-Sims, 1982; Pagelow, 1981) provides estimates ranging between 3 percent and 14 percent of married women, with much higher rates (about 35 percent) among battered women. Despite some variations in definitions by different researchers, marital rape can be defined the same way as any rape. Rape occurs when a person has sex with another by force and without her or his consent. Rape is "marital" simply when the attacker is the husband of the woman being attacked. Ironically, as Yllö and Finkelhor (1985) point out, marital rape is the most common form of rape; yet it remains the least acknowledged, and its victims remain the most silenced.

Many people believe that marital rape is a less traumatic form of rape because the woman knows her husband intimately and has had sex with him before. Yet, for exactly that reason, the woman whose husband rapes her may feel especially violated. As one battered woman (quoted by Finkelhor & Yllö, 1985, p. 118) poignantly recounted:

> The physical abuse was horrible, but that was something I could get over. It was like a sore that heals. When he forced me to have sex, that was more than just physical. It went all the way down to my soul. . . . He just raped me . . . my whole being was abused. . . . I feel if I'd been raped by a stranger, I could have dealt with it a lot better. . . . When a stranger does it he doesn't know me, I don't know him. He's not doing it to me as a person, personally. With your husband, it becomes personal. You say, this man knows me. He knows my feelings. He knows me intimately and then to do this to me. It's such a personal abuse.

Whereas the public may regard marital rape as an extension of sexual relations in the context of marriage, this misconception is based on a view of rape as a purely sexual act, rather than an act of power, violence, and degradation of a relationship. Women whose husbands rape them experience their major losses in the areas of control and trust. The rape threatens a woman's basic belief in her ability to form enduring relationships and to trust intimates. As Yllö and Finklehor (1985) point out, a woman raped by her husband has to live with her rapist, not "just" with a frightening memory of a stranger's attack. Being trapped in an abusive marriage leaves many women vulnerable to repeated sexual assaults by their husbands.

Research disputes the assumption that the aftereffects of marital rape are less serious than those of other forms of rape (Shields & Hanneke, 1983; Russell, 1982; Frieze, 1983). Feelings of anger toward the husband, low self-esteem, and avoidance of sexual relations were mentioned in all the studies. Frieze (1983) found that the more frequent the rapes, the more often the women blamed themselves. Six percent of those who were raped once blamed themselves, as compared to 20 percent who were raped often. Russell's study (1982) of a representative sample of over 900 San Francisco women shows that wife rape has the greatest long-term effect on the victim of all types of rape. "Fifty-two percent of the women raped by a husband and 52 percent of women raped by a relative . . . report that the rape(s) had a great effect on their lives, as compared with 39 percent of women raped by a stranger, 33 percent of women raped by an authority figure, 25 percent by an acquaintance, and 22 percent by a friend, date or lover" (p. 193).

Ironically, a woman who experiences marital rape still may maintain her social role as a loyal wife. Pressman (1989) asserts that even when a woman recognizes that her partner has the problem and that she is not the cause of the violence, she will remain silent about her situation to protect him from being criticized or ostracized by the community or family members. Battered women may tell their therapists about the rape, but only so that they can learn how to become better wives who do not provoke such behavior in their partners or how to help their husbands with their problems. This attitude enables battered women to maintain the belief that they have control over their partners' behavior and therefore can avoid further abuse.

The isolation of many rape survivors is reinforced by society's mistaken view that rape is a crime of sexual passion and therefore will have less impact on the sexually experienced woman. Wives and prostitutes are rarely mentioned in the literature on rape, not because of the infrequency of the assaults against them but because they are not thought of as entitled to the sympathy reserved for more innocent victims. And, in fact, few wives or prostitutes seek either legal or emotional support as a means of healing from the ongoing threat of continued rape. For these women, mere survival takes priority over an emphasis on healing.

The adult woman who has been raped may desperately want to get on with her life, in the hope that she can recapture the elusive normalcy of her previous existence. However, friends may distance themselves from her, in part because they feel awkward and in part because they do not know how to be comforting. And others in her life, wanting her to "get back to normal," may be intolerant or unable to understand her need to take many months or years to heal from the psychological injury of the assault. Legal proceedings, if any, can continue for many months, thereby preventing the woman from bringing closure to her emotional turmoil.

Adult Males

The adult male is not often thought of as a victim of sexual abuse. Such abuse, when it occurs, is considered an aberration of prison life (Cotton & Groth, 1984), a vicarious rape against women (Brownmiller, 1975), or a violent outgrowth of the homosexual subculture (Kaufman, 1984). Yet, even the sparse literature that does exist on male rape makes clear that it is a highly traumatic event for the survivors, regardless of the specific circumstances under which it occurs. Rape is for males, as it is for females, not primarily a sexually motivated act but, instead, an expression of aggression. The act of rape is an effort to demonstrate hostility, status, or domination and, as such, is especially threatening to males in our society, who are taught from a young age to defend themselves against aggressors.

Just as only a small percentage of women who are raped report their assault, even a smaller percentage of men will reveal that they have been sexually assaulted. Groth and Burgess (1980, p. 808) summarize three important barriers: societal beliefs that a man is expected to be able to defend himself against sexual assault; the victim's fear that his sexual preference may become suspect; and the fact that telling is highly distressing. If the male victim is gay, the fear that he may have to reveal his sexual orientation may deter him from seeking help and reporting his assault.

Thus, the losses that males face after a sexual assault are in many ways much like those faced by females: uncertainty about the safety of the environment; impaired feelings of identity and self-esteem; and disruption of social relationships, especially if one refuses to reveal the nature of the sexual assault. The male's feelings about himself as a competent male, as a capable sex partner, and as someone who can express his sexual needs openly may also be impaired.

In addition, the sexual assault on the male may impose emotional burdens not faced in the same way by a female. Since a male, by virtue of physical strength and social self-image, expects to be able to defend himself against danger, he suffers a tremendous blow to his manhood when he is rendered physically helpless. In submitting to a sexual assault, the male also feels that his sexual identity has been compromised, in that he has been forced to participate in a homosexual act.

A gay victim will not face the problem of compromised sexual identity, but the violence and exploitation of the rape experience may magnify existing feelings of vulnerability brought about by societal homophobia. Most men would view the seeking of help for such an assault as further confirmation of their helplessness and weakness; therefore, they may choose to de-emphasize their emotional needs even as they seek help for their physical injuries (Cotton & Groth, 1984).

In a study that compared fifteen male rape victims with one hundred randomly selected female rape victims over a three-year period, Kaufman (1984) found that typical male reactions differed substantially from those observed among female victims. One-third of the male victims failed at first to report the sexual component of their assault during the initial interview with emergency room staff, preferring to seek treatment solely for their nongenital trauma. Eighty percent of the

male victims appeared quiet, embarrassed, stoical, or withdrawn; in contrast, well over half of the female rape victims
expressed strong emotions.

This controlled emotional response to an assaultive incident may well reflect the socialization that males receive to be
stoic no matter how emotionally traumatized they may feel.
Therefore, professionals must not be misled by an initial withdrawn reaction and should, instead, understand it in the context of the disbelief and shock that the male is experiencing.
This emotional detachment, coupled with the reluctance to
report, may cause a male victim to present other symptoms in
reaching out for help and support.

A nurse speaks of her experience with a male who
sought medical care following a physical assault:

> I was taking a medical history and also trying to get Mr. Smith
> to tell me the extent of his injuries. He already had given a
> statement to the police, and I could tell he was worn out and
> having some trouble answering my questions. It was a quiet
> night in the emergency room, so I wasn't as rushed as usual,
> and at one point I asked if he had any questions I might be
> able to help with. To my surprise, he asked me if it is possible
> to get AIDS from being attacked. Immediately I thought to
> myself, "This man may have been raped." I sat back down,
> tried to keep the tension out of my voice, and asked if his
> assailant had attacked him sexually. When he looked down
> and nodded, I could sense his terror and despair.

Kaufman (1984) suggests that professionals should
maintain a high index of suspicion that sexual assault may have
occurred when a male presents himself as having been physically assaulted; when he appears emotionally withdrawn after
stating that he has been the victim of a crime; or when he has a
history of prior incarceration in jail or prison.

Given the reluctance of males to be open about their sexual assault experience, professionals will want to be especially
careful in their initial interviews not to add to the client's feelings of self-blame and humiliation. Kaufman (1984) emphasizes the importance of being nonjudgmental in framing questions; there should be no implication that the male survivor

was responsible for his assault, that he is gay, or that he did not try to fight off his attacker. Since, in fact, some male victims may be gay, and may be highly attuned to any remarks that might be construed as homophobic, the professional needs to be especially nonjudgmental in offering support.

Through the use of open-ended questions, the professional can encourage the client to talk about the physical and emotional impact of the assault. Since the survivor will find the recounting of his ordeal both distasteful and humiliating, questions concerning sensitive areas will need to be articulated carefully; otherwise, the client may believe that the professional suspects him of being untruthful or that the professional is being a voyeur. The professional will need to explain that, in asking for details of an experience, he is trying to understand how current problems in coping may relate to the assault suffered by the client.

The professional must demonstrate sensitivity, caring, and skill during the initial interviews, so that the male survivor will be more willing to engage in the long-term work necessary for any survivor of a sexual assault. As with females, the male should be viewed from a bio-psycho-social perspective, with special attention to the network of caring friends and relatives who can offer ongoing emotional support.

Middle-Aged and Older Women

In our society, there continues to be a prevalent misperception that older women do not get raped. Again, this misperception stems from an inability to understand that rape is not a crime of sexual passion but, instead, is an attempt to express anger, power, and hostility. Since our youth-oriented society does not generally view the older woman as a desired sex object, many prefer not to perceive her as the intended victim of a rapist. Moreover, because the literature is sparse on the occurrence of rape in older women, many people assume that this population of women over age fifty is relatively free from sexual assault. However, what is not taken into account is the underreporting of rapes by the older woman, because of feelings of shame and embarrassment. Estimates on underreporting in this age group range from 30 percent to as high as 95 percent (Law Enforcement Assistance Administration, 1977).

In comparison to younger women, the older woman is more likely to sustain serious injuries from her attacker and to have serious and prolonged emotional reactions following the rape. A younger woman probably will have more physical, emotional, and financial resilience than her older counterpart. Hicks and Moon (1984), in their study of the effects of sexual assault on older women, found that the majority of older rape survivors were assaulted in their homes and therefore had attendant feelings of invasion and insecurity. Twenty-one percent of the older women were raped by multiple offenders; only 9 percent in other age groups were victims of gang rapes. Sixty-three percent of older women had body trauma, compared to the overall incidence of 19 percent. Thirty-eight percent of older women had vaginal trauma; the overall incidence was only 5 percent. Therefore, professionals will need to take into account the older woman's heightened vulnerability, both at the time of the attack and subsequently as she seeks to recover from this terrible assault.

Although rape survivors of all ages can be expected to have many of the symptoms of the rape trauma syndrome, an older woman coping with the aftereffects of rape has special problems. The losses she faces will be in the areas of physical well-being and personal vulnerability, including feelings of helplessness and loss of control. Since declining health and a shrinking social network already may have affected her self-concept, the older woman confronts the aftermath of her rape as a massive trauma imposed on already existing developmental losses.

The beliefs of her generation make it difficult for the older woman, and her partner, to understand her victimization. Not only is she likely to have accepted the societal stereotypes of rape as a crime of sexual passion, but her feelings of modesty in the area of her own sexuality may make it difficult for her to talk about the details of the rape experience and her resulting emotional upheaval. Even using the term *rape* in reference to the assault may be abhorrent to her. Sexual acts such as fellatio and sodomy may be unfamiliar or disgusting to the older woman and may increase her personal feelings of revulsion and disgrace. Since many older women may have had a sexual relationship with only one man, the intrusiveness of the rape experience will be especially pronounced. If she is a widow, she may feel that the rape has forever spoiled her intimate memories of sexual experiences with her deceased husband; if her partner is still living, the aftermath of the rape may include sexual adjustments for both of them.

Like her younger counterpart, the older woman may have become accustomed to putting the needs of her family ahead of her own. Articulating her own needs, both to herself and to others, may be a source of guilt and anxiety, since she has gained self-esteem from her capacity to assist others and to function independently. Dependency needs resulting from the rape may feel threatening to the woman and to her family, because the balance of family dynamics has been disrupted and will need to be reassessed. Furthermore, many women in this age group have diminishing sources of emotional support, either because of widowhood, geographical separation from children and friends, or the deaths of close friends; therefore, the rape may intensify feelings of loneliness and emptiness. The woman's emotional resilience will be affected by the prominence of earlier losses and the extent of current social supports.

An eighty-year-old woman, raped and robbed six months ago, is still recovering from her injuries:

> The rape has changed my life forever. I used to have a nice little apartment downtown and could walk to do my shopping and errands. I had my cat and my TV for company. My church was just a few blocks away, and I would stop by for bingo games and social events as well as for Sunday services. Now, since the rape, my broken hip hasn't healed as it should and I'm stuck in this wheelchair. Having to give up my apartment and move to this nursing home was the worst of all. I can't keep my cat here, and I don't have room for all the scrapbooks and family pictures that comforted me at home. Sure, the folks

here are nice, but why should I have to change *my* life
because of that awful man and what he did to me? I try not to
let my hatred get me down, but how would you feel?

The decreased financial flexibility of the older woman
also represents a loss; she may now need to take costly security
measures that will enable her to feel safe, and the expenses of
medical care and counseling may be beyond her financial
means. Professionals must therefore make every effort to link
her with community services and financial support for which
she is eligible.

Therapeutic Implications for the Professional

Although the losses generated by a sexual assault or victimization will depend somewhat on the age or gender of the victim,
there are some common themes that professionals should be
aware of as they help victims become survivors.

First, the loss of a sense of personal safety is pervasive for
all victims. The professional will need to be sensitive first to
concrete interventions that will minimize the likelihood that
the victimization will occur again. Adults are most likely to be
concerned about physical security measures, such as locks, or
about the feasibility of moving to a new and safer environment
altogether. Some adults will not be able to alter their environment sufficiently to feel safe; the professional will need to advocate for clients who are unable or unready to make their living
situations safer, as in the case of victims of marital rape or
prison inmates.

Second, all these people have lost their feelings of personal competence and have acquired instead the role of a victim who feels guilty, damaged, and perhaps blamed. Therefore,
the professional must assure the client that the blame rests with
the assailant, that the client has accomplished a victory by surviving the assault, that it takes courage to seek out help, and
that everything possible will be done to help the client heal
from this traumatic experience.

Since victims of the rape trauma syndrome often use denial as a defense after the initial feeling of crisis dissipates, they may feel less need for professional support. Certainly professional help will bring painful reminders of the assault. The professional, on the other hand, should remain aware that these clients, in their efforts to achieve normalcy, will probably encounter equally painful reminiscences on their own and will also discover inevitable voids in their support networks. Therefore, the professional should maintain periodic contact with these clients. If they are able to perceive the professional as a caring and compassionate person, they may decide to undertake the long-term work on issues of loss and redefinition of self generated by the assault.

Third, victims of sexual assault often experience a loss of trust in relationships. If the assailant was someone whom the victim knew and trusted, she will certainly feel that her judgment about people is faulty. Again, the professional will want to remind the client that self-blame is not a constructive or a corrective way of viewing the situation but that perhaps the client can learn something from this experience to lower the risk of any subsequent assaults. Always with the blame resting firmly on the assailant, the professional can discuss with the client how to assess whether a relationship has earned her trust. The professional may also need to help the client acquire assertive communication skills and behaviors, so that she can be clear about her own needs and wishes and can make clear to others what she wants from a relationship.

A loss of trust in relationships can occur even if the assailant is a stranger. Many survivors find that their relationships with friends and loved ones change after the assault, in part because their friends may be incapable of comprehending the impact of the experience on the victim. Once the client discovers that her support network fails her at the very time she most needs to lean on others, she begins to question the sincerity of all relationships. She may test the professional as well, perhaps even inviting the rejection she feels she deserves in her role as victim. It will be challenging work for the professional to help her reconnect with familiar friends in new ways, as well as to encourage her to seek out new supports, particularly other survivors who are also struggling with the aftermath of a sexual assault.

A client's feelings of loss of control and powerlessness are completely expectable in the aftermath of the assault. Talking about the experience, which will help her articulate her terror, and receiving feedback from others, in which she is reassured that she is not to blame, can be immensely supportive—helping the client restore some order to the emotional chaos in which she finds herself. Survivors of sexual assault often have strong emotional reactions on the "anniversary" of the assault, so the professional should be sensitive to this phenomenon and explain its significance to the client. The feelings of loss of control are rooted in part in the perception that the world is no longer a safe place. The client must learn ways of living with this awareness without being paralyzed by fear. In addition to helping her talk about the experience, the professional may want to help her to use some techniques of behavior modification to desensitize her feelings of fear around situations reminiscent of the assault. The professional also will need to understand that symptoms such as flashbacks, nightmares, and hypervigilance are common manifestations of posttraumatic stress disorder.

Finally, losses that relate to sexuality are a common theme running through the recovery process of persons who have survived a sexual assault. One's identity as a sexual person is tarnished by an experience of sexual victimization. The individual feels robbed of the privilege to choose a desirable sexual partner, since the assault was forced on her. If she has lost her virginity because of the victimization, this may be another substantial loss. If she has learned dissociative behavior as a way of coping with repeated assaults, she may be unable to participate emotionally in future sexual relationships. If a male has been the victim of an assault, the normal adolescent confusion about sexual identity may be greatly magnified as he struggles to make sense of who he is as a sexual person. Some clients may attempt to submerge their sexuality altogether, both as a way of protecting themselves from flashbacks and as a way of hiding a part of themselves that they feel is damaged. The professional will want to help clients understand that such responses are expectable following an assault but that they have other choices besides continuing to live life with the self-definition of "sexual victim."

10

Adjusting to the Losses of Normal Aging

Although *aging* is a relative term, since people of whatever age are always growing older, in this chapter we will consider the issues faced by individuals beginning at about age fifty. That is the age when many women are coming to terms with menopause, when people of both sexes are acknowledging their changing body image, and when various other losses come with greater frequency than in the younger years.

The losses that occur at the latter end of the life cycle may eclipse sexual losses and may exacerbate feelings associated with losing a valued part of the self. In earlier chapters of this book, we have referred to losses that may occur in old age, particularly the unanticipated health problems that are difficult to contend with at any stage of the life cycle. However, some losses become almost expectable as one ages; cardiac disease, although not limited to the older person, certainly is more prevalent as people grow older and, for this reason, has been included in this chapter. Whether or not specific health conditions relate directly to sexuality, one's methods of coping with them will have an impact on the view of oneself as a sexual being. Indeed, as Viorst (1986) points out, it is the attitude toward our losses as much as the nature of these losses that will determine the quality of our old age.

These two older adults present dramatically different attitudes toward their sexuality:

Joe: "Sex? That's for the young folks, not for me! Besides, that's all you ever see in the movies or on the TV these days. I had all the sex I needed in my early years, and I guess you might say I've moved on to other less strenuous activities."

Thelma: "Life wouldn't be the same if I couldn't have sex. Mind you, I may not be as energetic as I was in my younger years, but it's still very important to me. I guess you could say that having good sex reminds me that all my parts are still working fine!"

The losses as we live past the middle years can include health, loved ones (through death, illness, or geographical distance), employment (including status, purposefulness, and financial stability), and one's home (which may encompass the move to a different community or into an institutional setting). With these losses also comes the sense that there are fewer choices over which one can exert control. The ways in which people approach these losses and cope with them will have an impact on how they view themselves with each passing year.

In addition to the concrete losses of old age, there are also the symbolic losses, many of which are associated with negative societal stereotypes. In American society, older people are often viewed as sexless, useless, powerless, and over the hill. Butler (1975, p. xi) writes of the double messages society communicates about its elderly: "We pay lip service to the idealized images of beloved and tranquil grandparents, wise elders, white-haired patriarchs and matriarchs. But the opposite image disparages the elderly, seeing age as decay, decrepitude, a disgusting and undignified dependency."

Thus, as people age, they may find themselves trying to cope with concrete losses that are exacerbated by the attitudes of others, who see them as incapable of managing their own lives with dignity. Most people cope with the losses of aging in the same ways that they have coped with other losses at earlier stages of the life cycle. Professionals working with older persons will want to inquire about earlier coping mechanisms, as a means of assessing the older person's resilience. In view of existing societal attitudes, the professional also will want to convey respect for the older person and to encourage self-determination at every opportunity.

Menopause

Menopause, or the cessation of menstruation, was depicted for years as a traumatic turning point for most women—a dreaded event accompanied by difficult physiological symptoms and the implication that a menopausal woman is "past her prime." More recently, however, many women have found that menopause does not deserve its negative reputation. The women's movement has shown them that menopause can be regarded as a transition rather than as an end; and medical options are available for reducing physiological discomforts associated with changing hormone levels (Sheehy, 1992).

Bart and Perlmutter (1981) highlight the social and cultural factors that influence women's experience during menopause. Lack of self-esteem rather than any hormonal changes seemed to account for the incidence of menopausal depression in this study. Bart and Perlmutter conclude that stress caused by social and cultural factors maximizes the distress and symptoms of menopause. Delaney, Lupton, and Toth (1988) cite a number of researchers who suggest that the negative symptoms associated with the menopause have less to do with hormonal change than with other coinciding midlife crises: children leaving, the death of a parent, economic problems, divorce, job dissatisfaction, sexual dissatisfaction, and so forth.

Thompson (1964) believes that the hazards of menopause are culturally induced. She reports that Chinese women have almost no menopausal problems, because older women in China are given power and respect as they reach maturity. Devereaux (1950) has noted a similar phenomenon among Mohave women. In that society, menopause is a sign of achievement; Mohave women are free to work, to flirt, and to be wise during their middle years. In stark contrast is the American stereotype, in which the menopausal woman is depicted as exhausted, irritable, unsexy, hard to live with, irrationally depressed, and unwillingly suffering a "change" that marks the end of her active (re)productive life (Boston Women's Health Collective, 1976).

For most women, however, menopause is not a severe or traumatic life event. Lowenthal and Chiriboga (1972) maintain that most women are matter-of-fact about it and handle the menopause experience as well or as poorly as they do their other life events. Lindemann (1984) cites research showing that only 25 percent of women see their physicians for menopausal symptoms. Neugarten, Wood, Kraines, and Loomins (1963) found that menopause was a major source of worry for only one out of four women in their study. Sixty-five percent of the women in this study said that menopause had had no effect on their sexuality; and of the remainder, 45 percent found sexual activity less important, and half thought that sexual relations were more enjoyable because menstruation and fear of pregnancy were removed.

In an effort to counteract the destructive attitudes surrounding menopause, Lindemann and Sheehy (1992) advocate consciousness raising as a means by which women can learn more about menopause from one another, communicate information about the medical controversies surrounding treatment of menopausal symptoms, and become empowered to live full and active lives after their reproductive years are past. Certainly, helping professionals will want to maximize women's positive views of themselves as they confront negative societal stereotypes connected with menopause. In addition, professionals can encourage health care organizations and social agencies to be responsive to the bio-psycho-social needs of women.

Male Midlife Changes

Males, too, experience changes in their bodies during the midlife years. Men's testosterone production begins to taper off around age forty, though not as suddenly as the female hormonal change. Physiological aspects of aging for many males include a slow regression of androgen-dependent tissues, such as the penis and scrotum. However, psychosocial rather than biological factors have gained credibility as explanations for diminution of sexual potency or loss of libido (Woods & Herbert, 1979). Masters and Johnson (1966) identified monotony in the sexual relationship or the feeling of being taken for granted as a common factor in the loss of interest in sexual performance. Other problems that interfered with male sexual activity included economic or career concerns, physical or mental fatigue, physical or mental illness of the individual or his spouse, and overindulgence in food or drink. In addition, some males retreat from coital activity rather than experience the feelings of failure or embarrassment associated with periodic difficulties in achieving sexual arousal.

In fact, age-associated changes in sexual responsiveness are expectable in the middle-aged male. Such changes may include a delay in achieving an erection, with the erection not being as full as the male experienced in his younger years. Pre-ejaculatory emission may diminish or cease, the expulsive force of ejaculation decreases, as does the volume of seminal fluid expelled. Older men also cannot repeat ejaculation a second time, because of a longer refractory period; sometimes it takes a day or more before they can have another erection. There is evidence that the involuntary nocturnal emissions during sleep persist well into the later years (Kahn & Fisher, 1969; Karacan, Hursch, & Williams, 1972). Masters and Johnson (1966), who studied 212 men aged fifty to eighty-nine, emphasize the importance of continued and frequent sexual experiences. They maintain that if elevated levels of sexual activity are maintained from earlier years and neither acute nor chronic physical incapacity intervenes, aging males usually are able to continue some form of active sexual expression into the seventy- and even eighty-year age groups.

Sexual Interest and Activity

Most studies show that women's and men's interest and participation in sexual interaction are highly dependent on early patterns of sexual expression (Nass, Libby & Fisher, 1981). A study of the factors influencing sexual activity and interest during middle and old age revealed that for men the most important variables were past sexual experience, age, subjective and objective health factors, and social class. Marital status, age, and the enjoyment derived from sex during younger years influenced women's sexual activity and interest during middle and later years (Pfeiffer & Davis, 1972). For persons of both sexes, general health problems can pose continuing hurdles to sexual fulfillment. Such problems include high blood pressure, cardiac illness, hardening of the arteries, arthritis, muscle and bone weakness, diabetes, depression, and hearing and sight problems. Problems associated with organic brain syndrome can also affect sexual relationships, because impairments interfere with memory, intellectual functions, spatial orientation, judgment, and the capacity to empathize with others.

However, many studies have shown that continued sexual activity can have a salutary effect on existing physical conditions. It provides good exercise while stimulating the sympathetic and parasympathetic nerves. Felstein (1970) points out the aerobic potential of sexual activity that raises the heart and breathing rates. Butler and Lewis (1976) state that the contractions of orgasm in women help maintain muscle tone in the vagina. For males, Masters and Johnson (1966) assert that continuing sexual responsiveness is enhanced by high levels of sexual activity. Nass, Libby, and Fisher (1981) quote clinicians who state that arthritis patients get several hours of relief from pain through sexual activity.

Many of the existing studies equate sexual activity with coitus. Yet, since physiological aging and various physical conditions present challenges to intercourse as a measure of sexual activity, we must understand sexual activity in a broader context. By broadening our perspective to include genital and nongenital caressing, tender gestures, love talk, and kissing, we can more easily support a comprehensive view of sexuality, rather than the performance-ethic frequency-count approach that is the focus of most sexuality research.

Sexual expression remains an issue for many older people who have no sexual partners, either because of illness, death, divorce, singlehood, or institutionalization. Whereas some single elders may be able to be sexually involved with another adult, they may be reluctant or unable to initiate sexual relationships with potential partners. According to the value system with which many elderly women grew up, the only acceptable sexual partner for a woman is a spouse. The persistence of this belief restricts older women more than it does their male peers. In a study by Pfeiffer, Verwoerdt, and Davis (1972), men were shown to be largely free from narrow ideas about acceptable sex partners. Ninety percent of the women in this study, but only 29 percent of the men, cited the loss or illness or absence of a spouse as their reason for stopping sexual activity. The men gave three reasons for ending their sexual activity: 14 percent cited personal loss of interest, 17 percent cited their own illness, and 40 percent thought they were unable to participate sexually.

The loss of a sexual partner also presents concerns for gay males. In Kelly's Los Angeles study (1977) of gay males aged fifty to sixty-five, 50 percent reported satisfactory sex lives; but for men over fifty-five, the number of lasting partnerships dramatically diminished due to the poor health or death of one partner. On the other hand, Friend (1980) indicates that the forty-three older gay males in his study continue to enjoy contacts with family and friends. The resilience that gay males have developed by coming out may have prepared them for the stresses and negative stereotypes of aging. Lesbians, too, typically have strong friendships with their lovers or with others in the lesbian community (Nass, Libby, & Fisher, 1981). Anecdotal accounts of longtime lesbians indicate that many continue their erotic activities well into their eighties (Beauvoir, 1973).

Despite earlier research findings, masturbation plays a highly significant role in the sex lives of many older people. Although many of today's elders were raised during a time that masturbation was perceived as a deviant activity and was actively discouraged during childhood, later sexual experiences have acquainted many older adults with the satisfactions of self-pleasuring. Nass, Libby, and Fisher (1981) point out that women can masturbate to orgasm even after vaginal atrophy, arthritis, or other changes make intercourse impossible, and men can masturbate to orgasm even after they can no longer achieve an erection.

Other factors also influence the sexual expression of elderly people. Some older males may engage in what Zilbergeld (1978) refers to as a "cycle of retreat" from sexuality, in which they avoid sexual expression due to their fears of failure. A poor self-concept, for men or for women, is likely to diminish their feelings of sexual attractiveness and may cause them to withdraw from potentially rewarding relationships. Kaas (1978) and Wasow and Loeb (1979) found that a majority of nursing home residents considered themselves sexually unattractive.

The patterns of a lifetime can also conspire to discourage sexual expression between partners. Masters and Johnson (1966) place boredom first in their list of six reasons for the older male's loss of interest in intercourse. Once sexual activity is performed as an obligation, with diminished spontaneity and tenderness, the possibilities for meaningful intimacy disappear. Conversely, the presence of hostility and tension in a relationship also can have a chilling impact on sexual expression. One's need for affection cannot be met by the same partner who is perceived as the source of decades of pent-up anger. In this situation, the partner who is the target of the hostility also becomes a barrier to expressions of tenderness and intimacy.

Lack of privacy also interferes with sexual expression of elders. Declining health or restricted incomes may make it necessary for some elders to share a residence with their grown children. For those older adults who are able to remain in their own homes or apartments, poor health may necessitate numerous visits from community caregivers, neighbors, and family. The frequent comings and goings of others will serve to restrict spontaneity of sexual expression. Older people living in nursing homes and in hospitals will have even less privacy, since staff schedules and medical procedures have priority over other patient needs. Discouraged already by physical ill health and possibly by feelings of sexual unattractiveness, elders in an

institutional setting also must confront attitudinal barriers of
the setting and staff. Nowhere are societal stereotypes about
the "sexless elderly" as apparent as in institutional settings. In a
series of studies of Wisconsin nursing homes, Wasow and Loeb
(1979) noted that administrators and others are extremely
resistant to considering the elderly residents' sexual interests—
even though roughly 80 percent of the elderly residents
responded "Yes" to the question "Should older people be
allowed to have sex?" In Kaas's study (1978) of five Detroit-area
nursing homes, nursing staff said that sexual activity between
residents should be reported! Clearly, such attitudes will firmly
discourage elderly residents from expressions of sexual intimacy or affection.

Cardiac Disease

Although heart attacks occur in adults of any age, the likelihood that one may occur increases with age. The heart, more
than any other organ, is a reminder of health, vitality, and, ultimately, mortality. Thus, when someone suffers a myocardial
infarction (MI), that individual and his entire family are
reminded suddenly of the precariousness of life, In the
immediate aftermath of MI, sexuality is a low-priority concern.
Nevertheless, as the individual contemplates his close brush
with death, returning to normalcy is also on his mind, even on
the coronary care unit.

Sam recalls his hospitalization experience:

> I can remember waking up one morning with an erection. A
> pretty young nurse was bringing in my breakfast tray and of
> course my fantasy was to invite her to close the door and hop
> into bed with me. I guess I knew that was pretty preposterous,
> so instead I flirted with her. She gave me a suspicious look and
> disappeared as fast as she could. I found myself wondering
> whether people who have had heart attacks are allowed to be
> sexy or are we just supposed to fade into the woodwork?

Cassem and Hackett (1971), who studied males on a coronary care unit, reported that several subjects were greatly con-

cerned about impotence. Themes related to sexual prowess and function were found in the men's conversations. Once the threat of death was no longer present, the males' behavior in many instances became sexually provocative.

On the other hand, many individuals with heart disease (and their partners) fear sexual activity. Hellerstein and Friedman (1970) studied forty-eight males who had had a myocardial infarction at least three months previously. The men in the study were white, middle-aged, middle- to upper-income individuals, and predominantly Jewish businessmen. Twenty of the forty-eight subjects indicated no change in frequency of orgasm after their myocardial infarction. However, in the other twenty-eight men, orgasmic frequency did decrease from 2.1 times per week one year before the attack to 1.6 times per week six months after the myocardial infarction. Asked to account for these changes, these men gave reasons such as change in sexual desire (eleven men), the woman's decision not to have sexual intercourse (seven), feelings of depression (six), fears (five), and symptoms of coronary disease (six). Not one of the subjects attributed the decrease in orgasmic frequency to impotence. Bloch, Maeder, and Haissly (1975) found similar reasons for decrease in sexual activity in their population of eighty-eight men and twelve women. They concluded that the most prevalent reasons for decreased sexual activity had to do with psychological aspects. Counseling about the advisability of sexual activity undoubtedly could have allayed some of the concerns of these men and their wives; yet, all too often, neither the patient nor medical personnel bring up this problem for discussion.

As Woods and Herbert (1979) report, conjugal sex with a partner of twenty years or more in the privacy of one's own bedroom demands only modest physical requirements (in the absence of congestive heart failure) and is similar to walking up one flight of stairs, walking briskly, or performing ordinary tasks in many occupations. Sheridan (1984) reports that exercise studies have demonstrated that the majority of patients can begin or resume sexual activity if they are capable of climbing several flights of stairs. For most patients, a rehabilitative program in which sexual activity is resumed just as physical activity is resumed will be appropriate. Marital intercourse appears to be less taxing to the heart than extramarital liaisons.

Clearly, the factors that influence resumption of sexual activity after myocardial infarction are a mixture of the biological, the psychological, and the social. The postcoronary individual wants answers to such questions as "Is it safe to resume intercourse? When? How often? What physical symptoms during coitus should be reported to the physician?" Medical personnel must be responsive to such questions as they discuss resumption of normal activities during convalescence. The occurrence of angina during or after intercourse, palpitation that occurs for fifteen or more minutes after intercourse, sleeplessness caused by sexual exertion, and marked fatigue the day after intercourse are significant indications of overexertion. During the patient's later checkups, professionals should make follow-up inquiries on sexuality; if possible, the partner should be included in these discussions, to eliminate misperceptions about any risks associated with sexual activity. An assessment of how the coronary has affected the individual's self-image is important, as is a sensitivity to anxiety felt by the individual about adequacy in resuming the roles that were important prior to hospitalization. It is also helpful to assess the partner's role during the recovery period, to determine whether there is any evidence of overprotectiveness (or excessive dependency of the cardiac individual). Professionals will want to be alert to signs of depression, anxiety, fatigue, or side effects of medication, since any of these symptoms can have a negative impact on the sexual expression and enjoyment of both partners.

Therapeutic Implications for the Professional

Viorst (1986) remarks that when we give up our sexuality, we give up the riches it brings us—sensual pleasure, physical intimacy, and heightened self-worth. Thus, when elderly people in many other ways understand from the world that they are diminished because of their age, it becomes harder and harder for them to fight diminution. As professional helpers, we have the opportunity to join hands with our elders in that fight. Some losses that come with age can never be retrieved. However, sexuality need not be numbered as such a loss. When sexuality is defined broadly to include tenderness, comforting, sensuality, intimacy, and pleasuring, it becomes accessible to many older citizens. However, barriers of societal stereotypes, institutional regulations, and personal inadequacies still remain for professionals to confront, so that elders can live out their later years without feeling sexually diminished.

PART 3

The Expanding Role
of the Helping Professional

11

The Bio-Psycho-Social Relationships of Sexuality and Reproduction

Professionals take pride in achieving expertise. Yet such expertise, while clearly desirable, at the same time has the potential to keep professionals narrowly focused on what they know best and less attentive to seeing the client comprehensively. This chapter challenges the reader to expand her professional role to look beyond what is familiar to areas that, although less familiar, are crucial to understanding the client's needs.

Most losses involve biological, psychological, and social dimensions. Whether we are concerned for the person who has just received a diagnosis of prostate cancer, the person who has been raped, the person who has experienced a miscarriage, or the person whose well-being is diminishing with advancing age, we must constantly strive to understand the unique meaning of each individual's experience. We must also be acutely aware of each individual's support network.

Because of the tendency toward specialization in professional education and in practice, most professionals encounter a substantial challenge when they attempt to bridge the gaps between the biological, the psychological, and the social in the lives of their clients. Physicians and nurses (with the exception of those concentrating on psychiatric problems) focus the bulk of their education on the biological; psychologists emphasize the psychological aspects of human behavior in their education; and social workers concentrate on social interactions among people and their environments. Clergy value the spiritual needs of the client, often making referrals to appropriate community resources when other areas of expertise are needed. Such specialization may be beneficial from the perspective of some clients, since they can be assured that the professionals with whom they work are knowledgeable about their specific areas of expertise. On the other hand, the focused attention promoted by specializations often prevents the professional from looking at the client as a whole person. Not only is the client in danger of being thought of as "the prostate case," but there is a tendency to emphasize problematic functioning, rather than appreciating the positive coping mechanisms generated by the client and his support network.

In spite of the diagnosis of a physical or psychiatric condition for a client, professionals must strive always to think of the human being behind the label. That human being must be appreciated in the social context: as a family member, a worker, a community member, and a person who may have meaningful relationships in many contexts. Psychological coping mechanisms also are variable. Many people in the midst of a crisis will appear to be functioning quite poorly, as compared with their precrisis coping behavior. Holmes and Rahe (1967) have documented the association between loss of meaningful relationships and the stress that ensues. The challenge faced by anyone who bolsters a client's flagging psychological resources is to help the client return to a previous level of functioning or to improve the client's capacity to weather future psychological threats. If the client has a physical disease or disorder, the professional will need to understand the effects of that disorder on the client's overall functioning. Most clients need time to absorb the impact of a diagnosis and, although they value the medical expertise available to them, will also want to know how the medical condition will affect the quality of their lives.

Because of the close associations between the biological, the psychological, and the social, professionals will want to improve their understanding of the client's needs and to work closely with other professionals who are involved in specialized areas of care. At some times, the professional will be a key player in the client's efforts to regain control over life; at other times, the professional will play a backstage role to others in the client's support network. Balancing these helping efforts will require not only careful assessment and ongoing case management but also conscientious teamwork and compassionate care for the client and significant loved ones.

A developmental perspective is especially helpful when we are considering sexual and reproductive losses. Not only does such a perspective enable us to understand how one's history can influence one's sexual expression and satisfaction, but we also become more sensitive to the impact of family values, spiritual teachings, and societal norms on the ways that people think about themselves as sexual beings. Biological expression is only one way of defining one's sexuality; psychological and social forces are also compelling as the individual's sexuality continually unfolds. When interruptions and disruptions in one's sexual expression occur at any stage of the life cycle, the helping professional will need to acknowledge the losses involved and help the client express grief at these losses as an integral part of the healing process.

The developmental psychologist Erik Erikson is especially attentive to the bio-psycho-social changes encountered throughout the life cycle. He poses developmental tasks faced by the person at each stage of the life cycle, in the belief that mastery of each task will enable the individual to progress to the challenges of the next stage. Individuals who are unable to master the specified developmental tasks are seen by Erikson as being at risk of certain difficulties. He articulates the challenges of tasks versus risks at each stage, as seen in the remainder of this chapter.

Infants and Toddlers

The infant's sexual drive is manifested primarily in sucking and in the wish for warmth and body contact. Feeding time for infants provides both the chance for body closeness and for the satisfaction of sucking, a powerful urge that the infant needs to satisfy. Just as they are interested in other parts of their bodies, infants also will explore their genitalia. Unlike the caregiver who says "Don't touch!" caregivers who use this exploration period as an opportunity to tell infants the names of their body parts will foster an openness in communication. They will also help the infant develop a sense of trust that caregivers value them enough to respond quickly and compassionately to their needs. Erikson (1963) maintains that the development of trust versus mistrust is the primary psychological task faced by the baby in its first year.

Gender identity, a feeling that one is male or female or ambivalent, probably begins with the awareness that one belongs to one sex and not to the other. Studies indicate that core gender identity, or the earliest and probably unalterable form of gender identity, develops in the normal child by the time he or she is about three or four years of age (Kleeman, 1971). However, during infancy and toddlerhood, the baby becomes aware of verbal and nonverbal cues about behavior and sex appropriateness as modeled by parents and caregivers. Toddler play is filled with imitation of adult role models. Not only does the toddler perform some of the actions that he or she identifies with a like-sexed adult, but the infant also learns to categorize himself or herself as a boy or as a girl and subsequently invokes more feedback from adults about the appropriateness of this role behavior.

Children

Although the period extending from age three until puberty involves a great deal of psychological maturation and social maturation, physical growth occurs more rapidly in almost every system except the reproductive system. The genital organs remain quiescent, and no changes are seen in the ovaries, testes, or breasts until puberty. Between ages two and three, children are usually toilet trained and develop an increased awareness of their genitalia. They continue to learn to identify body parts, with particular interest in vocabulary concerned with excretion. Masturbation, which began in infancy and was interrupted by the wearing of diapers, now occurs with more frequency. The responses of parents and caregivers to a child's self-stimulation will have an impact on the developing sense of self-esteem. Children at this age are particularly vulnerable to shaming experiences and may be the objects of shaming or ridicule for toileting accidents and sexual behavior or language in inappropriate places.

Erikson (1963) regards autonomy as an important developmental task at this time. Autonomy (versus the competing messages of shame and doubt) is closely linked with toilet training, as well as with general efforts by the toddler to test limits, to assert individuality, and to explore the world nearby. The family is still the primary social unit with which the child identifies; and during the third year and beyond, children become aware of and interested in the parental relationship, including their roles, sleeping arrangements, and bathing. In single-parent homes or in situations where the child spends many hours in day care, the child may need to become familiar with a number of people who are responsible for her care. The messages communicated to the child about her efforts at autonomy will either enhance or diminish her self-esteem.

Erikson identifies the development of initiative versus guilt as the primary task for children between ages four and five. Socially, children are interacting with an increasingly wide range of individuals, both children and adults. Fears of parental separation, fears about school experiences, and childhood fantasies about aggression and mutilation are common and often result in nightmares. Children's specific concern with genital mutilation is fueled by the awareness that boys' and girls' genitals are different. As children grow more confident and are able to balance the challenges faced at home and at school, they can accept the encouragement of adults to assume an increasing amount of initiative for their own work and play. Children who do not receive such encouragement may find that guilt predominates, along with the fear of failure.

Children between six and ten are in what Freud referred to as the latency period. In Erikson's view, children in this age group face the primary task of industry versus inferiority. This period is a time of consolidation of sexual and psychosocial

growth, in preparation for the hormonal surges of adolescence. However, although their sexual organs are quiescent,
children are very much aware of sexual issues. With the pre-
dominance of sexual language and content in the media,
children's curiosity about sexuality is fueled, and they seek
answers from a number of sources. If parents, caregivers, and
teachers are perceived as "askable," they may become a source
of information for children. Otherwise, the peer group
becomes the most trusted source of information about sexuality, and misinformation tends to result from the lack of adult
input. Children in this age group are absorbed in their work
and in their play, with differences in gender roles becoming
increasingly apparent. Scapegoating, social cliques, and interest in self-formed "clubs" occur during these ages, as children
seek to form increasingly close ties with their peers.

Problems and subsequent losses concerned with sexuality during this period of childhood often originate in interactions between children and adults. Sexual abuse and violence
in the home are two of the most troubling examples, both of
which communicate to the child a feeling of powerlessness.
The adult who has abandoned the expected role of protector
from harm is now held in fear by the child. This fear is compounded by the adult's communication to the child to keep
the abuse a secret—which, in turn, places the child in a further
powerless position. Sexual abuse of children, discussed in
detail in Chapter Eight, brings about devastating losses, both in
childhood and in adulthood.

Domestic violence also communicates messages about
the abuse of power, confusion about love and abuse, disregard
for women and their needs, and the use of violence as a solution for feelings of frustration. Whether the child in a violent
home is male or female, whether the child is physically abused
or not, there is considerable emotional abuse in the passive
and trapped role that a child is forced to play. The child's
observation of male dominance and female submission can
have a deleterious effect on that child throughout his or her
life. Fortunately, many schools are now implementing curricula
that seek to help children recognize that they are entitled to be

safe, that their bodies belong to them, that they can seek help from trusted adults, and that they can advocate for their own needs. Nevertheless, the experience of witnessing or being a victim of abuse makes long-lasting impressions on the child in the areas of self-concept, self-esteem, and the capacity to trust others.

Adolescents

Bio-psycho-social development proceeds at a dizzying pace during adolescence. Biologically, young people are challenged by hormonal influences that result in changing body contours, menstruation and nocturnal emissions, and new sexual urges. The association of breast and penis size with femininity and virility causes many adolescents to despair at their changing bodies. Eating disorders often begin during this developmental period, in part representing the adolescent's effort to gain control over body size and shape, in part also representing the adolescent's efforts to declare autonomy from family expectations. Generally, the biological changes that occur during adolescence result in anxieties about maturation. The coping strategies that adolescents develop to deal with new feelings and drives involve both interpersonal relationships and intrapersonal struggle.

Adolescence is often seen as consisting of two major stages. The first stretches from the onset of puberty to about ages fourteen through sixteen; psychologically, it is characterized by the push for independence from parents and attempts to resolve conflicts between the continuing need for childish dependence and the desire for a separate identity. The second stage is marked by the search for a mature identity, the quest for a mate, and the exploration of different sets of values and of occupational and other life goals (Chilman, 1989). Erikson points to the development of identity in the face of role confusion as a major task for the adolescent. The newly experienced sexual maturity activates questions about maleness or femaleness and about one's position in the peer group. In order to increase his sense of security, the adolescent attempts to band together with others who have similar characteristics and to fall in love. Both of these activities may be considered a means of testing one's identity (Erikson, 1963).

Socially, adolescents receive a number of conflicting messages. Although adolescents are physiologically mature and experience intense sexual drives, society does not sanction adolescent premarital sexual behavior. Thus, adolescents face the dilemma of strong repression of sexuality versus rebellion against sexual mores. Those who do engage in early sexual activity, as study after study has shown, are extremely likely to have poor school performance and low academic goals. Low achievement in school, especially when it is combined with problems at home, can undermine a young person's self-esteem, acceptance by the dominant peer group, and hopes for future educational-occupational success. Without high self-esteem, acceptance by one's peer group, and hopes for the future, an adolescent is much more vulnerable to such easy impulse gratification and escapist behaviors as early nonmarital coitus along with heavy use of drugs and alcohol (Chilman, 1989). Evidence points to an association between substance abuse, early unprotected coitus, and inconsistent use of contraceptives (Mindick & Oskamp, 1982; Jessor, Costa, Jessor, & Donovan, 1983).

Indeed, numerous problems, adjustments, and losses are encountered by male and female adolescents in the area of human sexuality: sexual abuse from strangers, acquaintances, and family members; the threat of sexually transmitted diseases, particularly AIDS; lack of access to accurate and reliable information about sex and contraception; unplanned pregnancies and difficulties in obtaining needed medical services; and confusion about sexual identity. These problems can either be helped or exacerbated by the adolescent's family. If parents and extended family members are supportive of the adolescent's struggles, this support often can enable the young person to achieve autonomy from the family as an outgrowth of maturation rather than rebellion. On the other hand, if the family members are preoccupied with their own difficulties, or if they overtly reject the adolescent's efforts to achieve an independent identity, role confusion, feelings of loss, and further struggles lie ahead as the adolescent grows toward young adulthood.

Young Adults

The boundaries of young adulthood are chronologically less clear-cut than those of earlier stages. Traditionally, its beginning is marked by the end of adolescence, and it usually ends when parenthood begins. However, since many adults are waiting until well into their thirties to begin families, and since an increasing proportion of adults are deciding not to have children at all, it is perhaps appropriate to identify the twenties as the young adulthood period.

Although biological changes are minimal during the twenties, preoccupation with one's body is often heightened as the young adult becomes interested in finding a mate. Middle-income young adults are increasingly aware of the importance of good health and nutrition, in part because of the emphasis on these subjects in high school and college and also because of society's preoccupation with health care.

Erikson (1963) specifies intimacy—in contrast to isolation—as a major task of young adulthood. Offer and Simon (1976) describe young adulthood as a period of maximum sexual self-consciousness. Young adults' sexual statuses become a part of their public statuses. Most make some kind of commitment to a relationship, whether marital or nonmarital. As a result, they have increased chances for regular sexual activity. But although sexual prohibitions are relaxed during the young adult years, the threat of sexually transmitted diseases, especially AIDS, may constrain free sexual expression. However, intimacy goes beyond sexual activity; the young adult must learn to give and receive love, decide whether or not to marry, and choose a marital or sexual partner (Duvall, 1971).

Socially, the relaxation in rigid sex roles has enabled both males and females to experiment with new behavior and roles unknown to earlier generations. Women now perceive options other than (or in addition to) motherhood, so that the world of work offers new opportunities for independence during the young adult years. Males are finding support for their efforts to share in or to perform traditional "female" roles and tend to view work as one of many activities in their lives, rather than as a sole definition of their identity.

During young adulthood, the individual usually consolidates a sense of sexual identity. Whether gay, lesbian, bisexual, or heterosexual, the young adult must learn about and adjust to the needs and desires of another person. Mutual decisions about acceptable variations in sexual expression are important. Guilt, shame, and hostility may be associated with sex unless each partner is sensitive to the concerns of the other. Intimacy, as Erikson perceives it, has to do with more than the presence of another person in a sexual relationship; it is concerned with the very core of the mutuality of that relationship, in which both partners are able to be fulfilled through meeting each other's needs.

Adults

Adulthood between the years of thirty and fifty is typically devoted to parenting and consolidating the relationship with a spouse or sexual partner. The task critical to this stage of the life cycle is generativity, as opposed to stagnation and self-absorption (Erikson, 1963). This task remains important in spite of high divorce rates, delayed ages of first marriage, later ages of beginning a family, and the slight increase in the numbers of couples opting for child-free living. For nonparents, generativity can be demonstrated in a variety of nurturing functions: with extended family, with young colleagues in the workplace, with community projects, or with neighborhood involvements. For single parents, the nurturing function can be so overwhelming that it eclipses the need to find and sustain a relationship with a new partner. For gay and lesbian couples who desire children, the challenges include conceiving or adopting a child, carving out a life-style as parents that is legally protected, and seeking societal acceptance for their choices in an era when the traditional nuclear family is no longer the norm.

Biologically, this period of adulthood involves the gradual process of aging, overtly apparent by wrinkles and gray hairs. Given the emphasis in our society on the desirability of a youthful appearance, some anxiety may be evoked as bodily changes prove to be markers of the inevitable march of time. Pregnancy brings about dramatic physical changes in the woman, which, in turn, have an impact on her own self-image and her sexual relationship with her partner.

Problems involving sexual or reproductive losses occur with some frequency during this stage of the life cycle. Infertility, including pregnancy loss, is an unanticipated source of stress for some couples. Pregnancy itself may be a source of stress in the sexual relationship, as couples accommodate to the woman's changing contour, feelings of well-being, and changes in sexual desire. Sometimes the joy in a pregnancy ends precipitously when a miscarriage or a stillbirth occurs. When pregnancy results in a healthy birth, the couple's attention focuses on the infant, so that they may have less time and energy to devote to each other. The fatigue of one or both parents, the lack of privacy that comes with children in the home, and the need to balance job and family needs, especially if there are economic pressures, can produce tensions that interfere with feelings of sexual fulfillment. When couples are out of touch with each other's needs, or when they are overwhelmed with other demands, the sexual relationship may suffer.

Middle-Aged Adults

The middle-aged adult (between fifty and seventy years old) faces a number of changes. According to Erikson (1963), the critical task for this portion of the life cycle is to resolve feelings of integrity versus feelings of despair. Accepting one's own life, rather than despairing over what it has not been, determines whether a person will feel successful or preoccupied with feelings of failure.

As Duvall (1971) points out, numerous demands are placed on adults during the middle years: emancipating adolescent children, making a comfortable home, achieving a peak in one's work efforts, maintaining relationships with aging parents, and developing satisfaction from use of leisure time, social responsibility, and friendship. In addition to these rather monumental tasks, men and women must accept and adjust to the physiological aspects of middle age and develop new satisfactions in their relationships with their partners (Woods, 1979b). Couples who have had children now have more time together as a couple and will need to reconsider their mutual interests and values as they become reacquainted with each other in nonparenting pursuits.

Biological changes during this period often become preoccupations of middle-aged adults, in part because they see in their agemates the onset of medical problems that they now fear they too may need to confront. A decrease in height, muscle mass, strength, and cardiac power may become noticeable during this period. Weight gain and changes in digestive capacity may also influence feelings of esteem and self-control. Women go through menopause and men experience a slow regression of androgen-dependent tissues, such as the penis and scrotum, as well as a diminished or complete loss of libido or disturbances of sexual potency (Woods, 1979b). However, with good physical health and an interesting sexual partner, both men and women can still enjoy a full and satisfying sexual relationship.

Problems and losses in sexuality during this time are complex. Some problems are caused by physiological disorders or by interactions of medications that a person may be taking. Other problems are more in the psychological sphere; in particular, depression over widowhood or other losses in the middle years may diminish an individual's interest in sexual fulfillment. Yet other problems in sexual functioning may be socially induced. Societal stereotypes present older adults as asexual; when sexuality is expressed in the middle years, it is often presented in a negative context ("that dirty old man!"). Some adults—especially widows, widowers, and individuals who live in institutional settings—accept asexuality as the norm and, in turn, surrender their sexual needs rather than making an effort to remain sexually active.

Older Adults

The life challenges faced after age seventy are essentially a continuation of those of the earlier stage, with increased risks of declining health, increased losses in one's peer group, increased dependence on others, and increased likelihood of coping with the serious illness or death of one's life partner. Role changes are inevitable with the illness or death of a spouse. Loss of a peer group following retirement can be especially threatening for those who have spent a lifetime in an occupational setting. Loss of the husband may force a woman to develop a social identity of her own, since social systems linked to her husband's occupation and economic group may become closed to her (Aguilera & Messick, 1982). Likewise, males whose spouses have died will need to learn household tasks that may be completely unfamiliar; they may also have to learn to initiate social relationships as they move past their grief and try to build a life as single persons.

Biological changes continue during the later years, even for adults who are enjoying good physical health: wrinkling of the skin, diminished acuity in eyesight and hearing, joint changes, decrease in height, and diminution of strength and muscle mass. Steroid starvation is responsible for continued atrophy of the breasts, vaginal walls, and external genitalia of the female. Similar atrophy occurs in the male in response to diminished testosterone levels, but its course is more gradual than in the female (Woods, 1979b).

Sexual problems in the later years tend to be strongly associated with other losses: loss of health, loss of a partner, loss of previous sexual responsiveness, and—for institutionalized people—loss of privacy. However, at this age, as well as during earlier phases of the life cycle, individuals need not accept researchers' narrow definitions of sexual functioning. Even when intercourse is not a rewarding or feasible outlet, the help-

ing professional should encourage both attitudes and environments that favor tenderness, kissing, self-stimulation, warmth,
closeness, cuddling, and other creative outlets for sexual
expression.

Validating Sexual Losses

In reflecting on the interrelatedness of biological, psychological, and social development across the life cycle, one must conclude that losses are an integral part of this development. Apart
from the expectable losses that occur across a life span, there
are also many unanticipated losses for which there is little preparation: infertility, sexual assault, and life-threatening illness, to
name but a few. In spite of the social support networks that may
be available to help people at times of loss, little attention is
likely to be given to the sexual losses that accompany other life
crises. Yet, because our sexuality provides a potentially rich
source of satisfaction, professionals must help clients discuss
sexual losses as they become ready to do so. Only by introduc-
ing sexual fulfillment as an area that deserves equal time can
the professional offer the client an important opportunity for
fuller healing after a loss.

12

Beyond the Individual Client: Community Action

Although most helping professionals are accustomed to viewing the needs of clients as amenable to individual, group, or family counseling, they should also keep in mind the community dimension within which sexual losses occur. It is in the community context that the professional has a wonderful opportunity to emphasize prevention, sensitive service delivery, and institutional change. Furthermore, since some sexual losses are a result of societally held stereotypes, the professional also will find many challenges in efforts to dismantle such stereotypes through community education and social action.

Community Education

All communities have a wealth of resources that people turn to when they are having difficulty with coping. Most professionals who serve as resources have had some familiarity with issues of sexuality and loss. However, there are two societally generated barriers to raising these issues with clients. First, given the general American predilection to "get on with life," professionals often move too quickly into the area of recovery without according ample time for grieving and working through a loss, sexual or otherwise. Furthermore, since sexuality in our society is regarded either as a private matter or, thanks to the mass media, as an arena for seduction and conquest, many clients find it awkward to broach the subject of personal sexuality, even within the context of losses. Both barriers can be overcome by community professionals if they make a conscious effort to confront their own feelings of awkwardness or discomfort that may be generated by the client's expression of anguish or by frank discussions of sexuality.

Another barrier is the professional's own attitude toward sexual loss as an area for discussion. Many professionals will take at face value the manifest problem—for example, chronic illness—and will not see the potential for inquiry about how the illness has affected the sexual fulfillment of the individual and his or her partner. Therefore, professionals will need to recognize the potential for sexual losses in the many and varied problems that clients, patients, and parishioners bring to their attention. As emphasized in earlier chapters, losses that have sexual components may include the loss of a loved one, the loss of a body part, the diminishing functioning of one's body, and the injury to self-esteem caused by a number of life crises.

The community professional who has become comfortable with problems of sexuality and loss, and who appreciates the many contexts in which sexual losses occur, has a great deal to offer to other professionals. We will consider the ways in which this expertise can be communicated.

In-Service Training

Most agencies welcome the opportunity to have other professionals talk with their staff about topics relevant to the agency's work. However, in-service training must be presented in a way that meets the needs of staff and does not communicate to them that they are doing an inadequate job. A good strategy is to ask the agency contact person to inquire of her staff whether they would be interested in participating in a session on loss and/or sexuality. If interest is expressed, then the contact person should ask all staff members to submit a list of questions or concerns that they would like the presenter to discuss.

When staff are involved in the process from the beginning, they are more likely to feel invested in the learning process. Furthermore, the professional offering the training will be able to shape her presentation to the concerns of the group and will run less risk of making an irrelevant presentation or one that is perceived as speaking down to her audience. It may be helpful to envision the initial session as a broad overview, with the possibility for future sessions to be more specifically focused. The use of disguised case studies (with confidentiality carefully protected) and role plays can be particularly helpful as professionals seek to understand the connections between theory and practice.

Since many participants in the in-service training experience will tend to think of a loss as a crisis for the individual, the educator will need to emphasize the impact of a loss on significant others in the client's life. As articulated in chapters throughout this book, by framing the loss as one that affects the system within which the client lives, the professional can focus on needs that are broader than the client himself and can offer support that extends beyond the individual.

Although the term *significant others* is usually construed to mean loved ones, it can also mean co-workers, medical staff, neighbors, and other people who interact with the client on a daily basis. The professional should encourage the client to communicate her needs clearly to significant others, thereby dispelling the awkwardness that often arises when a loss occurs. When the client is feeling caught in the service system, the professional can play a crucial role as advocate for the client. In an institutional setting in particular, where staff often have very low tolerance for the expression of anger from patients, the professional can explain the therapeutic aspects of anger in the healing process following a loss and can suggest to staff how they might respond constructively to angry outbursts. Such advocacy on behalf of one client has the potential for enabling the staff to understand better the needs of other clients who also are recovering from a loss.

Consultation

Some agencies, as well as professionals in private practice, appreciate knowing which professionals in the community have particular areas of expertise. Although these service providers may not believe that they need to know much about loss and sexuality, because of the presenting needs of their clientele, they at least should know where to turn when problems concerning loss and sexuality do show up. A consultant in this area can offer a theoretical framework for assessing the problem and can provide suggestions for additional reading to be carried out independently after she has departed from the specific consultation task.

However, as mentioned earlier, professionals often do not make connections between losses of a general kind and their impact on the client's sexual fulfillment. So, even when a consultant is asked to be helpful in a specific instance, he should first frame the issue of sexual loss in a broad context, so that the agency or practitioner seeking consultation can be aware of broader applications of the information conveyed by the consultant.

Professional Seminars

Seminars often are sponsored by local chapters of national professional organizations, such as the National Association of Social Workers or the American Psychological Association. Some communities have support groups that serve local helping professionals, offering periodic professional seminars on a variety of topics. This is clearly an excellent arena in which to share concerns about community coverage for specific counseling needs, as well as to sensitize professionals to the issues of loss and sexuality that may be present with their clients. Many professionals, especially those who utilize a crisis intervention model or a case management model, are alert for issues of loss, but they seek to move beyond the feelings associated with loss before the client is ready to complete the mourning process.

Support Groups

The consultant can also inform community professionals about the need to offer support groups for individuals who have experienced a loss. Such support groups could be offered for people grappling with infertility, AIDS, loss of a loved one (through suicide, divorce, illness), sexual assault, cancer, and numerous other health problems. Some institutional settings are ideal locations for client support groups (and probably for the staff who are trying to meet the needs of such clients). Any facilitator of such a support group should remain highly sensitive to sexual issues imbedded in the loss being discussed by the group. Once the group has built a feeling of trust in the facilitator and among its members, the facilitator can ask about the ways in which the members' sexual fulfillment has been affected by the loss they have endured.

Prevention of Violence and Oppression

Although some life crises are unable to be anticipated, others are more expectable and provide the opportunity for professionals to intervene on a preventive basis. Since Americans often tend to deny the sexuality of young people, most schools and parents wait until a child reaches puberty before (if at all!) acquainting the young person with information about sexuality. Likewise, because the youth culture is so highly revered in our society, little attention is paid to helping adults consider that aging is inevitable. Since one of the consequences of aging includes a variety of bodily changes, adults owe themselves good health care throughout their lives. However, the fast pace of adult life and the stressors that occur in the adult years (whether it be the hectic life-style of two-career families or the desperation of an unemployed parent) usually force other priorities ahead of preventive health care.

Prevention also needs to be practiced in the arena of oppression, where racism, sexism, homophobia, ageism, handicapism, and classism flourish. In addition, the acceptability of violence influences individuals, family members, and community groups when conflicts arise. The attitudes that promote violence and oppression are deeply rooted in American society, and professionals must be prepared to confront these attitudes and the values that give rise to them.

Violence

The high incidence of violence on television, in movies, in legal and governmental systems, and in communities influences the level of violence in families (Stith & Rosen, 1990). Straus (1977) asserts that societies that tolerate and even glorify violence outside the family can expect to have high levels of violence within the family. In addition to being besieged by the high incidence of violence in the mass media and in children's toys and games, parents are rarely encouraged to consider noncorporal forms of punishment or limit setting for their children. This absence of alternatives reinforces adults' beliefs that physical punishment is an acceptable way to deal with children who misbehave; it also enforces children's beliefs that adults who hurt them have a right to do so. As a result, the lines between what is appropriate discipline and what is abuse become blurred (Steele, 1976). The acceptability of violence gives rise to a society that accepts at many levels such phenomena in this book as sexual abuse, marital rape, acquaintance rape, and other forms of sexual violence.

Racism

The civil rights movement in this country focused public attention on discrimination against people of color and women and led to a reduction in overt discrimination. Nonetheless, racial tensions in urban environments and on college campuses appear to be on the increase, and the federal courts continue to narrow the mandate of earlier civil rights legislation. Twenty-five years after the passage of the Civil Rights and the Voting Rights Acts, the gaps in education, income, and health are increasing between whites and people of color. A disproportionate number of African Americans, Hispanics, and Native Americans do not have access to quality health care, either to prevent health problems or to treat them. The resultant experiences with sexual losses include soaring cases of AIDS and other sexually transmitted diseases; pregnancy loss attributable to lack of prenatal care; sexual assault, particularly in poor inner-city neighborhoods; and chronic illness of various kinds. As long as poverty and race are inextricably linked, professionals will face the major challenge of fighting for racial justice while, at the same time, advocating for quality service provision in traditionally underserved areas.

Sexism

The subordinate status of women in most of the world's communities, including the United States, is well recorded (Blumberg, 1978; Chafetz, 1984). Straus (1976) has suggested that physical force is the ultimate means by which subordinate groups are kept in their place. In the United States, women's work is devalued, as can be seen in pay inequities and the lack of women assuming leadership positions in business, government, and the legal system. Children who are exposed to these societal values are also influenced, especially when such values are reflected in family life. Women may remain in abusive homes in order to ensure that their children have financial support. Men who are disrespectful of the needs and rights of women believe that they own their wives and children and that they have the right to "use" their wives and children in any way that gratifies them. Such societal sexism has a devastating effect on the lives of many families, where males regard emotional, sexual, and physical abuse as an acceptable way of keeping women in subservient roles.

Homophobia

Fear and misunderstanding of homosexuality pervade our society (Berger, 1987; DeCrescenzo, 1983–1984; Paul, 1982). Lesbians, bisexuals, and gay men who are beginning to explore and accept their sexuality may experience ostracism and oppression by members of society who feel threatened by diverse forms of sexual expression. In particular, lesbian, bisexual, and gay youth, long an invisible part of American culture, represent a high-risk population for social, psychological, and health problems such as depression and attempted suicide (Hippler, 1986; Vergara, 1983–1984). Hippler (p. 42) reports that "homosexual youths are six times more likely to attempt suicide than are heterosexual youths." Oppression against homosexuals goes beyond exclusion and ostracism. Newspapers regularly report on crimes against homosexuals. As stated in earlier chapters of this book, the fear of being labeled homosexual prevents many males, both old and young, from reporting crimes involving sexual assault. Homophobia also interferes with society's validation of loving and caring relationships, denying a gay partner the right to hospital visits, next-of-kin benefits, and custody rights when the couple have raised a child together.

Ageism

Cultural values in the United States emphasize youth, work, independence, education, and progress; as a result, elderly citizens often are regarded as relatively unimportant (Kosberg, 1985). This societally held perception becomes a self-perception of many people as they age. The losses that come with age have been discussed in Chapter Ten, and some of those losses are inevitable concomitants of aging. What is not inevitable, however, is the loss of self-esteem that occurs when older Americans take on the self-image assigned to them by societal stereotypes.

Handicapism

In this country, where vigorous good health is revered, the presence of a handicap serves as a stigma. Others tend to feel awkward when interacting with someone who has a handicap; and the individual who has the handicap often is ignored by teachers and prospective employers, who fail to recognize his strengths; he also has difficulty in gaining physical access to many public places.

Older people may be subjected to oppression both because of their age and because of any handicap caused by frailty or health problems. Young people, especially if chronic health conditions limit their full participation in society, often feel ostracized and stigmatized. Nowhere is handicapism more emphasized than in institutional settings, where the resident loses virtually all self-determination and finds that others are constantly making decisions that affect her well-being. The supression of sexuality by residential and health care institutions (mentioned in Chapter Ten) makes people with handicaps feel that expression of their sexuality is somehow deviant and robs them of their right to be sexual beings.

Classism

Socioeconomic oppression affects one's view of sexuality from many perspectives. Many low-income young people are at risk of unplanned pregnancies and sexually transmitted diseases because they have left school or attend so sporadically that they never receive or fully understand educational information about sexual health. For women, educational attainment is correlated with an ability to delay one's first sexual experience. According to recent research (Harlap, Kost, & Forrest, 1990), women with ten or more years of schooling are less likely than those with seven to nine years of education to start a sexual relationship before their twentieth birthday (74 versus 93 percent).

Since, aside from families, schools are the central influence on the lives of most young people, their ability to perform well academically and the ability of schools to meet their needs are of tremendous importance. Low achievement in school, especially when it is combined with problems at home, can undermine a young person's self-esteem, acceptance by the dominant peer group, and hopes for future educational-occupational success. Without self-esteem, peer acceptance, and hopes for the future, an adolescent is much more vulnerable to such easy impulse gratification and escapist behaviors as early nonmarital coitus and heavy use of drugs and alcohol (Chilman, 1989).

In addition to their lack of positive school experiences, many low-income youth are called on to assume responsibility for younger siblings and to contribute to the family's income. It is not surprising that these young people consider themselves full-fledged adults who are ready to have sexual relationships. Sometimes a young person enters a sexual relationship in order to escape from an oppressive family environment; such a relationship often results in an unplanned pregnancy, forcing the young people to confront their readiness to become parents at an age when they have barely emerged from their own childhood. It is well known that young people and adults from low-income backgrounds may not have easy access to public health clinics and Planned Parenthood organizations, particularly in rural areas. Thus, needed services, both educational and health-related, often are unavailable to them.

The sexual lives of adults also are influenced by an environment where socioeconomic status limits opportunities for education, employment, housing, financial stability, and health care. In such an environment, sexuality may be suppressed by the stark issues of survival that are a part of everyday existence; or it may be curtailed by illness, including a sexually transmitted disease; or it may be overridden by feelings of depression or escape into alcoholism and drugs.

Professional Challenges

For helping professionals, the challenge to change societally held values and attitudes that have promoted racism, sexism, and the like can seem insurmountable. Therefore, professionals may want to join together, acknowledging shared barriers to the delivery of services, and carve out manageable efforts that can lower such barriers. Affected client groups also should be involved in this enterprise, so that they themselves can feel empowered at some level. Community organization strategies are ideal, whether the "community" is the size of a city block or a hospital ward. The impetus to use one's professional skills in new ways will come from the recognition that meaningful individual change cannot endure if the client must continue living in oppressive and exploitive circumstances.

Creating New Services

In these days of tightening budgets in human services, the idea of creating new services can sound ludicrous. Yet, such new services do not necessarily need to be separate from existing services; they can be integrated into a functioning network whenever possible. Below are some ideas for integrating services for people recovering from sexual and reproductive losses.

Institutions

Institutions can benefit from being more respectful of the sexual needs of their residents. Professionals on staff or in the community can offer to consult with institutional staff in order to determine their current practices and attitudes that encourage or discourage sexual expression by residents. Once the staff can come to some agreements on ways in which they can demonstrate respect for sexual expression of residents, the residents themselves can be encouraged to offer ideas about changes that would make them feel more comfortable about their sexuality. Such discussions can occur individually or in groups or resident councils, and are likely to focus on privacy, staff responses to couples who develop loving relationships, and other matters concerned with sexuality. Most of the changes requested are likely to be attitudinal (for example, knocking before entering a room, respecting a "do not disturb" sign, treating with adult respect the warm relationships and expressions of physical affection between residents). In some cases, residents with physical impairments may ask for help in getting into a comfortable position with a partner. Others may need help with toileting, prostheses, or appliances prior to spending time with a partner. Some residents also may need clear guidelines about what public behaviors—including appropriate expression of sexuality—are considered appropriate by others. In all these situations, the staff members in the institution must respect the residents' right to be sexual and must be willing to vary institutional routines to incorporate the time and privacy needed by residents to express their sexuality.

Professionals also must do everything possible to help staff prevent sexual abuse in the institution. Staff first must recognize that sexually exploitive or assaultive behavior will not be tolerated in the institution; second, staff must be alerted to indications by residents that they may be the victims of such abuse; any such acts should be promptly reported and investigated. In this connection, the professional may need to reiterate that the role of being a staff member never permits sexual acting out with residents.

Since everyone who resides in an institution has experienced multiple losses—whether of health, body parts, family, home, independence, or familiar routines—staff members also must be sensitized to the impact of such losses on the residents, so that they can be more understanding when feelings of bitterness, anger, depression, and resentment are expressed. Rather than denying the residents' rights to have such legitimate responses to loss, staff can be encouraged to think of empathic ways to respond to a resident who is recovering from the dynamics of grieving and the feelings associated with it. Alert and concerned professionals can meet with staff to help them understand that denial, anger, bargaining, and grieving can all be therapeutic responses to loss. In addition, discussion groups for residents—on such topics as transition into the institution, current events, hobbies, exercise, the life review, and coping with change—can enable them to find a variety of outlets for their feelings, as well as encouraging interpersonal interactions.

Crisis Services

Crises tend to be regarded as those unexpected events that occur outside the boundaries of existing agencies or beyond the expertise of these agencies. Sometimes the definition of crisis also alludes to the hour at which the crisis occurs and the lack of available services, short of police intervention, in the middle of the night. Battered women, suicidal or depressed individuals, sexual assault victims, and overstressed parents are all potentially in need of crisis services during hours that agencies are usually closed. In response to these crises, the community might establish a crisis telephone hotline, staffed primarily by volunteers who have been trained in crisis counseling, to help people connect with appropriate community resources. Existing agencies would undoubtedly support such an idea, once they were reassured about the screening and training of the volunteers, because it would increase the number of appropriate referrals; reduce potential burnout among staff whose clients contact them after-hours in emergencies; and reassure police that they would not be expected to have expertise in mental health. Clearly, the success of such an effort would rest on the hiring of a mental health professional with expertise in training and working effectively with volunteers.

OB-GYN Services

Given the number of times that a sexual loss will place a woman squarely before her obstetrician-gynecologist, it seems relevant to suggest that these professionals could benefit from a consultant to help them assess and intervene in the psychosocial needs of their clients. If such a consultant could be added to the office staff and housed in the same office building, so much the better. Regardless of physical location, the availability of a counselor to help women (and their partners) process sexual losses is crucial to the recovery process. Many physicians believe that they are able to be responsive to the emotional needs of their patients. However, regardless of their responsiveness, few physicians have the time to spend, or the expertise in grief and mourning, that is needed by a woman who has sustained any of the sexual losses described in this book. Also, many women are reluctant to engage their physician in their emotional coping efforts; so even if the physician has every wish to attend to her psychosocial needs, the woman may not feel comfortable extending the relationship in this direction.

Schools

These days, schools are expected to be many things to many people. No longer limited to the teaching of academic subjects, schools now provide social services, including health services. Health education has been broadened, particularly in the area of human sexuality, to include more than the traditional anatomy lessons of a generation ago. Acknowledging that half of all high school graduates are sexually active, educators are increasingly including information on values, decision making, and communication skills in their health classes, so that young people will have the tools to resist peer pressure and avoid gender stereotyping. In the health clinics established by a number of schools, students have an opportunity to discuss sexual health, as well as the common concerns of flu, strep infections, and sports injuries.

Because of the AIDS epidemic, many schools that previously did not offer courses in sex education are now providing them. Children in the lower grades are being given age-appropriate information about human sexuality to prepare them for the more complex information that will follow in the upper grades. The schools are also helping parents become sex educators of their children in this era of AIDS, when all adults are potential sources of information (or misinformation) for their children.

Professionals who want to have a positive impact in the schools will ally themselves with concerned parents, as well as teachers and their labor unions, to advocate for new services or for educational reform. Efforts at improving school services should not be limited to sex education. Since research has shown that women who remain in school longer delay the beginning of their sexual activity (Harlap, Kost, & Forrest, 1990), professionals should help the schools try to prevent young people from dropping out. Feelings of school failure often begin in the very earliest grades, when children do not gain the basic skills they need to progress with confidence to higher grade levels. For this reason, schools should be urged to begin diagnostic and remediation services in the earliest grades, rather than waiting until a child has failed a grade or fallen badly behind her peer group in subject mastery.

Colleges, too, have the potential to influence young people in their sexual behavior. To eliminate sexual assaults on campus, for example, a college can increase campus security; set clear policies on sexual harassment; limit consumption of alcohol on campus; hold personal-growth workshops that focus on communication about sexual concerns; provide campus escort services after dark; offer workshops aimed at preventing acquaintance rape; and provide dormitory discussion sessions on matters of sexual concern. Campus health services must be equipped to counsel students preventively on contraception and sexually transmitted diseases, particularly HIV, and also to respond quickly to such crises as unplanned pregnancies and sexual assault.

For freshmen, many of whom arrive at college still sexually undereducated, inexperienced, or naive, colleges can provide courses on human sexuality; dormitory discussions with campus resource people; films, role-plays, or theatrical productions, followed by discussion groups; or literature on a wide variety of topics.

Therapeutic Implications for the Professional

To a large extent, this chapter is concerned with both advocacy and empowerment. The professional whose clients have experienced sexual and reproductive losses must recognize that her efforts may be seriously limited by the social environment. Therefore, in addition to clinical work with client populations, the professional must consider extending herself into the larger social environment, both to prevent potential future losses and to sensitize others to needed services. Just as the professional may be an advocate on behalf of clients who have suffered important losses, she also must help clients articulate their own needs. Clients who feel empowered to make changes in their lives are well on the way to recovery after a loss. So professionals must tread a fine line between advocating on behalf of clients and enabling clients to feel empowered. In general, the more a client has been able to recover from the trauma of loss, the more energy he will have to bring about enduring changes in his own life and, perhaps, to ease the pain of a similar loss for someone else.

13

Guarding
Against Burnout

Just as relationships, ideally, should be ended in a careful and thoughtful way, I want to end this book about loss and grief by anticipating the need for comfort by the professionals who undertake this difficult work with clients. For—as much as we may speak about being objective and emotionally detached— most of us feel the pain of our clients and must find our own ways of coming to terms with it.

When we considered the expanding role of the helping professional in earlier chapters, the focus was on increasing the quality of service to clients. Yet it also is crucial to attend to *our* needs as professionals. We, who help our clients to become more resilient and self-sufficient, all too easily can forget that we need to replenish our energies, stimulate our intellects, and challenge ourselves to grow both personally and professionally.

Professionals in the human services are known to be at high risk for burnout (Pines, Aronson, & Kafry, 1981). Sometimes the emotional energy that they invest in their work with clients leaves them exhausted. Sometimes a client's apparent lack of progress leaves them feeling futile. This chapter will examine the ways in which professionals can increase their therapeutic helpfulness and avoid burnout.

Mastering a Knowledge Base

Sexual losses are complex, in part because they involve attention to two areas that Americans generally view as highly private. For this reason, practitioners must master a knowledge base that will enable them to discuss delicate subjects with clients in the most comfortable way possible.

Loss and Grief

Too often, the literature on specific losses emphasizes the client's need to cope with the loss and ignores the client's need to grieve for the primary loss and the secondary losses associated with it. In the area of grief and loss, the professional needs to know what life events constitute a loss, how that loss affects people at different stages of the life cycle, and how earlier losses affect an individual's ability to grieve a current loss and to heal from its pain.

The professional also needs to be alert for behavioral cues that are normal aspects of the grieving process. The client and others in the client's life may label as pathological certain behaviors that are, in fact, highly therapeutic when viewed in the context of working through one's grief. The practitioner may even need to remind herself that certain responses in the counseling relationship, such as regression and anger, must be taken in stride when loss is the theme of the work with the client. Only with a solid theoretical understanding of issues of attachment and loss can the practitioner convey confidence that the client is moving forward, in spite of the pain and discomfort involved in the journey.

Likewise, a professional who is familiar with the normal aspects of grieving will be able to realize when a client needs more support than the counseling relationship can provide. Serious depression, suicidal gestures, and psychotic thought processes must be recognized as beyond the realm of griefwork alone and should be regarded as a signal that more help may be needed than is available in the therapeutic relationship.

Crisis Intervention

A crisis—a period when accustomed coping mechanisms fail to be effective—is a turning point that offers the opportunity for either regression or growth. Practitioners who are not familiar with techniques of assessment and intervention at a time of crisis may want to consult the helpful books and articles on crisis intervention written for professionals (Aguilera & Messick, 1982; Janosik, 1984; Puryear, 1979; Hendricks, 1985; Hoff, 1978; Hoff & Miller, 1987; Gilliland & James, 1988). As with the literature on specific losses, however, the literature on crisis intervention ignores the importance of the grieving process. Crisis literature emphasizes helping the client return to a previous or more effective level of coping; the therapeutic focus is on stress management, control of affect, cognitive reorganization, task accomplishment, and resource utilization. Furthermore, crisis theory presents crisis as time-limited, in most cases being resolved in six to eight weeks.

It is important for the professional not to confuse crisis and mourning, since many clients experiencing a sexual or reproductive loss will demonstrate both. The initial challenge may be to help the client cope with the crisis represented by the loss; after some coping mechanisms have been restored, however, there may be a lengthy period of mourning. During this period, the client must be respected in his efforts to grapple with a changed self-identity, a diminished sense of life opportunities, and an altered belief about the future and what it holds. Sometimes an individual who has coped adequately with an initial serious loss will have less resilience when a subsequent less serious stress or loss occurs, so that the more recent stress appears to be the source of the crisis. Therefore, in taking a psychosocial history of a troubled client, professionals must assess the full impact of all losses being worked through. The period of mourning is necessary and therapeutic for many clients; it can be exhausting for professionals, many of whom will feel impatient for the client to get on with the griefwork so that they can see some positive outcomes of the intervention efforts.

Posttraumatic Stress Disorder

The literature on posttraumatic stress disorder (PTSD) includes studies of soldiers recovering from the Vietnam War, as well as studies of individuals exposed to various life-threatening events such as fires, serious traffic accidents, natural disasters, or criminal victimization, such as rape and other violent acts (Ochberg, 1988; Figley, 1978, 1989; Young, 1988; Chu, 1988; Eth & Pynoos, 1985).

Clients with PTSD have symptoms that include, but are not limited to, recurrent nightmares; intrusive thoughts or flashbacks of a traumatic event; phobic behavior or generalized apathy; and hypervigilance and other symptoms of increased arousal lasting longer than one month. Some clients experience bouts of amnesia surrounding the traumatizing experience or catastrophe. After an acute phase that includes anxiety symptoms, clients with PTSD tend also to display symptoms of depression, including somatic complaints (Figley, 1989).

Clients whose losses have been traumatic will need an intervention that utilizes an understanding of PTSD. Although loss may be the immediate precipitant causing a client to seek help, the appearance of the above symptoms should serve as a clue that the loss may be but the tip of the psychological iceberg. Many people who experience an external violent stressor event develop an internal style of psychic traumatization and may attempt to split off, forget, or unconsciously repress their memories of that event or events (Williams, 1990). Yet, later in life, these memories press for expression from their active memory storage center (Lindy, 1986). When these pieces start to reappear, perhaps as feeling states (anxiety) or intrusions (flashbacks, nightmares, behavioral reenactments), the self attempts to defend against them and tries again to repress the information, feelings, and fragments (Briere, 1989). The imagery disturbances frequently are associated with powerful emotions that lead to physiological hypervigilant reactions. Working with clients who have PTSD is highly challenging and involves more than the immediate issues of loss that may have been the initial reason for referral. Professionals working with clients who have PTSD symptoms should be well versed in the dynamics of this disorder and the appropriate intervention strategies before attempting to help clients uncover and deal with the painful memories associated with their trauma.

Human Sexuality

As emphasized in Chapter Eleven, which presents a life-span approach to human sexuality and reproduction, sexual functioning is truly a bio-psycho-social phenomenon. Because of the interrelatedness of mind, body, and intimate relationships, professionals dealing with cases of sexual loss frequently work collaboratively on behalf of a client. The various members of such a collaborative team must clearly understand their particular roles, so that interventions can be ordered in a timely fashion, keeping pace with the readiness of the client to take new risks. Understanding sexual development across the life span is important for professionals, as is an appreciation for the ways in which sexual assault can interfere with sexual functioning and self-esteem.

Family Dynamics

Rarely do sexual and reproductive losses occur in isolation from the family arena. The client's position in his family, the way in which the loss affects other family members, and the extent to which the family is able to offer support are all important components that will contribute to the healing process. In cases of incest or domestic violence, a family member may actually be the source of the client's anguish, and careful attention to family dynamics is critical to the client's decision about relating to or separating from specific family members. In many cases of sexual or reproductive loss, the family of the client needs as much help as the client.

In the best of all worlds, families want to be supportive of a member in pain, but issues of sexuality and loss are surrounded with such awkwardness in American society that family therapy may be needed to keep communication open. In other situations, family members may be nonsupportive because they fail to understand or are unable to respond to the client's feelings of loss. The professional needs to support the client in her feelings of entitlement to work through her losses, in spite of an unsupportive family environment. Helping the client identify her needs, express them clearly and assertively to other family members, and make careful decisions on how to take care of herself are all challenges to the professional.

The use of genograms, family sculpting, and family drawings will enable the professional to communicate in new ways with family members involved in counseling. A firm grounding in literature about family theory, family structure, and family communication patterns is critical if the family component is to be respected in the helping process.

Translating Knowledge into Skills

When utilizing the skills discussed in the following sections, the professional will need to be especially attentive to the importance of starting where the client is and treating that person as a unique individual.

Grief Counseling

Professionals who undertake grief counseling not only must have a theoretical understanding of the dynamics of grief but also must be able stay emotionally connected with the client through a painful process. Professionals set as their goal the task of helping clients move past their grief; yet this process is highly individualistic. Without even being aware of it, the professional can begin to feel impatient when the clients seem to require "too much time" to mourn the depth of their loss. Conversely, some clients do become "stuck" at some point in the mourning process, and here the professional must find a way of supporting the client to move forward and take new risks.

Worden (1982) provides nine guidelines that the counselor can follow in applying the skills of grief counseling:

1. Helping the survivor actualize the loss (by talking about the loss, the events leading up to it, and the client's feelings about it).
2. Helping the survivor identify and express feelings (in particular, feelings of anger, guilt, anxiety, helplessness, and sadness).
3. Helping clients structure their lives to accommodate the loss (for example, by learning new skills and building new relationships).
4. Facilitating emotional withdrawal that encourages the bereaved person to form new relationships. It is important for the person to be aware that premature intense attachment in a new relationship may preclude adequate resolution of grief.
5. Providing time to grieve.
6. Interpreting "normal" behavior (thereby reassuring the client who may be unsettled by the feelings of upset or distractibility that follow the loss).
7. Allowing for individual differences (using theory as a gentle guide, but not as a determinant of behaviors).
8. Providing continuing support (from the professional but also, when appropriate, from the family and the community).
9. Examining defenses and coping styles (avenues of coping that may be most effective in lowering distress and resolving problems).
10. Recognizing when a client's needs are beyond one's expertise or ability to help—and, consequently, referring the client to an appropriate individual or agency.

Lethality Assessment

As mentioned in Chapter One, a grieving client may be so despondent that the professional suspects he is considering suicide as a release from the pain. The professional then must ask the client whether he is considering suicide. Even if the client's answer is negative, he usually will appreciate the depth of the professional's empathy with his pain; furthermore, the asking of the question means that the professional is willing to discuss the topic if the client chooses to raise it at another time. If a client responds affirmatively to the question about suicidal thoughts or gestures, the professional should conduct a lethality assessment in order to determine the immediacy of danger for the client.

A lethality assessment consists of questions in four major areas:

1. *Specificity of the plan.* A client who specifies how, when, and where the suicide will take place should be considered at high risk for suicide. If the plan includes use of a highly lethal means, such as a gun, hanging, poison, carbon monoxide, or a car wreck, the client is in danger. If the time frame in which the client plans to kill himself is immediately or in a few hours, the professional must regard the suicidal intent as serious. The professional must ask whether the means for carrying out the suicide are available or close by; if so, the chance of lethality is high.

2. *Ambivalence about living.* Suicidal gestures within the past six months, especially if the attempts were highly lethal, suggest that the client is prepared to carry through on the plan. Likewise, if the client communicates no ambivalence about dying, has given away possessions, has made a will, and has no future-oriented plans, the lethality should be considered high.

3. *Changes in personality or behavior.* The professional should be concerned if a client becomes more seriously depressed or, conversely, if previous depression lifts. The deepening of depression may confirm for the individual that life is not worth living. The lifting of depression may cause the professional to suspect that the client has made a decision to carry out suicidal thoughts and is now no longer preoccupied with the emotional struggle of whether or not to live. The ending of the preoccupation

frees up emotional energy in the client, often giving her enough energy to carry out the suicidal plan.

4. *Long-standing depression.* A person who has been seriously depressed for a long time is at risk for suicide because over time there seems to be less and less reason to go on living. The fatalistic attitude that life is not worth living causes suicide to seem like a release from a meaningless or painful existence.

The professional whose client acknowledges suicidal intentions is bound to feel highly anxious about his ability to be helpful. Every professional who is working with a suicidal client must get additional consultation, both to ensure his ability to develop a safe intervention and to allay the inevitable anxiety caused by shouldering such a heavy professional burden alone. If the lethality is determined to be high, such consultation should be sought while the client is still present.

If the client insists on leaving while still in a highly lethal state, the professional should bargain for time—perhaps by asking the client to promise not to kill herself at least until they have met one more time. Surprisingly, clients who agree to this bargain usually carry through on their commitment to wait, although the professional should be certain to set a time within twenty-four hours for the next meeting. In that time, the professional will have been able to seek consultation and will have a clearer idea of what next steps are possible with the suicidal client.

Sex Counseling

Since sexuality is a subject that most Americans view as either highly private or highly risqué, the professional will need to be sensitive to the awkwardness of the topic when broaching it with clients. She should not—especially at the beginning of a relationship with an anxious client—treat the topic casually and attempt to interject occasional humor. Instead, she should convey empathy and an appreciation for the loss that has been endured. The professional can build further rapport by evidencing a matter-of-fact directness accompanied by an interest in hearing in the client's own words about the meaning of his loss.

Since sex counseling at some point is likely to involve the client's sexual partner, the professional must be able to encourage the couple to talk openly about their needs, and to encourage support and creativity as a means of coming to new levels of satisfaction with their sexual relationship. As has been mentioned in earlier chapters, the professional should keep the notion of sexuality broad and not limit it to intercourse and coitus alone. Couples then can be encouraged to consider a wide range of fulfilling experiences, including touching, massage, caressing, masturbation, hugging, kissing, and snuggling.

Family Counseling

As mentioned earlier, the members of a client's family often are seriously affected by his loss. The loss may be theirs as well, as in the case of a stillborn baby, or they may feel the loss in other ways—for instance, when grief and anguish claim the time and attention of a loved one who previously assumed major family roles. A loss in the family almost always means a reallocation of family roles and functions. The professional will want to use her family counseling skills to help family members express their grief, handle feelings of blame, express support, articulate needs, and draw together in new ways that respect the impact of the loss without disintegrating as a family unit. The crucial dimension for the professional to remember is that in family counseling the family as a unit must be regarded as the client, even though the needs of the family member with the loss may have precipitated the initial request for help.

Communication Skills

The professional must have sensitive communication skills when encouraging clients to talk about the delicate areas of loss and sexuality; she must also help clients master effective communication skills. Assertive communication techniques can be helpful for a client who is in touch with her needs but apprehensive about expressing them to health care professionals, family members, clergy, or colleagues. Other skills—especially effective listening, "I" messages, and clarifying meanings—are effective in use with loved ones and family members. Usually, the best way of teaching these skills to the client is to have the client role-play with the professional, using the new skills, before trying them out for the first time with others. In some cases, family members may be involved in the counseling sessions, and then the skills can be learned and practiced by the client and her loved ones, with the gentle coaching of the professional.

Termination Skills

The skill of terminating a relationship with a client has received relatively scant attention in professional literature (Shapiro, 1980; Fox, Nelson, & Bolman, 1969). For that reason, the professional may believe that successful reaching of therapeutic goals is a clear signal that the client is ready to end the relationship. However, several authors (Shapiro, 1980; Garvin, 1981) speak of the parallels between the termination of a helping relationship and the stages of mourning set forth by Elisabeth Kübler-Ross (1969). For the client who has felt the caring support and encouragement of the professional over the period of mourning his losses, termination of the relationship with this practitioner is likely to loom as a substantial loss.

Feelings associated with earlier losses may become more poignant and pronounced as the client contemplates losing the relationship that has sustained him through an intense period of emotional isolation. Therefore, the professional should introduce the topic of termination well in advance of its actual occurrence; anticipate feelings of denial, anger, bargaining, and mourning; encourage the client to become involved with appropriate community resources in advance of termination; and review carefully with the client the many gains he has made, in spite of work still needing to be accomplished. By attending carefully and sensitively to the skills involved in termination, the professional will enable the client to acknowledge his sadness at ending but also to take satisfaction in his accomplishments and, in turn, to transfer his new coping skills to other life situations, even without the ongoing support of the professional.

Gaining Personal Replenishment

Working with grieving clients can take its toll on the professional. Not only is there the inevitable feeling of helplessness as the counselor watches the client try to work through the heavy burden of pain, but there may also be a feeling of some impatience that the client needs to take so long to work through the many issues associated with her loss. In addition, since the professional empathizes with the client, he may become more aware of his own losses—especially if the client's loss is similar to one that he has sustained but not fully worked through. In fact, professionals should try to be sufficiently aware of unresolved losses in their own lives that they do not undertake work with a client who needs to process such a loss. Once the practitioner has successfully worked through a significant loss, he will be in a much stronger position to be a resource for the client, although there must always be a vigilance against inappropriate disclosure of personal information to a client whose issues initially seem so familiar.

Work with grieving clients can also make professionals aware that they themselves may face a similar loss at some future time. The resulting feelings of anxiety can interfere with the effectiveness of the counseling relationship. In such instances, the professional will need to bring his anxiety into consciousness and examine its causes, so that work with the client can progress. If the anxieties are either deeply rooted or a serious preoccupation, he should consider transferring the client to another worker, taking care to explain as frankly as possible to the client the reasons for the transfer.

As Worden (1982) points out, professionals might want to explore their own history of loss in order to become sensitive to unresolved issues and vulnerable areas and to recognize their own limitations—limitations that might prevent them from helping clients with certain specific losses. Although some work settings (such as hospices) make it impossible to vary the kinds of losses clients are facing, a professional should be cautious about working with too many clients at once who have problems that are highly draining. What is draining for one practitioner may be invigorating for another, so—again—the challenge is to know one's own strengths and limitations.

If the client is terminally ill and dies, the professional needs to acknowledge her own grief at losing this human relationship. Attending the funeral or memorial service is one way for the professional to gain a broader perspective on the person who has died, since others in attendance will remember happier and healthier times in the client's life. A funeral service also enables the professional to shed tears and reflect on the importance of the relationship and the sadness that comes with its ending. Helping family members after the death can sometimes be cathartic for the professional, but it also can be immensely draining and can prevent the professional from dealing with her own feelings surrounding the loss.

When feeling bereft, inadequate, or emotionally drained, the professional needs to find ways of getting support. Too often, we believe that we are invulnerable when it comes to feelings of sadness or pain or that, as professionals who help others recover from losses, we should be able to assuage our own pain. Sometimes this belief leads us to ignore our own pain altogether or to suppress it until it begins to interfere with the energy and emotional support that clients need from us. In addition, a number of professionals deal with their need for support in counterproductive ways. Some professionals change careers; some seek refuge in drugs or alcohol; some simply go through the motions of their work with clients and refrain from becoming any more involved than necessary.

So where are the sources of support when we need them? Since many professionals work in teams with clients who have sustained losses, team members can be a source of support against emotional burnout. Too often, professionals limit their discussions of a client's suffering to what *they* can do to alleviate the pain. They also need to acknowledge their own pain and to discuss their feelings with other involved staff who are also likely to be feeling helpless and impotent at various stages of their work with the client.

In some cases, talking with one's supervisor can be helpful, if that person has the depth of experience necessary to help the practitioner work through the feelings of sadness associated with client losses. Some professionals find that peer supervision, either with a partner or a small group, can provide the validation for one's pain. If clients' losses have stirred up unresolved loss issues in the professional, she should consider working these issues through in therapy, which would provide an opportunity for personal growth and professional growth to be linked.

The exhaustion of helping clients work through their losses can also be offset by other stimulating professional endeavors (Shapiro, 1982). A professional should consider expanding his skill base by requesting an opportunity to work with clients who have needs and problems that are unfamiliar. Such work provides a chance for continuing professional growth, which, in turn, can offset some of the feelings of emotional exhaustion caused by helping other clients work through their pain.

Many professionals who help clients confront losses could become resources for other agencies in their community. The professional might consider sharing his expertise through consultation or in-service training. Conversely, he might make use of other people's expertise by attending conferences or workshops, taking courses, and acquiring in-service training. This continuing education might be in the areas concerned with grief and sexuality, or it might be in new areas that the professional finds challenging. The hope here is that professionals will feel continuing challenge in their work, to offset the emotional exhaustion that comes from working with too many clients whose needs are especially compelling.

In Conclusion

In the process of writing this book, I have helped clients to grieve a number of sexual and reproductive losses, including cancer, pregnancy loss, infertility, and sexual assault. Each experience has been different, in part because each client is unique and in part because *I* change as a result of helping clients find new ways of moving ahead with their lives. But what I continue to recognize as a constant is the immense amount of emotional isolation caused by sexual and reproductive losses. In general, these clients are emotionally unprepared to face these losses and have never spoken with anyone who has sustained a similar loss. These special losses—resulting from sexual assault, infertility, chronic illness, or simply growing old—carry their own stigma in our society. There is an unspoken question that still lurks in the shadows: "What did you do to bring this on?" People simply find it easier to distance themselves by assigning blame than to listen to another's pain.

So—what with the lack of preparedness, the privacy that Americans accord to personal sexuality, the awkwardness felt toward someone who is grieving, and the unspoken assumption of others that the client probably deserves some blame for his condition—people who sustain sexual and reproductive losses are isolated indeed. To these isolated people we as professionals need to offer our skills and our compassion. It is sometimes overwhelming to contemplate the array of skills and knowledge necessary to help clients and their families. However, most professionals are well aware that expertise evolves, rather than being bestowed along with a diploma; and so we take whatever opportunities we can to learn from others. Our educational programs have stressed the importance of keeping up with the professional literature; our professional organizations have emphasized the need to attend conferences and workshops; and our own colleagues have often extended their expertise to us in consultations and workshops. In the midst of this learning, we also need to be aware of how much we learn from our clients. These are the people who muster strength and courage to face their pain, to grieve their losses, to connect with resources, and to move forward with their lives. And since each client is unique, we can learn from setbacks as well as from successes. The process of working with clients is one of helping them empower themselves, sometimes under circumstances that seem insurmountable. It is my hope that this book offers encouragement in meeting the challenge.

REFERENCES

Ageton, S. S. (1981). *Sexual assault among adolescents: A national survey* (Research Project No. RO1 MH31751). Washington, DC: National Institute of Mental Health.

Aguilera, D. C., & Messick, J. M. (1982). *Crisis intervention: Theory and methodology* (4th ed.). St. Louis, MO: Mosby.

American Psychiatric Association. (1987). *Diagnostic and statistical manual of mental disorders* (3rd ed., rev.). Washington, DC: Author.

Arnstein, H. S. (1978). *What to tell your child: About birth, illness, death, divorce, and other family crises.* Westport, CT: Condor.

Bart, P., & Perlmutter, E. (1981). The menopause in changing times. In B. Justice & R. Pore (Eds.), *Toward the second decade: The impact of the women's movement on American institutions* (pp. 93–117). Westport, CT: Greenwood Press.

Beauvoir, S. de. (1973). *The coming of age.* New York: Warner Books.

Benward, J., & Densen-Gerber, J. (1976). *Incest as a causative factor in anti-social behavior: An exploratory study.* New York: Odyssey Institute.

Berezin, J. E. (1982). *After a loss in pregnancy: Help for families affected by a miscarriage, a stillbirth, or the loss of a newborn.* New York: Simon & Schuster.

245

Berger, R. M. (1987). Homosexuality: Gay men. In *Encyclopedia of social work* (Vol. 1, 18th ed., pp. 795–805). Silver Spring, MD: National Association of Social Workers.

Bernstein, J. E. (1983). *Books to help children cope with separation and loss* (2nd ed.). New York: Bowker.

Bloch, A., Maeder, J. P., & Haissly, J. E. (1975). Sexual problems after myocardial infarction. *American Heart Journal, 90,* 536–537.

Bluebond-Langner, M. (1977). Meanings of death to children. In H. Feifel (Ed.), *New meanings of death* (pp. 47–66). New York: McGraw-Hill.

Blumberg, B., Golbus, M., & Hanson, K. (1975). The psychological sequelae of abortion performed for genetic indication. *American Journal of Obstetrics and Gynecology, 122,* 799–808.

Blumberg, R. (1978). *Stratification: Socioeconomic and sexual inequality.* Dubuque, IA: Brown.

Borg, S., & Lasker, J. (1981). *When pregnancy fails: Families coping with miscarriage, stillbirth, and infant death.* Boston: Beacon Press.

Boston Women's Health Collective. (1976). *Our bodies, ourselves* (2nd ed.). New York: Simon & Schuster.

Bowlby, J. (1961). Process of mourning. *Journal of Psychoanalysis, 42,* 317–340.

Briere, J. (1989). *Therapy for adults molested as children: Beyond survival.* New York: Springer.

Brownmiller, S. (1975). *Against our will.* New York: Simon & Schuster.

Burgess, A. W. (1985). Sexual victimization of adolescents. In A. W. Burgess (Ed.), *Rape and sexual assault* (pp. 123–138). New York: Garland.

Burgess, A. W., & Holmstrom, L. L. (1974). Rape trauma syndrome. *Journal of Psychiatry, 131,* 981–986.

Burgess, A. W., & Holstrom, L. L. (1979a). *Rape: Crisis and recovery.* Bowie, MD: Brady.

Burgess, A. W., & Holmstrom, L. L. (1979b). Rape: Sexual disruption and recovery. *American Journal of Orthopsychiatry, 49,* 648–657.

Burgess, A. W., & Holstrom, L. L. (1985). Rape trauma syndrome and posttraumatic stress response. In A. W. Burgess (Ed.), *Rape and sexual assault* (pp. 46–59). New York: Garland.

Burnham, W. R., Lennard-Jones, J. E., & Brooke, B. N. (1977). Sexual problems among married ileostomists. *Gut, 18*(8), 637–677.

Bury, M. (1982). Chronic illness as a biographic disruption. *Sociology of Health and Illness, 4,* 167–182.

Butler, R. N. (1975). *Why survive?* New York: HarperCollins.

Butler, R. N., & Lewis, M. I. (1976). *Sex after sixty.* New York: HarperCollins.

Caplan, G. (1964). *Principles of preventive psychiatry.* New York: Basic Books.

Cassem, N. H., & Hackett, T. (1971). Psychiatric consultation on a coronary care unit. *Annals of Internal Medicine, 75,* 9–14.

Chafetz, J. (1984). *Sex and advantage: A comparative macrostructural theory of sex stratification.* Totowa, NJ: Rowman & Allanheld.

Chilman, C. S. (1989). Some major issues regarding adolescent sexuality and childbearing in the United States. In P. A. Meares & C. H. Shapiro (Eds.), *Adolescent sexuality: New challenges for social work* (pp. 3–26). New York: Haworth Press.

Chu, J. A. (1988, December). 10 traps for therapists in the treatment of trauma survivors. *Dissociation,* pp. 24–26.

Collins, J. A., Garner, J. B., Wilson, E. W., Wrixon, W., & Casper, R. F. (1984). A proportional hazards analysis of the clinical characteristics of infertile couples. *American Journal of Obstetrics and Gynecology, 148,* 527–532.

Comarr, A. E. (1966). Observations on menstruation and pregnancy among female spinal cord injury patients. *Paraplegia, 3*(4), 263–272.

Comarr, A. E. (1971). Sexual concepts in traumatic cord and equina lesions. *Journal of Urology, 106,* 375–378.

Cotton, D. J., & Groth, A. N. (1984). Sexual assault in correctional institutions: Prevention and intervention. In I. R. Stuart & J. G. Greer (Eds.), *Victims of sexual aggression* (pp. 127–155). New York: Van Nostrand Reinhold.

DeCrescenzo, T. D. (1983–1984). Homophobia: A study of the attitudes of mental health professionals toward homosexuality. *Journal of Social Work and Human Sexuality, 2*(2–3), 178–183.

DeFrain, J. (1986). *Stillborn: The invisible death.* Lexington, MA: Lexington Books.

Delaney, J., Lupton, M. J., & Toth, E. (1988). *The curse: A cultural history of menstruation.* Urbana: University of Illinois Press.

Devereaux, G. (1950). The psychology of feminine genital bleeding: An analysis of Mohave Indian puberty and menstrual rites. *International Journal of Psychoanalysis, 31,* 168.

Dlin, B. A., & Perlman, A. (1971). Emotional responses to ileostomy and colostomy in patients over the age of 50. *Geriatrics, 26,* 112–118.

Doka, K. (Ed.). (1989). *Disenfranchised grief.* Lexington, MA: Lexington Books.

Doron, J. (1980). *Conflict and violence in intimate relationships: Focus on marital rape.* Paper presented at the meeting of the American Sociological Association, New York.

Duvall, E. M. (1971). *Family development.* Philadelphia: Lippincott.

Ellis, E. M., Calhoun, K. S., & Atkeson, B. M. (1980). Sexual dysfunction in victims of rape: Victims may experience a loss of sexual arousal and frightening flashbacks even one year after the assault. *Women and Health, 5,* 39–47.

Erikson, E. (1963). *Childhood and society* (2nd ed.). New York: Norton.

Eth, S., & Pynoos, R. S. (1985). *Post-traumatic stress disorder in children.* Washington, DC: American Psychiatric Association.

Federal Bureau of Investigation. (1980, 1981). *Uniform Crime Reports.* Washington, DC: U.S. Department of Justice.

Feldman-Summers, S., Gordon, P. E., & Meagher, J. R. (1979). The impact of rape on sexual satisfaction. *Journal of Abnormal Psychology, 8,* 101–105.

Felstein, I. (1970). *Sex in later life.* West Drayton, Middlesex, United Kingdom: Penguin.

Figley, C. R. (1978). Psychosocial adjustment among Vietnam veterans: An overview of the research. In C. R. Figley (Ed.), *Stress disorders among Vietnam veterans: Theory, research, and treatment* (pp. 57–70). New York: Brunner/Mazel.

Figley, C. R. (1989). *Helping traumatized families.* San Francisco: Jossey-Bass.

Finkelhor, D. (1979). *Sexually victimized children.* New York: Free Press.

Finkelhor, D. (1985). Sexual abuse of boys. In A. W. Burgess (Ed.), *Rape and sexual assault* (pp. 97–109). New York: Garland.

Finkelhor, D., & Yllö, K. (1983). Rape in marriage: A sociological view. In D. Finkelhor, R. Gelles, G. Hotaling, & M. Straus (Eds.), *The dark side of families: Current family violence research* (pp. 119–130). Newbury Park, CA: Sage.

Finkelhor, D., & Yllö, K. (1985). *License to rape: Sexual abuse of wives.* Troy, MO: Holt, Rinehart & Winston.

Fox, E. F., Nelson, M. A., & Bolman, W. M. (1969). The termination process: A neglected dimension of social work. *Social Work, 14*(2), 53–63.

Freud, S. (1961). Mourning and melancholia. In J. Strachey (Ed. and Trans.), *The standard edition of the complete psychological works of Sigmund Freud* (Vol. 14, pp. 237–258). London: Hogarth Press. (Original work published 1917.)

Friedman, R., & Gradstein, B. (1982). *Surviving pregnancy loss.* Boston: Little, Brown.

Friend, R. A. (1980). GAYing: Adjustment and the older gay male. *Alternative Lifestyles, 3,* 231–248.

Frieze, I. (1983). Investigating the causes and consequences of marital rape. *Signs, 8,* 532–553.

Gager, N., & Schurr, C. (1976). *Sexual assault: Confronting rape in America.* New York: Gosset & Dunlap.

Garmezy, N. (1981). Overview. In *Adolescence and stress* (DHHS Publication No. ADM 81–1098). Washington, DC: National Institute of Mental Health.

Garvin, C. (1981). *Contemporary group work.* Englewood Cliffs, NJ: Prentice-Hall.

Geiser, R. (1979). *Hidden victims: The sexual abuse of children.* Boston: Beacon Press.

Giarretto, H. (1976). The treatment of father-daughter incest: A psycho-social approach. *Children Today, 5,* 2–5, 34–35.

Giles-Sims, J. (1982). *Wife-battering: A systems theory approach.* New York: Guilford.

Gilliland, B. E., & James, R. K. (1988). *Crisis intervention strategies.* Pacific Grove, CA: Brooks/Cole.

Gochros, H. L. (1992). The sexuality of gay men with HIV infection. *Social Work, 37,* 105–109.

Goodwin, J. (1982). *Sexual abuse: Incest victims and their families.* Boston: John Wright.

Greil, A. L. (1991). *Not yet pregnant: Infertile couples in contemporary America.* New Brunswick, NJ: Rutgers University Press.

Grollman, E. A. (Ed.). (1967). *Explaining death to children.* Boston: Beacon Press.

Groth, A. N., & Burgess, A. W. (1980). Male rape: Offender and victims. *American Journal of Psychiatry, 137,* 806–810.

Harlap, S., Kost, K., & Forrest, J. D. (1990). *Preventing pregnancy, protecting health: A new look at birth control choices in the United States.* New York: Alan Guttmacher Institute.

Hellerstein, H., & Friedman, E. H. (1970). Sexual activity and the post coronary patient. *Archives of Internal Medicine, 125,* 987–999.

Hendricks, J. E. (1985). *Crisis intervention: Contemporary issues for on-site interveners.* Springfield, IL: Thomas.

Herman, J. (1981). *Father-daughter incest.* Cambridge, MA: Harvard University Press.

Herman, J. (1985). Father-daughter incest. In A. W. Burgess (Ed.), *Rape and sexual assault* (pp. 83–96). New York: Garland.

Hicks, D. J., & Moon, D. M. (1984). Sexual assault of the older woman. In I. R. Stuart & J. G. Greer (Eds.), *Victims of sexual aggression* (pp. 180–196). New York: Van Nostrand Reinhold.

Hilberman, E. (1976). *The rape victim.* New York: Basic Books.

Hippler, M. (1986, September 16). The problems and promise of gay youth. *Advocate,* p. 42.

Hirsch, M. B., & Mosher, W. D. (1987). Characteristics of infertile women in the United States and their use of fertility services. *Fertility and Sterility, 47,* 618–625.

Hoff, L. A. (1978). *People in crisis.* Reading, MA: Addison-Wesley.

Hoff, L. A., & Miller, N. K. (1987). *Programs for people in crisis.* Boston: Northeastern University Custom Book Program.

Holmes, T., & Rahe, R. (1967). The social readjustment rating scale. *Journal of Psychosomatic Research, 11,* 213–218.

Hysterectomy and its alternatives. (1990, September). *Consumer Reports,* pp. 603–607.

Ilse, S., Burns, L. H., & Erling, S. (1984). *Sibling grief . . . After miscarriage, stillbirth or infant death.* Wayzata, MN: Pregnancy and Infant Loss Center.

Insler, V., Potashnik, G., & Glassner, M. (1981). Some epidemiological aspects of fertility evaluation. In V. Insler & G. Bettendorf (Eds.), *Advances in diagnosis and treatment of infertility* (pp. 165–177). New York: Elsevier Science.

Jackson, E. N. (1965). *Telling a child about death.* New York: Dutton (Hawthorn Books).

Janosik, E. H. (1984). *Crisis counseling: A contemporary approach.* Boston: Jones & Bartlett.

Jessor, R., Costa, E., Jessor, S., & Donovan, J. (1983). The time of first intercourse: A prospective study. *Journal of Personality and Social Psychology, 44,* 608–626.

Kaas, M. J. (1978). Sexual expression of the elderly in nursing homes. *Gerontologist, 18,* 372–378.

Kahn, E., & Fisher, C. (1969). REM sleep and sexuality in the aged. *Journal of Geriatric Psychiatry, 2,* 181–199.

Karacan, I., Hursch, C. J., & Williams, R. L. (1972). Some characteristics of nocturnal penile tumescence in elderly males. *Gerontology, 27,* 39–45.

Kaufman, A. (1984). Rape of men in the community. In I. R. Stuart & J. G. Greer (Eds.), *Victims of sexual aggression* (pp. 156–179). New York: Van Nostrand Reinhold.

Kelly, J. (1977). The aging male homosexual: Myths and reality. *Gerontologist, 17,* 328–332.

Kleeman, J. A. (1971). The establishment of core gender identity in normal girls. *Archives of Sexual Behavior, 1,* 103–116.

Kliger, B. E. (1984). Evaluation, therapy, and outcome in 493 infertile couples. *Fertility and Sterility, 41,* 40–46.

Kosberg, J. (1985). Victimization of the elderly: Causation and prevention. *Victimology: An International Journal, 10,* 376–396.

Koss, M. P. (1985). The hidden rape victim: Personality, attitudinal, and situational characteristics. *Psychology of Women Quarterly, 9,* 193–212.

Koss, M. P., Gidycz, C. A., & Wisniewski, N. (1987). The scope of rape: Incidence and prevalence of sexual aggression and victimization in a national sample of higher education students. *Journal of Consulting and Clinical Psychology, 55,* 162–170.

Kübler-Ross, E. (1969). *On death and dying.* New York: Macmillan.

Lalos, A., Lalos, O., Jacobson, L., & van Schoultz, B. (1985). Psychological reaction to the medical investigation and surgical treatment of infertility. *Gynecologic and Obstetric Investigation, 20,* 1–9.

Lamb, E. J., & Leurgans, S. (1979). Does adoption affect subsequent fertility? *American Journal of Obstetrics and Gynecology, 134*(2), 138–144.

Law Enforcement Assistance Administration. (1977). *Sourcebook of criminal justice statistics.* Washington, DC: National Criminal Justice Information and Statistical Services.

Lewis, E., & Page, A. (1978). Failure to mourn a stillbirth: An overlooked catastrophe. *British Journal of Medical Psychology, 51,* 237–241.

Lindemann, C. (1984). Women's health/sexuality: The case of menopause. In L. Lister & D. Shore (Eds.), *Human sexuality in medical social work* (pp. 101–112). New York: Haworth Press.

Lindemann, E. (1944). The symptomatology and management of acute grief. *American Journal of Psychiatry, 101,* 141–148.

Lindy, J. D. (1986). An outline for the psychoanalytic psychotherapy of post-traumatic stress disorders. In C. R. Figley (Ed.), *Trauma and its wake: Traumatic stress theory, research, and intervention* (Vol. 2, pp. 195–212). New York: Brunner/Mazel.

Lowenthal, M. F., & Chiriboga, D. (1972). Transition to the empty nest: Crisis, challenge, or relief. *Archives of General Psychiatry, 26,* 8–14.

Lystad, M. (1982). Child sexual abuse: When it happens in the home. *Response, 5,* 5-7.

McCarthy, B. W. (1990). A cognitive-behavioral approach to the treatment of incestuous families. In S. Stith, M. B. Williams, & K. Rosen (Eds.), *Violence hits home: Comprehensive treatment approaches to domestic violence* (pp. 179–193). New York: Springer.

McGuire, L., & Wagner, N. (1978). Sexual dysfunctions in women who were molested as children: One response pattern and suggestions for treatment. *Journal of Sex and Marital Therapy, 4,* 11–15.

Mahlstedt, P. (1985). The psychological component of infertility. *Fertility and Sterility, 43*(3), 335–346.

Marris, P. (1974). *Loss and change.* New York: Random House.

Masters, W., & Johnson, V. (1966). *Human sexual response.* Boston: Little, Brown.

Mazor, M. D. (1984). Emotional reactions to infertility. In M. D. Mazor & H. F. Simons (Eds.), *Infertility: Medical, emotional, and social consequences* (pp. 23–35). New York: Human Sciences Press.

Menning, B. E. (1977). *Infertility: A guide for the childless couple.* Englewood Cliffs, NJ: Prentice-Hall.

Miller, W. R., & Williams, A. M. (1984). Marital and sexual dysfunction following rape: Identification and treatment. In I. R. Stuart & J. G. Greer (Eds.), *Victims of sexual aggression* (pp. 197–233). New York: Van Nostrand Reinhold.

Mindick, B., & Oskamp, S. (1982). Individual differences among adolescent contraceptors: Some implications for intervention. In I. R. Stuart & C. F. Wells (Eds.), *Pregnancy in adolescence: Needs, problems, and management* (pp. 140–176). New York: Van Nostrand Reinhold.

Mooney, T., Cole, T., & Chilgren, R. (1975). *Sexual options for paraplegics and quadriplegics.* Boston: Little, Brown.

Mooney, T., Cole, T., & Chilgren, R. (1975). *Sexual options for paraplegics and quadraplegics.* Boston: Little, Brown.

Moos, R. H., & Tsu, V. D. (Eds.). (1977). *Coping with physical illness.* New York: Plenum.

Mosher, W. D. (1982). Infertility among U.S. couples, 1965–1976. *Family Planning Perspectives, 14,* 22–27.

Mosher, W. D. (1987). Infertility: Why business is booming. *American Demographics, 9,* 42–43.

Nadelson, C. C., & Notman, M. T. (1984). Psychodynamics of sexual assault experiences. In I. R. Stuart & J. G. Greer (Eds.), *Victims of sexual aggression* (pp. 3–17). New York: Van Nostrand Reinhold.

Nadelson, C. C., Notman, M. T., Zackson, H., & Gornick, J. (1982). A follow-up study of rape victims. *American Journal of Psychiatry, 139,* 1266–1270.

Nagy, M. (1965). The child's view of death. In H. Feifel (Ed.), *The meaning of death.* New York: McGraw-Hill.

Nass, G. D., Libby, R. W., & Fisher, M. P. (1981). *Sexual choices.* Belmont, CA: Wadsworth.

National Crime Survey. (1981). *Criminal victimization in the United States, 1979.* Washington, DC: U.S. Department of Justice.

Neugarten, B., Wood, V., Kraines, R., & Loomins, B. (1963). Women's attitudes toward the menopause. *Vita Humana, 6,* 140–151.

Ochberg, F. (Ed.). (1988). *Post-traumatic therapy.* New York: Brunner/Mazel.

Offer, D., & Simon, W. (1976). Sexual development. In B. Sadock, H. Kaplan, & A. Freedman (Eds.), *The sexual experience* (pp. 128–141). Baltimore: Williams & Wilkins.

Orbach, C. E., & Tallent, N. (1965). Modification of perceived body and of body concepts. *Archives of General Psychiatry, 12,* 126–135.

Orfirer, A. P. (1970). Loss of sexual function in the male. In B. Schoenberg, A. Carr, D. Peretz, & A. Kutscher (Eds.), *Loss and grief: Psychological management in medical practice* (pp. 156–177). New York: Columbia University Press.

Pagelow, M. (1981). *Woman-battering: Victims and their experiences.* Newbury Park, CA: Sage.

Parkes, C. M., & Weiss, R. S. (1983). *Recovery from bereavement.* New York: Basic Books.

Parrot, A. (1985). *Comparison of acquaintance rape patterns among college students in a large co-ed university and a small women's college.* Paper presented at the meeting of the National Society for the Scientific Study of Sex, San Diego, CA, November 1985.

Parrot, A. (1988). *Coping with date rape and acquaintance rape.* New York: Rosen Publishing Group.

Parrot, A. (1989). Acquaintance rape among adolescents: Identifying risk groups and intervention strategies. In P. A. Meares & C. H. Shapiro (Eds.), *Adolescent sexuality: New challenges for social work* (pp. 47–62). New York: Haworth Press.

Patten, S. B., Gatz, Y. K., Jones, B., & Thomas, D. L. (1989). Posttraumatic stress disorder and the treatment of sexual abuse. *Social Work, 34,* 197–203.

Paul, W. (1982). Social issues and homosexual behavior. In W. Paul, J. D. Weinrich, J. C. Gonsiorek, & M. E. Hotvedt (Eds.), *Homosexuality: Social, psychological, and biological issues* (pp. 29–54). Newbury Park, CA: Sage.

Peretz, D. (1970). Development, object-relationships, and loss. In B. Schoenberg, A. Carr, D. Peretz, & A. Kutscher (Eds.), *Loss and grief: Psychological management in medical practice* (pp. 3–19). New York: Columbia University Press.

Pfeiffer, E., & Davis, G. C. (1972). Determinants of sexual behavior in middle and old age. *Journal of the American Geriatrics Society, 20,* 151–158.

Pfeiffer, E., Verwoerdt, A., & Davis, G. C. (1972). Sexual behavior in middle life. *American Journal of Psychiatry, 128,* 82–87.

Pines, A. M., Aronson, E., & Kafry, D. (1981). *Burnout: From tedium to personal growth.* New York: Free Press.

Pressman, B. (1989). Treatment of wife abuse: The case for feminist therapy. In B. Pressman, G. Cameron, & M. Rothery (Eds.), *Intervening with assaulted women: Current theory, research, and practice* (pp. 21–45). Hillsdale, NJ: Erlbaum.

Puryear, D. A. (1979). *Helping people in crisis: A practical, family-oriented approach to effective crisis intervention.* San Francisco: Jossey-Bass.

Rando, T. A. (1984). *Grief, dying, and death: Interventions for caregivers.* Champaign, IL: Research Press.

Rando, T. A. (Ed.). (1986). *Loss and anticipatory grief.* Lexington, MA: Lexington Books.

Rando, T. A. (1988). *Grieving.* Lexington, MA: Lexington Books.

Rochman, S. (1990, September). In the dark: Emphasis on AIDS as a disease of gay males has dangerous implications for women. *Ithaca Times,* pp. 9–13.

Rogers, C. M., & Terry, T. (1984). Clinical intervention with boy victims of sexual abuse. In I. R. Stuart & J. G. Greer (Eds.), *Victims of sexual aggression* (pp. 91–104). New York: Van Nostrand Reinhold.

Rowan, E. L., & Rowan, J. B. (1984). Rape and the college student: Multiple crises in late adolescence. In I. R. Stuart & J. G. Greer (Eds.), *Victims of sexual aggression* (pp. 234–250). New York: Van Nostrand Reinhold.

Russell, D. (1982). *Rape in marriage.* New York: Macmillan.

Salzer, L. P. (1991). *Surviving infertility.* New York: Harper-Collins.

Schultz, L. G. (1980). *The sexual victimology of youth.* Springfield, IL: Thomas.

Seltzer, V. L. (1987). *Every woman's guide to breast cancer.* New York: Viking Penguin.

Selye, H. (1956). *The stress of life.* New York: McGraw-Hill.

Shapiro, C. H. (1980). Termination: A neglected concept in the social work curriculum. *Journal of Education for Social Work, 16*(2), 13–19.

Shapiro, C. H. (1982). Creative supervision. In W. S. Paine (Ed.), *Job stress and burnout* (pp. 213–228). Newbury Park, CA: Sage.

Shapiro, C. H. (1988). *Infertility and pregnancy loss: A guide for helping professionals.* San Francisco: Jossey-Bass.

Sheehy, G. (1992). *The silent passage: Menopause.* New York: Random House.

Sheridan, M. S. (1984). Sexuality and chronic illness. In L. Lister & D. Shore (Eds.), *Human sexuality in medical social work* (pp. 67–81). New York: Haworth Press.

Shields, N., & Hanneke, C. (1983). Battered wives' reaction to marital rape. In D. Finkelhor, R. Gelles, G. Hotaling, & M. Straus (Eds.), *The dark side of families* (pp. 131–148). Newbury Park, CA: Sage.

Silbert, M. H. (1984). Treatment of prostitute victims of sexual assault. In I. R. Stuart & J. G. Greer (Eds.), *Victims of sexual aggression* (pp. 127–155). New York: Van Nostrand Reinhold.

Simos, B. G. (1979). *A time to grieve.* New York: Family Service Association of America.

Steele, B. (1976). Violence within the family. In R. E. Helfer & C. H. Kempe (Eds.), *Child abuse and neglect: The family and the community* (pp. 3–23). Cambridge, MA: Ballinger.

Stith, S. M., & Rosen, K. H. (1990). Overview of domestic violence. In S. M. Stith, M. B. Williams, & K. Rosen (Eds.), *Violence hits home* (pp. 1–21). New York: Springer.

Straus, M. (1976). Sexual inequality, cultural norms, and wife-beating. *Victimology, 1*(1), 54–76.

Straus, M. (1977). A sociological perspective on the prevention and treatment of wifebeating. In M. Roy (Ed.), *Battered women* (pp. 194–239). New York: Van Nostrand Reinhold.

Strauss, A. (1976). *Chronic illness and the quality of life.* St. Louis, MO: Mosby.

Thompson, C. M. (1964). *Interpersonal psychoanalysis: The selected pages of Clara M. Thompson.* New York: Basic Books.

Vergara, T. L. (1983–1984). Meeting the needs of sexual minority youth: One program's response. *Journal of Social Work & Human Sexuality, 2*(2–3), 19–38.

Verkauf, B. (1983). The incidence and outcome of single-factor, multifactorial, and unexplained infertility. *American Journal of Obstetrics and Gynecology, 147,* 175–181.

Viorst, J. (1986). *Necessary losses.* New York: Ballantine.

Walsh, F., & McGoldrick, M. (1991). Loss and the family: A systemic perspective. In F. Walsh & M. McGoldrick (Eds.), *Living beyond loss: Death in the family* (pp. 1–29). New York: Norton.

Wasow, M., & Loeb, M. (1979). Sexuality in nursing homes. *Journal of the American Geriatrics Society, 27*(3), 73–79.

Weinberg, K. (1968). *Incest in problems of sex behavior.* New York: Crowell.

Williams, M. B. (1990). The treatment of the traumatic impact of family violence: An integration of theoretical perspectives. In S. Stith, M. B. Williams, & K. Rosen (Eds.), *Violence hits home* (pp. 330–352). New York: Springer.

Woods, N. F. (1979a). Adaptation to hospitalization and illness. In N. F. Woods (Ed.), *Human sexuality in health and illness* (pp. 272–286). St. Louis, MO: Mosby.

Woods, N. F. (1979b). Sexual adaptation to changed body image. In N. F. Woods (Ed.), *Human sexuality in health and illness* (pp. 323–344). St. Louis, MO: Mosby.

Woods, N. F. (1979c). Sexual adaptation to trauma: Paraplegia. In N. F. Woods (Ed.), *Human sexuality in health and illness.* (pp. 345–363). St. Louis, MO: Mosby.

Woods, N. F. (1979d). Sexuality throughout the life cycle: Young adulthood through aging. In N. F. Woods (Ed.), *Human sexuality in health and illness* (pp. 55–72). St. Louis, MO: Mosby.

Woods, N. F., & Herbert, J. M. (1979). Sexuality and chronic illness. In N. F. Woods (Ed.), *Human sexuality in health and illness* (pp. 287–322). St. Louis, MO: Mosby.

Worden, J. W. (1982). *Grief counseling and grief therapy: A handbook for the mental health practitioner.* New York: Springer.

Wu, R. (1973). *Behavior and illness.* Englewood Cliffs, NJ: Prentice-Hall.

Yllö, K., & Finkelhor, D. (1985). Marital rape. In A. W. Burgess (Ed.), *Rape and sexual assault* (pp. 146–209). New York: Garland.

Young, M. A. (1988). Support services for victims. In F. M. Ochberg (Ed.), *Post-traumatic therapy* (pp. 330–351). New York: Brunner/Mazel.

Zellman, C. L., Johnson, P. B., Giarrusso, R., & Goodchild, J. D. (1979, September). *Adolescent expectations for dating relationships: Consensus and conflict between the sexes.* Paper presented at the meeting of the American Psychological Association, New York.

Zilbergeld, B. (1978). *Male sexuality: A guide to sexual fulfillment.* Boston: Little, Brown.

INDEX

Loomins, B., 187

Loss, 3–4; with aging, 184–186; with AIDS, 79–88; and bio-psychosocial development, 212; with cancer, 67–79; coping with, 37–44; definition of, 4; developmental, 8–10; of external objects, 7–8; grief following, 28–37; with infertility, 94–96; knowledge about, 230; of part of self, 5–7; with rape, 180–183; reawakened earlier, 12; reproductive, 108–124; response to, 13–21; secondary, 10; of significant person, 4–5; symbolic, 11–12; and therapy, 21–22. *See also* Pregnancy loss

Lowenthal, M. F., 187

Lupton, M. J., 186

Lystad, M., 159

M

McCarthy, B. W., 145

McGoldrick, M., 80

McGuire, L., 166

Maeder, J. P., 193

Mahlstedt, P., 96, 97, 98, 100

Marital rape, 171–174

Marris, P., 4, 36, 37, 51

Mastectomy: consolidation phase with, 35; organization for, 14; symbolic losses with, 11. *See also* Cancer

Masters, W., 188, 189, 191

Mazor, M. D., 92, 93, 97, 100

Meagher, J. R., 166

Memorializing, with stillbirth, 140–141

Men: cancer in, 39–40, 77–79; elderly, 190–191; hospitalization of, 53; midlife changes of, 187–188; and miscarriage, 118–119; rape of, 177–180; sex-role conditioning of, 18. *See also* Fathers; Gay males

Menning, B. E., 93

Menopause, 186–187

Messick, J. M., 211, 231

Midlife changes, of males, 187–188

Miller, N. K., 231

Miller, W. R., 167

Mindick, B., 206

Miscarriage, 115–121

Moon, D. M., 178

Mooney, T., 63

Moos, R. H., 51, 52

Mosher, W. D., 92, 94

Mourning, 24

Myocardial infarction (MI), and sexuality, 192–194. *See also* Heart attack

N

Nadelson, C. C., 147, 167, 171

Nagy, M., 136

Nass, G. D., 188, 189, 190

National Association of Social Workers, 216

National Cancer Institute, 67

National Crime Survey, 159

National Survey of Family Growth, 91–92

Nelson, M. A., 239

Neugarten, B., 187

Notman, M. T., 147, 167, 171

O

OB-GYN services, 225–226

Objects, external, loss of, 7–8

Ochberg, F., 232

Offer, D., 207

Oppression, prevention of, 217–222

Orbach, C. E., 60

Orfirer, A. P., 5

Oskamp, S., 206

P

Page, A., 142

Pagelow, M., 171

Paraplegia, 62–65

Parkes, C. M., 4

Patten, S. B., 148

Paul, W., 219

Peretz, D., 4

Perlman, A., 61

Perlmutter, E., 186

Pfeiffer, E., 189, 190

Pines, A. M., 229